GOLD CORD

THE STORY OF A FELLOWSHIP

AMY CARMICHAEL

CHRISTIAN · LITERATURE · CRUSADE
Fort Washington, Pennsylvania 19034

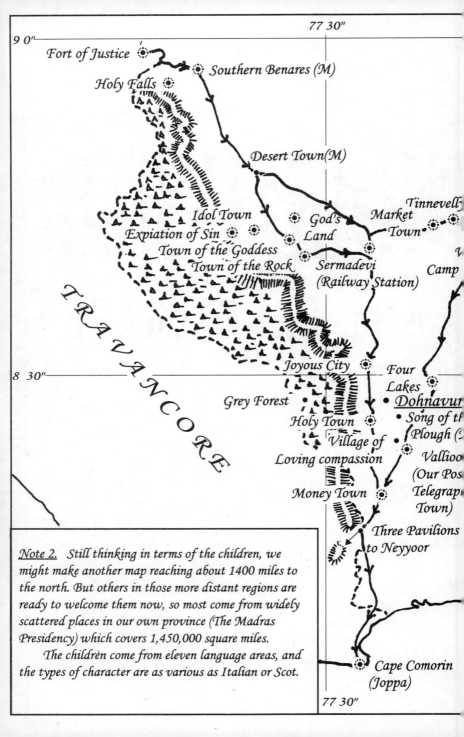

77 30"

9 0"

Fort of Justice

Holy Falls

Southern Benares (M)

Desert Town (M)

Idol Town

Expiation of Sin

Town of the Goddess

Town of the Rock

God's Land

Tinnevelly

Market Town

Sermadevi (Railway Station)

Camp

T R A V A N C O R E

Joyous City

Four Lakes

8 30"

Grey Forest

Dohnavur

Holy Town

Song of the Plough (S)

Village of Loving compassion

Vallioo (Our Post Telegraph Town)

Money Town

Three Pavilions to Neyyoor

Note 2. Still thinking in terms of the children, we might make another map reaching about 1400 miles to the north. But others in those more distant regions are ready to welcome them now, so most come from widely scattered places in our own province (The Madras Presidency) which covers 1,450,000 square miles.

The children come from eleven language areas, and the types of character are as various as Italian or Scot.

Cape Comorin (Joppa)

77 30"

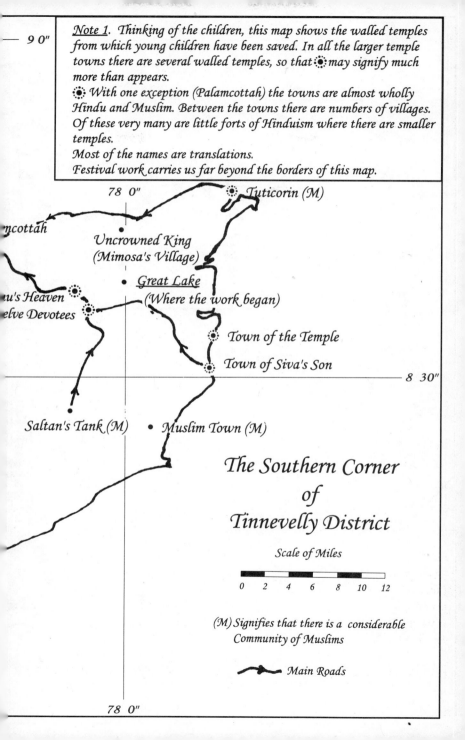

— 9 0"

Note 1. Thinking of the children, this map shows the walled temples from which young children have been saved. In all the larger temple towns there are several walled temples, so that ⊙ may signify much more than appears.

⊙ With one exception (Palamcottah) the towns are almost wholly Hindu and Muslim. Between the towns there are numbers of villages. Of these very many are little forts of Hinduism where there are smaller temples.

Most of the names are translations.

Festival work carries us far beyond the borders of this map.

78 0"

⊙ *Tuticorin (M)*

mcottah

*Uncrowned King
(Mimosa's Village)*

⊙ *Great Lake
(Where the work began)*

u's Heaven ⊙
elve Devotees ⊙

⊙ *Town of the Temple*

⊙ *Town of Siva's Son*

8 30"

Saltan's Tank (M) • *Muslim Town (M)*

The Southern Corner
of
Tinnevelly District

Scale of Miles

0 2 4 6 8 10 12

*(M) Signifies that there is a considerable
Community of Muslims*

Main Roads

78 0"

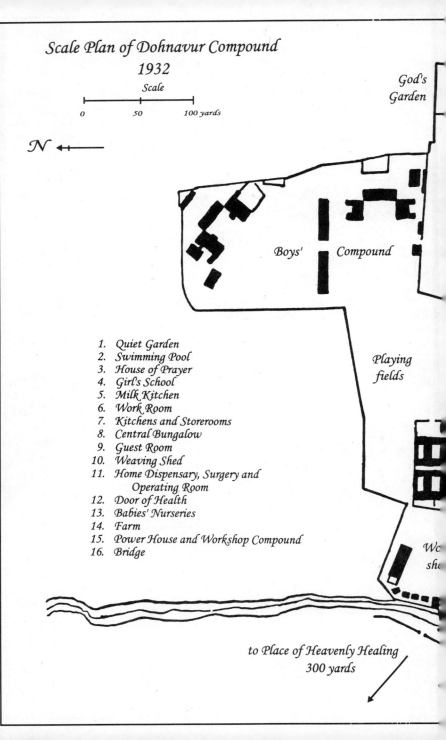

Scale Plan of Dohnavur Compound
1932

Scale

0   50   100 yards

N

God's
Garden

Boys'   Compound

Playing
fields

1. Quiet Garden
2. Swimming Pool
3. House of Prayer
4. Girl's School
5. Milk Kitchen
6. Work Room
7. Kitchens and Storerooms
8. Central Bungalow
9. Guest Room
10. Weaving Shed
11. Home Dispensary, Surgery and
      Operating Room
12. Door of Health
13. Babies' Nurseries
14. Farm
15. Power House and Workshop Compound
16. Bridge

Wc
sh

to Place of Heavenly Healing
300 yards

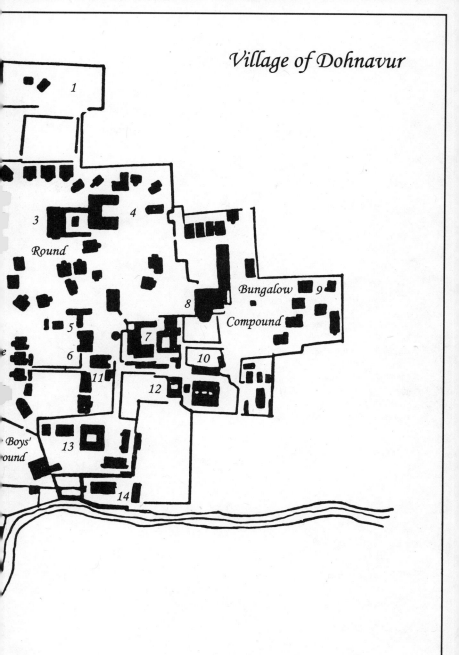

Village of Dohnavur

1

3
Round

4

5

6

7

8

Bungalow
9
Compound

10

11

12

Boys'
ound

13

14

Village of Chettimerdu
(Hindu)

CHRISTIAN LITERATURE CRUSADE
U.S.A.
P.O. Box 1449, Fort Washington, PA 19034

with publishing programs also in:
GREAT BRITAIN
51 The Dean, Alresford, Hants., SO24 9BJ

AUSTRALIA
P.O. Box 419M, Manunda QLD 4879

NEW ZEALAND
10 MacArthur Street, Feilding

ISBN 0-87508-068-5

First published 1932
This American edition 1996

This printing 1999

Reprinted by permission of The Dohnavur Fellowship

Cover design: Skip Mable Studio

Printed in the United States of America

Foreword

Why Written

The Dohnavur Fellowship is a group of Indian and European men and women who work together in the South of India. Its friends wanted to know how it began (just what is hardest to tell, because without foolish fuss it is impossible to escape the personal). And they asked for something that would link up the stories already written; the beads should be strung on some sort of cord, they said. (That is why some of the Dohnavur books are mentioned along with their years.) Others asked for another kind of cord. "What holds you together?" they asked; and we answered, "A gold cord."

Then our publishers asked for something; a religious document they called it. We knew that nothing so formal was likely to evolve, and a Tamil proverb came up, laughing: "Does one make a song about pulling up a handful of greens?" It would be hateful to do that, so we answered with a brief Tamil verb which conveniently means can't or won't, according to feeling.

But one morning early, before the crush of the day, a quiet private word ended this ineffective unwillingness. And so, in scattered hours, the writing has been done, helped by the comradeship of the whole Fellowship, and the tireless patience of several who searched the dull typescript for slips, helped to correct the proofs, and made the index.

Its Setting

A tragic page of history. There is not a date but is linked to great events in one or in many of the nations, or to those overwhelming distresses that the very names Armenia, Russia, China, Central Asia, suggest. And all that has happened in India is never out of mind. But the story holds to a single course. It looks across the open frontier to the heavenly Country whose forces move unseen among us; for they are the things that matter most, "and the life of the spirit has no borders."

Its Special Word
From an old Gaelic Rune:

> Jesu, Son of the Virgin pure,
> Be Thou my pilgrim staff,
>   Throughout the lands,
>   Throughout the lands,
> Thy love in all my thoughts,
>   Thy likeness in my face,
> May I heartwarm to others
>   And they heartwarm to me,
> For love of the love of Thee,
> For love of the love of Thee.

In comradeship,
Amy Carmichael

Dohnavur Fellowship,
Dohnavur,
S. India.

Contents

Antony is speaking:
The vision of the holy ones is not fraught with distraction: for they will not strive, nor cry, nor shall anyone hear their voice. But it comes so quietly and gently that immediately joy, gladness and courage arise in the soul. For the Lord who is our joy is with them, and the power of God the Father. And the thoughts of the soul remain unruffled and undisturbed, so that it, enlightened as it were by rays, beholds by itself those who appear.

Whenever ye . . . are afraid, your fear is immediately taken away, and in place of it comes joy unspeakable, cheerfulness, courage, renewed strength, calmness of thought.—St. Athanasius' *Life of St. Antony* (fourth century).

1.

From prayer that asks that I may be
Sheltered from winds that beat on Thee,
From fearing when I should aspire,
From faltering when I should climb higher,
From silken self, O Captain, free
Thy soldier who would follow Thee.

From subtle love of softening things,
From easy choices, weakenings,
(Not thus are spirits fortified,
Not this way went the Crucified)
From all that dims Thy Calvary,
O Lamb of God, deliver me.

Give me the love that leads the way,
The faith that nothing can dismay,
The hope no disappointments tire,
The passion that will burn like fire,
Let me not sink to be a clod:
Make me Thy fuel, Flame of God.

1. Gold, Silver, Precious Stones

On a hot September day in 1918, some happy Indian children set out to trace their mountain river to its source. After the rains in June and in October, the river is a glory of rushing water pouring down a deep ravine; but in dry, burnt-up September, it is shallow and, from below, bare boulders as big as cottages looked like the steps of a giant staircase. It would be easy, we thought, to find the source.

It was a joyful, though a scorching, climb. Sometimes the shadowy forest on either side drew back a little and there were open sunny bays where the people of the woods come down to drink. Often the moist ground near the water was pitted with tiny hoofprints, and once there was the more exciting spoor of tiger. "Perhaps even now they are watching us, seeing everything we do," whispered the children, and they were aware of delicious shivers and hesitations. It was thrilling to think that the forest was full of eyes, and "they" quite near and watchful. But never the tip of a tail was seen that day. The birds warned the monkey people, and the monkey people warned the other people, long before the queer blue creatures crawling up the riverbed approached. Only the brave Malabar thrush, who whistles like a schoolboy trying to find a lost tune, waited till the curious blue appeared over the top of a boulder; then, with a sharp cry of surprise or disapproval, he flew off.

The children found new delights—fairy falls and fairy pools and caves and dear growing things, great ferns and cushions of moss; but the source they did not find. A tree had crashed through the forest just where the banks were too steep to climb and the undergrowth was too entangled to penetrate. The trunk was covered with orchids, and was a beautiful thing, but it barred the way. Below it was a deep, clear pool. The children knew that, far beyond, above the fringes of the forest, the real source must lie out under the sky in a lonely loveliness, with only the wind and the whispering rushes and the marsh flowers to tell it of the ways of the world below. But they could not go up there.

*   *   *   *   *

We have been asked to tell of the beginning of our Fellowship, why it shaped as it did, and how it came to be a little thing committed to the hand of God. We cannot go back to the beginning. So we begin at the pool below the tree that leans across the river.

*   *   *   *   *

It was a dull Sunday morning in a street in Belfast thirty-three years before the day when the children climbed their mountain stream. My brothers and sisters and I were returning with our mother from church when we met a poor, pathetic old woman who was carrying a heavy bundle. We had never seen such a thing in Presbyterian Belfast on Sunday, and, moved by sudden pity, my brothers and I turned with her, relieved her of the bundle, took her by her arms as though they had been handles, and helped her along. This meant facing all the respectable people who were, like ourselves, on their way home. It was a horrid moment. We were only two boys and a girl, and not at all exalted Christians. We hated doing it. Crimson all over (at least we felt crimson, souls and body of us) we plodded on, a wet wind blowing us about, and blowing, too, the rags of that poor old woman, till she seemed like a bundle of feathers and we unhappily mixed up with them. But just as we passed a fountain, recently built near the curbstone, this mighty phrase was suddenly flashed as it were through the grey drizzle:

"Gold, silver, precious stones, wood, hay, stubble—every man's work shall be made manifest: for the day shall declare it, because it shall be revealed by fire; and the fire shall try every man's work of what sort it is. If any man's work abide—"

If any man's work abide: I turned to see the voice that spoke with me. The fountain, the muddy street, the people with their politely surprised faces, all this I saw, but saw nothing else. The blinding flash had come and gone; the ordinary was all about us. We went on. I said nothing to anyone, but I knew that something had happened that had changed life's values. Nothing could ever matter again but the things that were eternal.

From this pool flowed the stream that is the story. There are so many stories already in the world, and so many are splendid and great, that it is difficult to believe it can be worth the telling. But if only I can tell it under direction, it will carry at least one quality of clear, running water—sincerity.

2.

Before Gordon left Cairo on an expedition perhaps as hazardous as any man in this world ever undertook, he sent a short and characteristic letter to his sister:

"26 January 1884—I leave for the Sudan tonight. I feel quite happy, for I say, If God is with me, who can or will be hurtful to me? May He be glorified, the world and the people of the Sudan be blessed, and may I be the dust under His feet."—*Gordon and the Sudan*, by Bernard M. Allen.

Now let me burn out for God.—Henry Martyn.

God, hold me on with a steady pace.—Robert Murray McCheyne.

2. Influences

There must still be many on earth who remember Keswick in the nineties. Perhaps they remember, too, a little old Bible, familiar to thousands as the only Bible the beloved chairman ever used. Many a beautiful Bible he bought for others; but for himself he wanted nothing better than that shabby, podgy little volume, with its penciled, "Robert Wilson, 1858."

In that same little old Bible, which is with me now, pasted on a blank fly-leaf is a fragment from a letter: "Follow no voice, not mine or any other which is not His. My soul, wait thou only upon God, for my expectation is from Him." Week by week, from March 3, 1893, till power to write failed, came the letters, written with a fine pen upon thin paper, that followed the fortunes of the Convention movement in Britain and overseas, and always somewhere there were words of loving wisdom, counsel, encouragement to keep first things first. These letters, that followed me to China, Japan, India, and the life that lay behind them, are among the influences that have molded our Fellowship.

Other words follow down the years—sometimes odd words. I was staying at the China Inland Mission House,

Shanghai, en route for Japan, when, one morning after breakfast, the veteran missionary, Mr. J.W. Stevenson, Deputy Director of the C.I.M., rose from his seat at the end of one of the long tables, a tall figure in Chinese dress, with shaved head and queue. He stood for a moment silent, then, "And there was much rubbish," he said.

Everyone understood. Part of the C.I.M. compound was not quite finished, and where there is building there is rubbish. "People will try to discourage you. They will say, 'Oh, your converts are all rice Christians.' Don't be discouraged. Of course there is rubbish—there always is where anything is being done. Don't stop because of the rubbish; get on with the building."

On board ship, crossing form China to Japan, I heard another of those words that stick like burrs. I was traveling alone, and, much against my will, had been put in the first class. This was the first-class talk: "A missionary? Oh yes, you'll have a very good time; missionaries really have, you know."

But in the Matsuye band led by Barclay F. Buxton, saint and soldier, there was something that would have surprised those friendly first-class passengers. No one in Matsuye had any desire for the life they had described. And yet in every land it is possible to slip into that life. God hold us to that which drew us first, when the Cross was the attraction, and we wanted nothing else.

India (for a breakdown in Japan led to India) is a kind land to a new arrival, though how people so tired (the white faces strike a newcomer) and so often, as it seemed, over-driven too, had time to be kind was always a marvel to me. But presently questions began to float up, like bubbles slowly rising from the bottom of a pool, and they did not break and vanish as bubbles do.

"Yes, it's a bit of a shock," said a nice old missionary one day, when the talk turned to the state of things in the Church in general. "It's rather a drop from a missionary platform to this. But one gets used to it. At first you feel it's no earthly use to stay out at all; then you remember it's as bad at home, and you get accustomed to it and jog along peacefully. But I'll own it's a bit of a shock." It was; and I soon came to know that to many of us when we first come out there is "a bit of a shock," and then gradually we "get accustomed to it," and even content. But somehow we seem to lose something in the process—the fine edge of the spiritual, perhaps—and sometimes we strangle our souls. And so, what was offered as comfort turned to a rankling thorn. Is there any real comfort in remembering that things are as bad at home? And should we get accustomed to it? At such times that calm C.I.M. word about the rubbish and about getting on with the work had a steadying effect; for, though there was rubbish everywhere, there was good building too.

And yet should there be so much rubbish? Our Lord had prepared us for some, but not for so much. The wheat seemed to be often crowded out by the tares. He had said, "Let both grow together until the harvest." Was it that we did not know enough to know which was which? That must often be so, but there was another side to the puzzle, and it could not be forgotten. This habit of using evident tares as "mission agents" (an odious word, for should we not be colleagues?) what of that? "Spiritual men for spiritual work," was far more slogan than fact. What of the people to whom the preacher had nothing to give? "The hungry sheep look up and are not fed"—it was that often. "I never suspected him of conversion," was the report of a missionary on one whom he had to accept or refuse, "but by all means let us give him the benefit of the doubt." And he was made a catechist. But what of the hungry sheep? Where did their benefit come in?

Just before I came to India, the brave Danes, after patient waiting, had tried to clear their fields of salaried tares, and they had pensioned off those men and women who were manifestly not commissioned by the Spirit. The air was full of talk about this action, and many blamed it.

Within a short time those workers had been absorbed by the surrounding missions.

All this meant much to me, for I had been taught the Lord's will for me personally in this matter, in connection with the work of a little mission-hall in Ireland. The book of Ezra, chapters three to six, had shown the way I must go. By holding to this line (that of using as builders only those who had a spiritual call to build), the work is sure to be hindered for a time—"Then ceased the work of the house of God"—but in the end it goes on. And as to supplies, the command of the King is: That which they have need of, let it be given them day by day without fail.

As years pass, one learns to fear to be unjust. Anything hasty grows to appear unsure, and all generalizations unfair and often untrue. But there are impressions which deepen, and sometimes, with sympathetic joy, we see others moved to the same ends. At the time of writing, nearly forty years after these influences first began to work, an Indian woman is trying single-handed to lead the mission of which she is a member back to the ways of the Acts of the Apostles. She is considered unpractical—always the word for anything that crosses the usual. God's dreamers are always "unpractical"; but in the end some of their dreams come true.

And now, in a place quite unlike a city street on a rainy day, another great truth was made vital. It was the grave of the pioneer missionary, Ragland. It lies on a bare plain in North Tinnevelly, near a small, ruined house. The day had been hot, we (the Walkers of Tinnevelly and I) had had a rackety journey and a walk on a glary white road. Nobody seemed inclined to speak, the stifling heat discouraged speech, and we hung about the ugly little ruin and the depressing tombstone like wet socks put out to dry, to quote a perfect word for the feelings of hot, limp people at the end of a blistering day. It did not seem the moment for anything inspiring to happen; but suddenly

Mr. Walker, Ragland's spiritual successor, broke the tired silence with words that are associated with Ragland:

"Of all plans of ensuring success, the most certain is Christ's own—becoming a corn of wheat, falling into the ground and dying:

"'Verily, verily, I say unto you, Except a corn of wheat fall into the ground and die, it abideth alone; but if it die it bringeth forth much fruit.'"

Forgotten then were the heat, the fag of life—forgotten was everything. For a minute we stood in silence, and I know that the prayer rose then from the depths of our hearts: Lord, give it to us to live that life and to die that death, and to bring forth fruit unto life eternal.

In those days a spirit of concern was abroad in the land. Ragland's influence had not quite passed, and Walker of Tinnevelly was in the full might of his power. He stood for the highest always and everywhere. And there were others all over India who clearly discerned the true nature of that which shows so well on paper, but must bring tears to the angels' eyes if such glorious beings can weep. Sometimes, in our little corner, the stiffness that confined the weekly mission prayer meeting was broken through, and fustiness fled, and there was a quickening and freedom and fresh air. It was not discouragement that moved these men: it was sorrow, and, though I knew so little then, I was wholly with them. This ice and this formalism, how melt them? How kindle these dry sticks? One hardly ever saw in the churches or in their network of organization anything approaching a fellowship with our Lord's Cross and Passion. The love that should fuse us all together was simply not there.

Why was it so? People referred me to the Epistles of St. Paul and quoted Westcott about our habit of unconsciously clothing the early centuries in light. This was salutary. But there was no way to evade the questions that persisted: Why are these things so? Is the reason some lack in us? Do we love the people enough? Does the love of the heavenly Lover pour through us to them? Very early in Tamil reading one comes upon a proverb, "As the thread, so the garment; as the mother, so the child." Was this lovelessness only ourselves multiplied?

We grovel among trifles and our spirits fret and toss.
And above us burns the vision of the Christ upon the Cross.

Did the vision burn above us? There were some who had shone in the missionary sky like those great white stars that hold us in wonder, so pure and so glorious do they appear among the hosts of lesser stars. Part of the joy of missionary life is to learn to know (through the most vital of missionary biography) the starry souls who shine now in other skies, and there were some shining like that among us then. But as a company of people set apart for a special purpose, we were, it seemed to me, just dim. There did not appear to be anything burning about us. We were decorously smoldering, we were not vehement flames (were we aflame at all?) and I knew that I burned most dimly of all.

"I realize that I have scarcely begun. I do not think I would dare to call myself a missionary yet." (A South Indian missionary wrote this recently in a private letter which I am allowed to use because it speaks the thought of more than one earnest heart.) "I have stood, as it were, on the edge of His sea of suffering, and have hastily diverted myself with something else, lest He should call me to enter that sea with Him. And yet there is nothing I long more to do. To me there is no more tragic sight than the average missionary. A Hindu bowing down to his idol leaves me unmoved beside it. We have given so much, yet not the one thing that counts; we aspire so high, and fall so low; we suffer so much, but so seldom with Christ; we have done so much, and so little will remain; we have known

Christ in part, and have so effectively barricaded our hearts against His mighty love, which surely He must yearn to give His disciples above all people."

Far more than anything in these to whom we were sent, this dullness, this dimness in ourselves came with a sharp surprise. India is a land where it is fatally easy to live easily.

Those were ignorant years, but the thoughts that came colored that which was to be, and so they belong to the story of our gold cord. And a little old poem that I have rarely heard quoted, one of Traherne's, written some time before 1674, so persisted in recurring that I copy it now:

> His earnest love, His infinite desires,
> His living, endless, and devouring fires,
> Do rage in thirst, and fervently require
>   A love 'tis strange it should desire.
>
> We cold and careless are, and scarcely think
> Upon the glorious spring whereat we drink,
> Did He not love us we could be content:
>   We wretches are indifferent.
>
> 'Tis death, my soul, to be indifferent;
> Set forth thyself unto thy whole extent,
> And all the glory of His passion prize,
>   Who for thee lives, who for thee dies.

"*'Tis death, my soul, to be indifferent*"—that is surely a deathless word.

3.

I pray God to keep alive a band of Puritans, for they are the ones that make the best missionaries all the world over. Surely what we want now is more fire. I do not see much sign of it, the fire that comes from tribulation and persecution I mean. Would that the Union (Cambridge Christian Union) had not such an easy time of it now! Let us promote a foreign campaign again. Where are the prophets with the vision of the world's need? Let them arise and call the Movement to go forward.

He himself, in the singleness of his purpose, stripped his life, with something of sternness, of all that was superfluous or unrelated to the work in hand.

His subordination of all things to the single aim was absolute.

Better a thousand times effective peculiarity than ineffective ordinariness.—*D.M. Thornton: A Study in Missionary Ideals and Methods*, by W.H.T. Gairdner.

To set out walking (the aorist marking a new departure) in a way worthy of the Lord *to all meeting of His wishes* (Col. 1:10).—Bishop Moule: *Colossian Studies*.

Renew our force, O Lord, that waging
A tireless war against the foe,
We may together forward go,
Undaunted by his angry raging.

O Spirit of Power and Love, enfold us,
O valiant Spirit of Discipline,
Turn Thy bright face on us and shine,
And shame our dullness, and uphold us.

Thou hast not given the spirit of fear:
The word is strong, be of good cheer,
And Thou art here.

3. To All Meeting of His Wishes

One evening, towards the close of 1898, three Indian sisters and I were on our way from a town which was then, and is now, given up to idolatry. In the river that flows by the town, while groups of Brahmans stood on the flat roofs of their houses and stared down disapprovingly, Walker of Tinnevelly had baptized a young man who was to become a power in the district. This man had asked us to take his wife home with us and teach her how to win souls. He followed our wagon now as it trailed along, and coming close up to its open end, he said to his wife, "Give me your jewels. What does a winner of souls want with jewels?" The girl unfastened her earrings, chains and bangles, and gave them to him, smothering her astonishment. In this simple way what was known as the jewel question was born. For, as the girl gave her jewels to her husband, I saw an expression of intense interest pass over Ponnamal's face (I quote now from the story of her life):

> And she told me that, on the evening before, while she was speaking in the open air, she had overheard a child say to her mother that when she grew up she would "join that band and wear jewels like that sister" (herself). The words had smitten Ponnamal. She felt this was the last

impression she wished to leave upon anyone's mind; she
had gone to her Lord about it, and the answer that came to
her was this:

"Thou shalt also be a crown of glory in the hand of the
Lord, and a royal diadem in the hand of thy God." She did
not argue as to the meaning of these words. She saw in a
flash herself, unjeweled, a marked woman among her own
people, an eyesore, an offense. But, and the joy of the
thought overwhelmed her, not so to the Lord her God.

When we went home she took off her jewels. How
minute, how inoffensive the words appear now, set down
in one short sentence, but every syllable in them burned
for Ponnamal and for us who stood with her.

A few—very few, but to the startled and indignant eyes
that watched, it was ominous—"inebriated with divine
love, eager to forsake and defy the spirit of the word,"
stripped themselves of every weight that they might the
less laden run the race that was set before them. One who
had a long struggle with herself told me that she had never
gone to sleep at night without her hand on the gold chains
she wore round her neck. "If I had loved my Saviour more,
I should have loved my jewels less," she said. The last to
do this difficult thing had a hard time afterwards: she was
taken from us by her people and suffered many things.
(She was, in fact, slowly done to death by her "Christian"
husband.) None of us touched on the subject except when
privately asked what we felt, but it was impossible to
speak without seeming to allude to it.

How vividly, as I write, an afternoon meeting in a
church in the country comes back to me. The place was
full, for we were in the middle of a mission; and, to the
Indian Christian, meetings are a sweet delight. Before me
sat rows of women, and, the village being rich, the lobes of
their ears, cut into large loops, were laden with ornaments.
But to me it had been given that day to look upon Christ
crucified.

Far, far from me was any thought of the women's golden
toys; all eternity was round me, and that common little
building was the vestibule thereof. Then, as I spoke, I saw
a woman rise. She told me afterwards that she could not
bear it. Time, and the scorn of time and its poor estimates,
how trivial all appeared! "I saw Him," she said, "naked of
this world's glory, stripped to the uttermost; and I went
and made an ash-heap of my pride." It was Pearl—she

who was to become my sister and comrade both in labor
and in arms.

This new abandonment of obedience made an immense
difference. Things impossible before were now undertaken
without a thought. The women were free from a thousand
nets that had entangled their feet with invisible threads. Is
there any limit to what God is prepared to do for the one
who loves His Son well enough to meet His lightest wish?
"After these things"—renunciation of the choices of time—
the word of the Lord came unto Abraham in a vision,
saying, Fear not, I am thy shield and thy exceeding great
reward. After these things—not dissimilar—the word was
the same here.

Fifteen years later, as she lay slowly dying of cancer,
Ponnamal, recalling those days, said, "It was to me a new
emancipation. A new sense of spiritual liberty is bound up
in my mind with that experience; it affected everything in
such an unexpected way; it set my spirit free. I could not
have done this new work (the work for the temple children) if it had not been for the new courage that came with
that break with custom and from bondage to the fear of
man."

Then the father of a young convert, a man of fine character who had allowed his daughter to be with us (sheer
miracle this), hearing of what was going on, sent a message to her to this effect, "If I hear that you have taken off
your jewels I will come for you." Arulai (Star is her name
in other stories) knew that if he took her away he would at
once have her married to a Hindu. Such a life would have
been death to her. It was a tremendous decision that she
made at the foot of the Cross that day. But nothing anyone
could say could shake her. She had seen her Beloved, her
Redeemer. On His brow was a crown not of gold, but of
thorns. His hands and His feet were not jeweled, but
pierced. She had seen Him. Could she follow Him adorned
with gold?

We were to go to camp that night. She and I were
traveling by bullock cart, and her father was to wait by the
roadside and take her home if she was not wearing her

jewels. How slowly that cart crawled, but the minutes ran. Our hearts were tense; we hardly spoke. We lay very close together on the mattress spread in the cart. Would we ever be together again?

A tall form loomed up through the darkness. The cart stopped. A hand was thrust into the cart. "Your father could not come. He sent me," said an old voice. It was Star's grandfather.

"For my father, this parcel," she said, slipping into his hand the little parcel of jewels.

The cart went on. What happened then in the invisible world? We do not know. We only know that something must have happened, for Star was left with us to be our fellow-warrior in the years to come.

So much about so little? It did not seem little to the church. Sermons were preached about it. The vernacular press published articles on the subject, and the district rang from end to end with absurd stories about what we had done—we whose influence it was held was responsible for the deplorable affair. For no one recognized the finger of God in this touch on the women's jewels, and the men whose prestige it affected (the richer the jewels the greater the honor to the family) were exceedingly annoyed.

Straight into the turmoil of these excited feelings came, in February 1899, F.B. Meyer from England. He stayed with us. We told him nothing. Missioners speaking through interpreters are not expected to probe very deep. They preach to appreciative congregations and go away blessed by all. But F.B. Meyer had been struck by the bedecked Christian women of the South. He had also come full upon caste and debt—both prickly subjects—and when he pleaded that the whole burnt-offering might be laid on the altar, he named them explicitly as hindering things, instead of skating round them and giving, what all India loves, "a spiritual address." His words were an offense. His sensitive spirit felt this acutely. Years afterwards he wrote to us that he had been sorely tempted over that series of meetings. And small wonder. He had spoken plain words, and the devil never forgives plainness of speech.

To us who were left to bear the brunt of the blame after this most unpopular mission was over, came a great calm. We saw the road clear before us; the only thing was to go on. Two or three fellow-missionaries and a few Christians were one with us in spirit, and that was cheer. But we learned to go on unaffected by approval or disapproval. For the matter of the jewels was only one of a series of tests and disciplines; and we proved the truth of words that we read much later: "There is always something more in your nature which He wills to mark with the Cross."

It was thus the heavenly Builder laid the foundations of our Fellowship in obedience in very small matters, and that "meeting of His wishes" which does not wait for an explicit command: a wish is enough for one who loves. And because his wisdom chose thus to deal with us, it has seemed right to tell it just as it occurred.

Because of that, yes chiefly because of that, we have told it. But a question comes and will not be quieted: What might it not mean for others if all of us who are seeking after a country of our own, a better Country, that is, a heavenly, lived more like pilgrims here? Those little Indian handfuls of gold turned to golden handfuls of help for a faraway province in China. The Lord to whom all lands lie spread open like a map, and the covered poverty too, perhaps in some little house at our very door, has ways of showing where He needs that precious thing which is wasted now, like the treasure of seed not sown, but only stored.

4.

And when thou com'st thy tale to tell,
Smooth not thy tongue to filèd talk.
—Shakespeare.

Going from city to city, tired and weary, always to meet with sharp opposition and cynicism, and ever new proofs of the vast and hideous oppression, is like running one's breast upon knife points, always beginning afresh before the last wound is healed.

One thing we know, and that is, that all this cruelty and sin, this blinding and misleading of souls, this selfish profligacy, this slaughter of the innocents, this organized vice, this heavy oppression, is hateful in the eyes of the Holy God, and we know that it must perish before the light of His countenance, when the arm of the Lord shall be revealed and when His own arm shall bring salvation. Even out of the depths therefore we will praise Him, and rejoice for the day that is coming.—Josephine Butler.

4. The First Child

Once, out on the rough grass that stretches beyond a noted temple near the sea a thousand or more miles from Dohnavur, we came on a group of women surrounding a five-legged calf. One by one the women were dropping silver coins on the back of the calf. As each coin fell, the little animal shivered. The falling of the coins tickled it; the shiver was merely that, but to the women there was something mysterious in it. So they worshiped, folding their hands and bowing. And the owner of the calf gathered up the coins with a smile, extraordinarily like the enigmatical smile of Mona Lisa.

Farther down on the grass we saw more animals with added limbs; each had its attendant who swept up the silver gains.

Grass, withered and brown, but still innocent grass; air clear and blue; sky cloudless; sea clean and glorious—but behind each little calf we saw a stark and cruel thing: an operation without an anesthetic on two animals, the one from which the limb was cut, the creature on to which it was grafted. The law forbids this operation to be done in public. No one asks where it is done or what is done, if only it be not done in the open street.

And no one asks what has happened to make a normal boy or girl one who will be abnormal, demoniacal. And no one asks where the deed was accomplished or the series of deeds that ends in the forming of character, earthly, sensual, devilish.

In that town, which exists for the temple, there are secret corners. The temple itself is a secret. Once, long ago, someone went up the steps and in through the door which opens on a wide street. He told what he saw. It was never forgiven. Now only worshipers may go up those steps and through that door.

The temple itself is not imposing. It is not like our towered temples of farther south. An immense wall surrounds it; but from what can be seen from without and from photographs taken from adjacent roofs, it appears a squat structure or conglomeration of structures clustered together, and reminds one of nothing so much as the monstrous Indian spider which hangs its web from branch to branch of forest trees, and lies in wait in the middle. The web is strong enough to hold little birds. From such webs our children are disentangled, bright birds and butterflies indeed.*

We would have been as others who see without seeing and never dream of what is being done out of sight if it had not been for what was caused to happen on March 6, 1901. I will tell it briefly, for it has been told before.

Pearleyes, a child of seven, whose father, a thoughtful and scholarly Hindu landowner, had recently died, was allowed by her mother to pay a visit to women of whose occupation that mother knew little. They were servants of

---

* Nothing written here or elsewhere in this book or in any Dohnavur book is told in forgetfulness of the sins of the West. We all live in glass houses. Not one of us can throw stones. And we do not forget what Indian men and women are doing to end the wrongs that still persist. If what we write be read in the spirit which urges the writing, then India's own sons and daughters will be strengthened in their work by a new force of prayer and sympathy.

the gods, women belonging to a temple sacred to Perumal, one of the incarnations of Vishnu, in a village called Great Lake. This meant that each had been "married to the god," and that meant deified sin. In this child they saw one who could be trained to live that life, and they let her see things likely to accustom her to iniquity; and thus, according to the Tamil saying that what is not bent at five will be unbendable at fifty, tried to bend the mind of this child to their purposes.

But Pearleyes recoiled from it all. Perhaps a natural perversity of character had something to do with it; but far more surely a certain purity of spirit and instinctive horror of every false way worked within her, and she fled from the evil house. Her home was in Tuticorin, a town on the southeast coast, two days' journey by cart from Great Lake. How could so young a child go so far alone? It would take much more than two days to walk there. She trudged off bravely. Friendly carters gave her a lift occasionally, and at last that valiant little thing found her mother's house in the big and wicked town, one of the Sodoms of this province; and she flung herself into her mother's arms, sure of safe haven there.

But the temple-women had followed. They threatened the mother with the wrath of the gods. Her husband had been a devout Hindu. He had been famous as a reader and expounder of the religious poetry of his nation. The fear of the gods was upon the mother. She tore her little child's arms from her neck and pushed her back to those women, and they carried her off in triumph.

This decided them to marry her to Perumal as soon as possible, and Pearleyes overheard their conversation and thought that the idiom "tied to the god" meant that she would be tied with ropes to the figure of the idol she had seen in the far recesses of the temple. Terrified, she made up her mind to risk any punishment and tried to escape again.

But she was jealously watched—such children are of

value to their possessors. There were eyes everywhere.

One day—it was a day of terror for that helpless child—she crossed the stone-paved floor of the temple court and, going into the dark inner cell where the idol was set, threw herself down and prayed to Perumal to let her die.

At that time we were in Dohnavur, on the western side of the district, and were about to return to Great Lake, our old center in the east where previously we had been itinerating. We left Dohnavur on March 4, traveling, as was usual then, by night, to escape slow travel through the heat. We arrived at our old house on the 6th. That evening something happened in the temple-house in the village of Great Lake. What happened?

Does the story, so familiar that it has ceased to be fresh and vivid to us, tell what happened there? And behold an angel of the Lord, saying, Arise up quickly. Pearleyes saw no angel, heard no voice, but someone must have touched her and said, Follow me. For she followed, and no one saw her. Down the village street she walked, past the temple walls, and no one stopped her. Across the stream, through a little grove of palms and on to the village beyond she ran, and then stood waiting. There a kindly woman found her, like a lost lamb looking for its fold, and she took her home for the night.

But she dared not have kept her an hour longer. "If you had not come I would have taken her back to the temple-house," she said. "An evil place is the temple-house. It is good that you are back."

The child told us things that darkened the sunlight. It was impossible to forget those things. Wherever we went after that day we were constrained to gather facts about what appeared a great secret traffic in the souls and bodies of young children, and we searched for some way to save them, and could find no way. The helpless little things seemed to slip between our fingers as we stretched out our hands to grasp them, or it was as though a great wave swept up and carried them out to sea. In a kind of desperation, we sought for a way. But we found that we must know more before we could hope to find it. To graze upon the tips (of herbage) is the Tamil expression for superficial knowledge. It we were to do anything for these children it was vain to graze on the tips of facts; it took years to do more than that.

When at last we had learned things of which we were sure, we told them. We could not tell them fully. And why should we? We told what we could and left the rest to intuition and a compassionate imagination.*

The things that we saw haunted us. They are endurable now only because, as time goes on, something is being done towards their ending, and because of the certainty of their utter annihilation at the coming of the King of Righteousness. "With cause that hope sustains thee"—(often the words spoke). "Dagon must fall." And after the children came, we learned to live two lives. The haunted one was pushed far underneath. Gaiety, not spectres, should walk in the children's world. Sometimes we felt as though the things that we had seen and heard had killed forever the laughter in us. But children must have laughter round about them. Some guests to Dohnavur see nothing but the laughter side, the joy of flowers and babies; but a few see deeper, and it is for such this book is written and to such the word will come, "Inasmuch as ye have done it unto the least of these ye have done it unto Me." We discovered

---

* "We dare not do more than allude to the fact that children are brought up and kept in many of the idol temples for the vilest purposes," wrote the Rev. William Pakenham Walsh in 1862. We came upon his little old book in 1910. But in 1927 something more than allusion appeared. *Mother India* and *Slaves of the Gods* tore veils form the face of things. The author of those books had to suffer. She did not care how she suffered if only woman or child could be helped thereby. She did not profess to show India as a whole. Great beautiful fields of Indian life are untouched. She told what is harder to tell, because the one who tells it is misunderstood even by those whom she seeks to serve. Of the heart behind they know nothing. We who love India and yet love truth, we understood.

nothing by asking questions. To ask was to close every
door. To be foreign in dress, food or ways would have
been to lock those doors, the only doors to knowledge. We
learned by quietly sharing as much as we could in the life
of the people, by listening, not by questioning. Ponnamal,
one of the three Indian sisters of those early days, used to
travel with me, and together we stayed in some wayside
shelter, often only a roof on pillars, or with a convert girl
who had married and lived in a temple town. Once we
camped in a cow barn in a city slum, and Ponnamal, who
had never slept on a dirty floor, comforted herself by
remembering Bethlehem. Wherever a mat could be spread
on the ground, there we stayed for as long as we could
stand the noise and glare and heat and smells.

I wrote to missionaries all over the Province, trying to
find some way to reach the children; but no one could tell
me of any way. Some questioned their existence: Government blue-books occasionally alluded to them, but busy
missionaries have no time to read blue-books. We ourselves knew nothing of those books till long after we were
embarked on the work. But there were two who wrote
words of valiant comradeship: one an S.P.G. missionary to
whom had been given a child who would have been sent
to a temple had he not taken her; the other an American
woman who was very deeply moved. But neither she nor
he could suggest anything hopeful. I had one other memorable letter. It was from the daughter of a Government
official. She had saved a child who had grown up to break
her heart, but she was quick with sympathy. Her letter
was a treasure to me. So, a little later, was one from an
L.M.S. veteran. These four letters were all the human cheer
that was granted in those early days. The thing that we
wanted to do appeared to be impossible. It was all disappointment, and never a little one saved. But is it in vain,
says the old Tamil proverb, if the heart of God's servants
burn and smoke? No, it cannot be in vain.

5.

Do you know that lovely fact about the opal? That, in the first place, it is made only of desert dust, sand, silica, and owes its beauty and preciousness to a defect. It is a stone with a broken heart. It is full of minute fissures which admit air, and the air refracts the light. Hence its lovely hues, and that sweet lamp of fire that ever burns at its heart, for the breath of the Lord God is in it.

You are only conscious of the cracks and desert dust, but so He makes His precious opal. We must be broken in ourselves before we can give back the lovely hues of His light, and the lamp in the temple can burn in us and never go out.—Ellice Hopkins.

5. Under the Olive Trees

And now a great urgency was upon us. We thirsted for the strong succor of prayer for the children. We were still itinerating, camping in different parts of the district, seldom for long in one place, learning all we could wherever we went, becoming daily more burdened.

We were camping in Dohnavur,* then a bare, sunburnt spot out on the plains under the mountains to the west, a huddle of huts and small houses round a fairly big, whitewashed church with, beyond low mud walls, an old ramshackle bungalow built of mud bricks and visibly falling to pieces, when two friends, Ella Crossley and Mary Hatch, whose work was at that time a power in Ancoats, Manchester, came to stay with us.

They asked me to tell what I could of things just as they were. There was no time to sit down and write a book—there never has been time for anything so leisured—but they suggested putting together some home letters al-

---

* Rhyme *Doh* with No,
  Rhyme *na* with Ah,
  Rhyme *vur* with poor.
  Ur is the same word as in Ur of the Chaldees, found all over India and meaning city, town, village.

ready written, and so *Things as They Are* began with the
ordinary missionary day of the time before the first little
temple-child came. But it soon reached the place where
words seemed of no use at all.

"What thou seest, write." But how? How write anguish?
It cannot be written. It can only be felt. "Desperate tides of
the whole great world's anguish?" No, not of the whole
world's. Only God could endure that. India's anguish was
enough for one human heart. How draw others in to share
even a pulse-beat of that grief?

On a day when any words that I could find seemed
wholly inadequate, on a page torn from an old exercise-
book something was written down, with no thought of
print:

> Thou shalt have words,
> But at this cost, that thou must first be burned,
> Burned by red embers from a secret fire,
> Scorched by fierce heats and withering winds that sweep
> Through all thy being, carrying thee afar
> From old delights. Doth not the ardent fire
> Consume the mountain's heart before the flow
> Of fervent lava? Wouldst thou easefully,
> As from cool, pleasant fountains, flow in fire?

And so at last words came. But they seemed like words
of straw. To the Mighty One a mere blade of grass is a
weapon—this Tamil proverb became the special word of
the Dohnavur books as each went out. And now that we
are a community, with a single heart and purpose, we
bring each book or booklet, in English or in Tamil, to the
Mighty One before it goes out, and again after it returns to
us from the press and, laying it on the floor in our midst,
we pray,

> Take this book in Thy wounded hand,
>   Jesus, Lord of Calvary,
> Let it go forth at Thy command,
>   Use it as it pleaseth Thee.

Dust of earth, but Thy dust, Lord,
  Blade of grass in Thy hand a sword,
Nothing, nothing unless it be
  Purged and quickened, O Lord, by Thee.

A few years afterwards, Mr. F.R. Hemingway of the Indian Civil Service asked for notes about the facts we had discovered. He had been at first indignant, believing the book (*Things as They Are*) to be untrue. But he was as honest as he was brave, and he began to search for himself, and soon discovered the truth. He became our strong friend, and stood by us to the end. "Let them be as dry as dust," he said, speaking of the notes he wanted—"just the facts." I wrote them down as dustily as I could, but they were terrible reading. He put them before the Governor of the Madras Presidency, who was horrified. He had no idea that such things could happen under the roofs of the city where he lived and of many another city in South India, and in many an innocent-looking country town and village. How end them? He could see no way.

In Bombay and Calcutta reformers were at work, but the subject bristled with difficulties, and action at that time appeared to be impossible. Mr. Hemingway, who had beloved children of his own, could not forget. "Write a Jekyll-and-Hyde story," he said; "this thing must be smashed." Again and again Government asked for information and once a long telegram from Simla demanded it urgently. It was always given, but privately; Government promised not to mention us, lest publicity should make it harder for us to save children. And slowly things began to move; they are still moving. A distinguished Indian woman has of late been chief mover in South India. But we have learned since *Things* was written that something more powerful than the best-framed law is needed. Whatever the law, the rescue of the children must go on in quietness.

We had found that the children in peril belonged to five groups; and, in spite of what has been done to end the

wrong, this is true still, over large tracts of country. For
India is vast, and peopled by many millions. Superficial
writing is folly. To say that an evil is rapidly disappearing
does not make it disappear. But it charms the devil, who is
never so pleased as when he and his doings are under-
rated or ignored.

Children are dedicated to the temple because of a vow,
or in obedience to a family custom, or in order to escape
from some social entanglement caused, for example, by an
out-of-caste alliance. Often a poor widow or a deserted
wife of good family, faced with the impossibility of marry-
ing her child suitably, marries her to the god. Sometimes
lack of money to perform the death ceremonies required
by the caste tempts a mother to part with her child for her
husband's sake. And whenever a caste child is without
protectors, there is danger. In certain parts of India caste is
not considered, but in the South it is.

Everywhere there are men and women on the watch for
these children. The sale of a child is illegal; but money is
not passed in public, and the necessary proof cannot be
obtained. The woman who buys the child calls it her own
daughter, and can easily get witnesses to prove the relationship. We have rarely known a temple-woman to adopt
only one child. Most have several; and there were thousands of temple-women in this single Presidency. It was
(and it is) an overwhelming thought.

But do numbers paralyze sensation? We saw a child of
six one day. She was brought to try to draw our little girl
away from us. She was a gentle thing, with large, soft
brown eyes and the daintiest, prettiest ways. She looked
wistful—not unhappy, only wistful—and there was the
aloofness of one already set apart. We stretched out our
hands to her; she smiled as though across a deep ravine.
We could not go to her. She could not come to us. We
never saw her again; but we heard that she became a very
noted servant of the gods.

There was another. We were not conscious of any space

between us. She sat on my knee, and looked up with smiling eyes. But she disappeared. We found her at last. And now there was a chasm. She shrank away, her little face shadowed by horror and fear. She had been married to the god of the temple of Joyous City, six miles from Dohnavur. They had fastened a garland of pink flowers round her neck, and told her it was her birthday. But under the flowers was a small gold token that meant marriage to the god. A priest touched it in blessing; the soft pink petals were not sweeter than the gentle little face.

It is unbearable. I know it. It feels cruel to tell of it. And yet how can the reader cross the sea and walk in this new road with us without at least some knowledge of the road? I do not want to harrow for harrowing's sake, but I do earnestly desire to draw the heart that can care for a child into fellowship, and hold it fast to the road's end.

People, in their kindness, used to try to distract us from this that could not be forgotten. To be with them, hearing their talk, so clear and friendly, reading their books, looking at their pleasant things, was like being in some clean green field full of blessed flowers. But every now and then the face of the field would fall in and uncover a vault below; and in the vault chains and darkness and the souls of young children.

One night—we cannot forget it because the face of the field peeled off so suddenly, and the vault was so hatefully black—we found ourselves in the presence of one of the men who control this secret traffic. Half animal, half demon, not man at all, he sat, a coiled mass of naked flesh, in a huge armchair, watching us with snakelike eyes, and waiting in silence for us to speak. The window-shutters of that upper room were closed, though the night was hot; the room was full of sickly fumes; a yellow flame flickered in an corner. It was an evil room. We could not speak, but turned defeated and, climbing down the steep and slimy stairs, escaped into the cleaner air of the street. We had heard that he was a great sadhu, this Jeer—lately head priest of a Benares temple—and had hoped that he might be one to whom we could appeal. Such hopes are froth.

But words are froth too; the desolation of the children who had no deliverer, the wrong that we could not redress, the fear, the cold deadness of forced sin, how little of this could be shown then, can be shown now.

At last a day came when the burden grew too heavy for me; and then it was as though the tamarind trees about the house were not tamarind, but olive, and under one of those trees our Lord Jesus knelt, and He knelt alone. And I knew that this was His burden, not mine. It was He who was asking me to share it with Him, not I who was asking Him to share it with me. After that there was only one thing to do: who that saw Him kneeling there could turn away and forget? Who could have done anything but go into the garden and kneel down beside Him under the olive trees?

6.

He comforteth them that are losing patience.—
Ecclesiasticus 17:24.

Will not the end explain
The crossed endeavor, earnest purpose foiled?
The strange bewilderment of good work spoiled,
The clinging weariness, the inward strain,
Will not the end explain?

Meanwhile He comforteth
Them that are losing patience. 'Tis His way:
But none can write the words they hear Him say
For men to read; only they know He saith
Sweet words, and comforteth.

Not that He doth explain
The mystery that baffleth; but a sense
Husheth the quiet heart, that far, far hence
Lieth a field set thick with golden grain
Wetted in seedling days by many a rain:
The end—it will explain.

6. Dead Babies

A few days after that hour under the olive trees, our first baby was brought to us straight from the hands of a temple-woman. She was a little, fragile, creamy-colored thing, like a delicate wax doll. Soon afterwards two more came. The bar that had kept them from us was down at last.

A Swedish pearl-fisher has told of the finding of his first large pearl. "I sat there for hours holding this precious thing as if I were nursing a baby [that's what pearlers call them, babies] and fairly seeing visions." We, too, saw visions—visions of these three grown up. Within a year all three babies died.

Before that, Mr. Walker, who had been home on short furlough, had returned. He had to leave his wife, as she was not well enough to come back so soon, but he brought my mother with him, and she took the little ones into her arms as though they had been her own grandchildren. All will go well now, we thought; but she, who had brought up seven children, was baffled by the delicacy of these tiny infants. It was a different matter when our children's children came—beautiful healthy things—but that joy was years distant then. We did not know till we learned it by sorrowful experience that many of these sent to us had not had a fair chance. The shut-up life of the girl-mother, the sorrow shadowing the child born after its father's death (as these first three had been and others were) heavily handicaps the little life. The distressing death ceremonies, the severe penance meted out so unsparingly to the widow, her own abandonment to grief—these miseries do not make a healthy background for any young life; nor does the still darker shadow of wrong that lay behind some.

And yet, as we try to answer the question, What holds you, Indian and English, so very close together? we count those days among the most binding. "Fear is a cold thing," said my mother one night, when a quick call sent me flying to the nursery and the hot night seemed to shiver. Anxious vigils, the chill of fear, the rain of tears, of such strange things gold cords are made. And they are made of hope, the hope that refuses to despair. We were often tempted to despair. "But what hast thou lacked with me that, behold, thou seekest to go to thine own country? And he answered, Nothing; howbeit let me go in any wise." It was often like that. There was nothing lacking in the love that we folded round the children, but we could not undo what had been done before they came to us, nor could we create suitable food. We had no doctor. No foster-mother would help us in those early days—"It was not the custom"—and there are some children who cannot thrive on any artificial food. One night, in desperation, I went to the Christian quarter of the village at our eastern gates. (On the western side there is another village, it was wholly Hindu then.) It was Christmas Eve, the village church was lighted up and people were carrying palm branches and strings of colored paper for decorations; the birthday of the Child was in everyone's thoughts. In my arms was a sick baby. I held it close and tried to soothe it as I sought for some mother who, for love of that little Child, heaven's gift of love to us, would help this piteous baby whose weak wails smote my heart. But I could not find one. It seemed too sad to take it back uncomforted that Christmas Eve.

And now to the world in general looking on, not unkindly, we appeared to be failing badly. Where were our hopes? Dead with the dead babies, withering with the withering children? We could not give up—it never came into our minds to do so—but we were sometimes sorely tempted to discouragement, and then always what held us in confidence and peace was some word that was given to us and that we kept in the midst of our heart, a word that was life to us and health to all our flesh. *Fear not, little flock, for it is your Father's good pleasure to give you the kingdom,* was one of these words of life and health. When all looked hopeless, we looked back to it: *Remember the word unto Thy servant upon which Thou hast caused me to hope.* A few years later, a sensational lawsuit dragged us into the public gaze and set tongues talking for hundreds of miles all round our quiet, hidden home. Publicity is the worst possible thing for work of this sort. For months afterwards it was harder than ever to save the children. Doors opened after long toil one by one were silently, stealthily shut. Had unseen alert watchers been warned to beware? It seemed so, and as child after child whom we all but had in our arms was spirited away we had moments of keen distress. Then another scripture came, and with great might succored us: *Shall the prey be taken from the mighty, or the lawful captive delivered? But thus saith the Lord, Even the captives of the mighty shall be taken away, and the prey of the terrible shall be delivered: for I will contend with him that contendeth with thee, and I will save thy children.* Who can fathom the consolation of such a word? Earnestly then our hearts answered, *Confirm to Thy servant that promise of Thine.**

And it was confirmed, though it was never easy to find the special child that we exist to save—the child in temple

---

* Psalm 119:38 (Kay).

peril—and as we could not take all who needed care, we had to try to keep to those for whose rescue we were specially commissioned; but more than one baby fold was opened about that time, and many little ones as needy as these of ours were gathered by others into safety.

With the coming of each new child we learned a little more of the private ways of this dreadful underworld of India; but it was a long time before all the secret sources of traffic in the bodies and souls of children were uncovered, and as we penetrated deeper and deeper into the under life of the land, and came upon things that were hateful even to know, we learned what F.H. Meyers meant by fierce and patient purity: "Yea, Lord, I know it, teach me yet anew with what a fierce and patient purity I must confront the horror of the world." We can only touch evil by virtue of the cleansing blood. Nothing but the white fires of God's holiness suffice for such contact. Move out from the full stream of Calvary and you know yourself not only defenseless, but stained.

Once our friend, F.R. Hemingway, keen to give us a little relaxation, and knowing how we cared for books, sent one which was partly a study of the seamy side of life in the West. We could not read it. We had enough to do with such contacts in the ordinary way of duty, and we told him so. He sent us Lanöe Falkoner's lovely little, almost unknown, *Cecilia de Noel* then, and the life of Edward Burne-Jones by his wife, and other good things. Such friends and such books were like cool winds, for they carried us into new air. In the Life of Burne-Jones we came upon an arresting paragraph:

> He spoke of the joy his art had given him, of how he had striven for beauty and good work in it, and had hoped to influence his fellow-creatures in both these directions, but that he had to recognize how small, if not absolutely nothing, his influence had been. It was like a summing up of his whole life (Mr. Hallé writes), and as we sat in the dusk, his white face and the solemnity of his voice gave me a feeling

of awe. I tried once or twice to combat his views, but he would have none of it. Did I not see, he said, that the people who professed the greatest admiration for his work were equally enthusiastic about that whose principles he held in the greatest abomination? To this I had nothing to answer, as I knew it to be true. Such bitter draughts of seeming failure are poured out in all ages for those to whom the work is appointed of carrying on the lasting traditions of the world.

I hardly know why this sentence clung to memory; we had never thought of influencing others in the Burne-Jones sense of the word, and we had not sought their approval—though sympathy, when it came, was such a cheer that the least little word or look was treasured. And our case was different too, for we had no canvases crowded with beauty to offer to anyone—*Not as though I had already attained*, was written in large letters over everything we touched. It is written there still. And yet something in the words made them unforgettable. They struck down to reality.

Perhaps in a sense not in the least understood then, they forecast what we were to find in the days when people would be kind to us and interested, and pleased, and yet not really in sympathy and not truly understanding. To count on such for cooperation was to be disappointed.

It was well to be forewarned. For the work was to develop upon lines that would not find general acceptance, and we had to learn the unchangeable truth: Our Master has never promised us success. He demands obedience. He expects faithfulness. Results are His concern, not ours. And our reputation is a matter of no consequence at all.

It was in truth a fight, and a prayer that we met in later years was ours in spirit then:

> What though I stand with the winners,
>   Or perish with those that fall?
> Only the cowards are sinners,
>   Fighting the fight is all.

Strong is my foe, who advances,
    Snapped is my blade, O Lord;
See their proud banners and lances—
    But spare me the stub of a sword.

DUST

God's walking the blue sky-roads today:
See, how lovely the dust of His feet.
"Clouds of dust," we say down here
As it whirls through our troubled atmosphere
And we walk in the thick of it, but up there,
"The clouds are the dust of His feet," they say.

Do the angels say, when they look at the crowd
And the crush on the roads of this dusty star
As we toil along, nor strong, nor fleet,
And overwhelmed by the secular,
"How lovely the dust of their feet"?

7. He Took a Towel

Near the little jungle village of Dohnavur, in the old wreck of a compound (haunted by flocks of noisy goats) that surrounded the decrepit, three-roomed bungalow, there were four cottages. In these, in the year 1902, the Divinity students of the C.M.S. were to be bestowed, and in that house they were to be taught by one of the finest men the Church Missionary Society has ever sent to India. "Life is either a feast or a fast," was one of his sayings, and for him it was more fast than feast. But A.N.C. Storrs had broken down, and to his friend, Walker of Tinnevelly, was committed the training of those men.

There was no thought then of their staying in Dohnavur for more than a year, but the children had begun to come, and children cannot be carted about. So the Walkers made the place their headquarters, and we continued, to our great comfort, to live with them there. But in this I anticipate. When the first child came, we were, as I have told, together in Great Lake; but when the burden became so heavy that it had to be taken up, as Chapter 5 tells, the Walkers were at home. On their return they came to Dohnavur, and thereafter made it the center of their work.

After the work for the children developed we under-

stood why this special place had been chosen for our
home. It is several miles from the road, and in those days it
was even more inaccessible than it is now, so it was not
only safer for the children than a town would have been, it
was good for us too; for we were free to serve without too
many interruptions. It was healthy (that is, for the tropics); there was no malaria. It was beautiful, too, because of
the mountains to the west of the village. These mountains
were a wonderful help. They were so unchangeably strong
and tranquil and serene that just to look at them strengthened us. Often, caught and tangled in the throng of things,
we used to stop and let their calmness enter into us, and
we prayed that we might serve with "a quiet mind." It was
not a question of choice with us now. If we were to go on
at all, we must have a quiet mind. We had already seen
more than one missionary break down, not because of the
climate or the work, but because of a wearied, fretted
spirit too rushed to dwell in peace. So this prayer was not
for a spiritual luxury but for sheer necessity, and as the
children grew up we taught it to them, and tried to help
them also to serve Him with a quiet mind, so that in all our
rooms there would be peace.

We soon found that everything must go down before
the claims of the children. Everything personal had, of
course, gone down long ago, but now every missionary
call had to be subordinated to these new demands.

And yet, at the beginning, we were often tempted on
this point. The new work seemed poorer than the old. The
district where we had itinerated is twice as large as Wales
and twice as populous, and farther afield opportunities
had begun to open and, apart from the ordinary routine of
mission work, calls had begun to come from many parts of
the Madras Presidency and beyond. Could it be right to
turn from so much that might be of profit (evangelistic
tours, convention meetings for Christians and so on) and
become just nursemaids? "Jesus, knowing that the Father
had given all things into His hands, and that He was come

from God and went to God; He riseth from supper and laid aside His garments; and took a towel and girded Himself." *He took a towel*—the Lord of Glory did that. Is it the bondservant's business to say which work is large and which is small, which unimportant and which worth doing? The question answered itself, and was not asked again. It was a foolish question, for the Master never wastes the servant's time.

Children tie the mother's feet, the Tamils say, and Bishop Paget said, "With the venture of faith there is need of self-discipline and of effort." Babies are truly a venture of faith and, in India at least, they tie the mother's feet. For there are no "Nannies" here, and we had seen enough of the difficulties of some missionaries, who had to use ayahs, to teach us that we could not be too careful of our children's earliest years. So we let our feet be tied for love of Him whose feet were pierced.

Once an I.C.S. friend asked us to join him in camp on the Dohnavur mountains; he had bearers, tents, everything ready, he said. But we could not possibly go. His answer to our letter saying so was a huge hamper of maidenhair fern from that delectable camp. We never found that we lost a friend because of things like this.

And now, because in many places people were moved by the spirit of pity, as the trees of the wood are moved by the wind, and because our fellow-missionaries, especially in one of the cities of South India, cared enough to put the need of these little ones far before their own comfort and ease, a number of children were sent to us, and we were soon so greatly requiring help that I wrote a round-robin to the pastors, asking if they had any women wholly devoted to our Lord and separate in spirit from the world who were likely to be free for such work. "Not only have we no women, but we do not know even one woman of the kind you want," was, in effect, the answer of all. And some added, "This is something contrary to our custom," which was a gentle way of expressing frank disgust. It was true. The care of young children is not among the "honorable" occupations of South India.

Once a widow, who seemed to be the kind we could use, consulted her pastor, but was advised not to offer. "Too demeaning," he said. He did not mean it unkindly. He was, and is, our friend. An elderly widow did venture to come, and we welcomed her with warm hope. But one weekday morning, at the busiest hour, the village church began to ring its bell for some extra service, and she came to me at once. Her face wore its Sunday expression, and she had her Bible and Prayer Book under her arm. Five distracted babies for whom she was responsible were on a mat on the floor at her feet urgently demanding bottles and, because of their lamentations, I could hardly hear what she was saying. I got it at last. "I wish to go and do God's work," she said, and left us forthwith to cope with her five and our own too, and we saw her face no more. "God's work" meant to go to church and to teach or preach. To work with your hands is not "God's work" in this part of the East, even though our Lord Jesus worked with His hands in a workshop for years. "God didn't make you all mouth," we used to say to such a one. She would turn a shocked and sorrowful eye upon us. "All mouth!" It sounded irreligious, almost blasphemous.

One day, and I happened to be in the middle of writing one of these nursery pages, I turned to watch a baby play on the floor of my room. In his hands, held out straight in front of him as though he wanted all the world to look, was the small grey quarterly, published by the Officers' Christian Union, with its name, *Practical Christianity*, printed in large letters on its face. The boy was smiling that superb smile of the pleased baby. Practical Christianity had his complete approval.

I suppose such a thing existed somewhere at the date of this chapter, but it was very hard to find if, combined with it, what is usually called the spiritual were wanted too. (Not that we recognize the distinction, any more than the

Officers' Christian Union does.) And so, because we wanted our children to be taught other-worldly ways from their cradles, we were short-handed. And yet we had often to spare someone from the nurseries, for, now that we were on the track, the journeys to save the little ones in danger grew more and more frequent. There were no motors then to make travel quicker and easier, and sometimes the difficulties were increased by passport regulations in districts where plague was raging. Once a confused telegram told of the little party in quarantine, and no way of getting suitable food for two poor babies (did the agitated senders of that telegram look for bottles of milk by wire?) and it told, too, of language complications, for no one there knew Tamil. But both those babies survived, and have grown up to be fellow-workers. It was worth that journey, with all its vicissitudes, to save them. Floods, great heat, crowded trains when a festival was being held somewhere—and in South India there is at least one important festival every month—all these and many other difficulties have to be endured or overcome in such a work. And the sleepless care required is something any mother will understand. Sometimes there were temple scouts in the train. Many a time large sums have been covertly offered for a little child on her way to us. "You can say that it died, and that you had to get it buried on the way."

But we learned to watch for loving providences, and never once were any of us hindered by accident, or overtaken by pursuers after a child whose guardian, drawn by some large offer of money, had changed his mind. Nor did any of the threatened court cases, which at first were frequent, prosper. We always got, if possible, a paper signed by the child's guardian before we took it; but sometimes to press for that would have been (and would be still) to risk losing the little one. And in any case the paper was worthless in a court of law, except to prove our *bona fides*.

It was about this time that a word was given which was

to become, like *Gold, silver, precious stones* and *Except a corn of wheat fall into the ground and die*, part of our spiritual treasure.

It came in this way. A friend, upon whose understanding comradeship and sympathy I had counted very much, did not feel able to give either. Someone more suitable should do this special work, she said. How natural that was, and how true, for I knew that I was not suitable.

But no one else was free to do it—"I tell you that, if these should hold their peace, the stones would immediately cry out." How strangely Bible phrases come sometimes, rising unbidden, unexplained, perhaps apparently irrelevant, but somehow they still the soul.

But fear can hamstring the soul. And presently fear crept up, and a devastating sense of unfitness and insufficiency, and I saw our tiny company strung out like a little row of noughts on a sheet of paper. But "Thou art worth ten thousand of us"—an inadequate comparison, fitting the earthly David, bathos as applied to the Lion of the tribe of Judah, and yet it carried truth. What did it matter if we were noughts? It was for the Lord our God to write the figure to head that row of noughts. He Himself was the Figure. And we saw our calling, how that we were truly of no account ("like to a shell dishabited") that no flesh should glory in His presence.

Nothing anyone thought of us could reach lower down than that, no one could ever count us less than we were. But he that is down need fear no fall. He that is down cannot get between God and His glory. And we knew then that there was nothing that He could not do through us if only we were nothing.

It was then that a prayer came that we have often used since in our Fellowship life,

> Oh, we're too high, Lord Jesus, we implore Thee,
>   Make of us something like the low green moss
> That vaunteth not, a quiet thing before Thee,
>   Cool for Thy feet, sore wounded on the Cross.

And it was then, too, that those fathomless words became our very own: "God hath chosen the foolish things of the world to confound the wise; and God hath chosen the weak things of the world to confound the things which are mighty; and base things of the world, and things which are despised, hath God chosen, *yea, and things which are not*, to bring to nought things that are: that no flesh should glory in His presence."

8

(Brother Aymon and Brother John are talking over the future of the Franciscan Order. Aymon believes that compromise will lead to larger influence. John, that if this way were followed the sons of Francis would, as time passed, become a new monastic order, conformed to set tradition, living on easy terms with the unchallenged way of the world. With such orders the world has no quarrel.)

But in the gospel of Francis and, John believed, in the gospel of Christ, there was a different element: an element so disturbing that the world would forever reject it but never forget it; that the Church would waver forever between patronage and persecution.

"Yours is the present, Father, for the world will only ridicule us—or crucify; nor have we the visible power for good that you will have. But I think the future is ours. And Lady Poverty shall welcome us all to her mountain."

To Aymon's question about the future of the world, John stammered, wilting a little: "I think the Church and the world will be one."

Aymon's patience was exhausted. He spoke with sharp authority: "Come down from that mountain."

And, as to Father Philip when first he became a novice, John repeated, "I have heard another voice."—*Brother John*, Vida D. Scudder.

There are some who would have Christ cheap. They would have Him without the cross. But the price will not come down.—Samuel Rutherford.

8. Come Down From That Mountain

And yet, all through this time of death and dearth and difficulty, the conviction that we were in the way and that our Lord was leading us became more and more certain, and nothing could shake it.

I cannot help connecting this with something that happened on the day the last of the first three babies died. When she left us, and I gathered her little things together and folded them up to put them away, it seemed as though I were folding up all my hopes. But, standing there in the courtyard of that first nursery, in the twilight, with the small white things in my hands, I stopped, arrested by the near sense of that Presence that is never far; and the Presence shone in the dimness and there were words I could understand. And I knew that we were to keep that date month by month thereafter, as a day of prayer for all the imperiled children of India wherever they be.

The day was January 6, 1905. We forgot, at the moment, that the sixth of the month was the date of the deliverance of our first little girl, Pearleyes. We may forget dates: God does not. That date has been observed by us ever since, and by all who stand with us in the battle for the children. When Satan heard, or read, or in some other way became familiar with the ninety-first psalm, did the fourth verse baffle him? "He shall cover thee with His feathers and under His wings shalt thou trust"—"With His feathers shall He create a fence for thee," is Kay's rendering of that music. And all that had been so strong to discourage and even to trample out of existence that little faint beginning was "turned to the contrary." (Often since the days of Esther that word has found similar delightful illustration.) So covered, and so fenced, what could his malice accomplish against us? Nothing, nothing at all.

We soon learned why fasting is so often associated with prayer ("Food may hinder the spirit in its battle with the powers of darkness," perhaps because it is sometimes so interrupting) and we found a way to plan so that, if there were the desire, it might be followed without fuss or comment. But we never made any rules for ourselves, nor did we follow the rules of others. We found our Lord's enough; and often then, and since, the word for a day that we had meant to spend apart has been, "Is not this the fast that I have chosen? To loose the bands of wickedness, to undo the heavy burdens and to let the oppressed go free and that ye break every yoke?" Where there are little children and the sick and sorrowful to help, this is often the word.

One of the earliest lessons we learned together was that before asking for anything we should find out if it were according to the mind of the Lord. The kind of prayer that is a pouring out of the heart is different. This, that was definite petition, intercession, needed preparation of a special kind. It needed time—time to listen, to understand, to "wait," as the word is so often in the Psalms. For "this is the confidence that we have in Him that *if we ask anything according to His will He heareth us*: and if we know that He hear us whatsoever we ask, *we know that we have* the petitions that we desired of Him." The more we pondered over all that is said about prayer in the only book in the world that can speak with authority about it, the more we found to make us ask to be filled with the knowledge of

His will before offering petitions for a desired good. When we were in doubt about His will (as we often were and are) and had not liberty to ask for a clear sign, there was the prayer of prayers ready framed for us: Thy will be done, whatever that will may be. But when we are meant to know our Lord's wishes, we must be shown what they are before we can lay our prayer alongside, and often our first prayer was for spiritual understanding and direction in prayer:

> That which I know not teach Thou me.
> Who, blessed Lord, teacheth like Thee?
> Lead my desires that they may be
>   According to Thy will.
>
> Kindle my thoughts that they may glow,
> And lift them up where they are low,
> And freshen them, that they may flow
>   According to Thy will.

We did not know Julian, the dear Anchoress of Norwich, then; but later we knew her, and found this that we were learning had been written down by her five hundred years before: "I am the Ground of thy beseeching," she wrote, as she believed the words came to her from her Lord Himself. "First it is My will that thou have it; and after I make thee to will it; and after, I make thee beseech it; and thou beseechest it. How should it then be that thou shouldst not have thy beseeching?"

Our first "beseeching" after the children came is as distinct now as it was on the day it was framed. The thought came to make a little place for our Lord Jesus where He could walk about ungrieved. So we asked Him if we might do this, and with it in mind we tried to make our field into a garden and to fill it full of clearness and love, so that when He turned in at our gate He would feel at home with us. How good it would be, we used to say one to another, to be a little green place for Him here on the hot plain.

Up till about this time "we" has meant a few Indian sisters and one who did not feel foreign but, indeed, related to them. We would gladly have continued as we were, adding from time to time to our number from the women of India, but we could not find any prepared to come. So we began to look towards England. Of late years many have asked if we definitely thought out the Fellowship and, as it were, made it. No, we did not. It was simpler than that. We were shown what to ask. We saw a pattern, that was all; anyone might have seen it, many have seen it. I write of it only because some have wanted to know how it came to be.

First, then, the spiritual substance of all that we saw was loyalty. David's mighty men, who broke through the hosts of the Philistines and drew water from the well of Bethlehem because David longed for it, told us what to ask.

And as we went on thinking over this, we knew that such loyalty meant everything that heart could ever wish. To love our Captain so makes for a perfect comradeship. "And the three brake through": they knew that they could count upon one another without reserve to the end. We had learned already that unhindered prayer together was not just expedient but vital, and nothing kills that kind of prayer so swiftly as even the lightest flicker of uncertainty in one about another. Perhaps that was why we were first shown the crystal quality of loyalty, for our prayer-life together was to become the chief thing with us all. And it meant depth of conviction about certain matters, and singleness of mind, the opposite of a scattered life which effects nothing: "Better plough deep than wide," the Tamil says. It meant peacefulness, too, and something that Buchan in one of his stories calls an "immortal lightheartedness." And this was worth having; for though India can teach us patience, she does not know the secret of a spontaneous gaiety for which nothing in the circumstances that surround the man or woman in whom these bright fountains rise can possibly account. And when she sees it, she is sometimes drawn to ask whence the springs flow which feed those fountains.

With the freshness of young leaves and buds these thoughts opened during those spring days of life in India, and we saw how beautiful the pattern was, and how reasonable. And now, after sultry years, there is no fading in that freshness. We have not found this that was shown easy to follow. It often appears to us that there is nothing except our private walk with God which is more detested and assaulted by the devil than just this beautiful happy thing, the loyalty that is the basic quality of vital unity.* As to others, we made one careful rule: the absent must be safe with us. Criticism, therefore, was taboo. I could not forget the first time when, as a missionary (not expecting to meet it), this snake crossed my path. It was by the sea, on a grey morning after storm, while the waves were still sullen and fell on the shore with a heavy thud, without life and without resilience. Just so these words fell upon me that day. Many years later, a week or two after the little book called *But* went out from the Dohnavur Fellowship, *Blackwood's Magazine* brought us this (Farmer is writing about Dr. Johnson): "I can excuse his dogmatism and his prejudices; but he throws about rather too much of what some Frenchmen call 'The Essence of But.' In plain English, he seems to have something to except in every man's character." And a recent *Punch*: "Do you know that girl?" "Only to talk about." The Essence of *But* is distilled death: it carries the chill of death. I remember, that day by the seashore, wondering if, in the New Testament sense, love, fervent, stretched out, "growing and glowing," was to be found anywhere on earth. And yet what other way of life

---

* The words "vital unity" are from Westcott's note on St. John 17:22. This unity, he says, is something far more than a mere moral unity of purpose, feeling, affection; it is in some mysterious mode which we cannot distinctly apprehend, a vital unity.

could satisfy the heart that was set on living in the ungrieved presence of its Lord? The very thought of Him shames unkindness. It cannot abide before His clear countenance. He held His friends to the highest. Love that does this is love indeed. Lord, evermore give us this love.

It is easy to write of the pattern now; it was not easy to hold to it then, when we had no one to help us. But one day, when the pressure to change it a little was very insistent, a memory glanced, like light on steel, upon a word spoken by Hudson Taylor in a quiet room in Keswick, in talk with Robert Wilson, Convener of the Convention, who had just been reading from the letter of the secretary of a missionary society. The secretary thought that his society "would not refuse" an offer from a man who believed what was taught at the Convention. "I think we would put it differently," Hudson Taylor said, in his unpretentious way. That year the teaching had gone deep. This shows it:

> But all through life I see a Cross,
> Where sons of God yield up their breath:
> There is no gain except by loss,
> There is no life except by death,
> And no full vision but by Faith
> Nor glory but by bearing shame,
> Nor Justice but by taking blame;
> And that Eternal Passion saith,
> "Be emptied of glory and right and name."

Be emptied of glory and right and name. Men whose hearts rose with a bound to the clarion call of such words—these, and these only, were the men Hudson Taylor wanted and, God helping him, was determined to have. And the friends understood each other. The shining head of the older man bent in grave acquiescence and his keen blue eyes smiled. He, too, would have "put it differently."

We were wanting what Hudson Taylor wanted. Years afterwards, when the second volume of his life was published, we found it all there. And we put whole paragraphs in the Notes that we were preparing for those who wished to offer to the Fellowship. Still later, in H. Maynard Smith's *Frank Bishop of Zanzibar*, we found the same word, though set in a different frame: "It is not the language of compromise which grips a man's soul and inspires a faith which can remove mountains." "For him there was only one way of service—it was the way of the Incarnation—a man must make himself one with those whom he wished to serve."

All this, said David about the building of the Temple, have I been made to understand in writing from the hand of the Lord. As though in writing that the passing of the years made plainer, this was the pattern that was shown to us on the Mount. "Come down from that mountain," cried the voices about us. Sometimes they spoke with sharp authority. But, like Brother John, how could we? We had heard another voice.

9.

O Lord, my heart is all a prayer,
　　But it is silent unto Thee;
I am too tired to look for words,
　　I rest upon Thy sympathy
To understand when I am dumb;
　　And well I know Thou hearest me.

I know Thou hearest me because
　　A quiet peace comes down to me,
And fills the places where before
　　Weak thoughts were wandering wearily;
And deep within me it is calm,
　　Though waves are tossing outwardly.

Patience and comfort—words whose common use falls far short of their Biblical meaning. For in Scripture "Patience" is the patience which travels on and labors on, and "Comfort" is the comfort which not only consoles, but animates and empowers.—Bishop Moule.

Day unto day, Lord, speaketh in light,
And in the darkness night unto night;
Never a dark but somewhere a song
Singeth the whole night long.

Oh precious things put forth by the moon—
Let not the heat and hurry of noon
Silence the silver song that I heard.
Stifle the low sweet word.

9. Racing Winds and a Small Nest

On the other side of the hills in South Travancore, a day and a half distant by bullock-cart journey, is the London Missionary Society's medical mission, Neyyoor. The thought came to open a nursery there to which we could send the more delicate babies. And the doctors made this possible. It was the first of countless helps that we were to receive from the staff of that hospital and from other medical missions. The Lord of Compassion will not forget them when He says "Inasmuch."

The road to Neyyoor is sometimes unsafe for carts; as the little party journeyed in charge of Ponnamal on that September day in 1905, a hurricane tore across the plain. Many carts were overturned, among them were our three. Nurses and babies were flung out in frightened, bruised heaps, and all breakable things were smashed, such as the earthen vessels filled with boiled water for the babies' food. But no limbs were broken, and not quite all the water was spilled.

From that time on, these journeys were frequent—we came to know every slow mile of the road; but it was not love's labor lost. The lives of many of our children were saved by the tireless kindness of the always kind staff of that hospital.

The year that followed is memorable because of the terrible cholera which called all of us who could do anything to the villages about Dohnavur. Night after night we were in the little stricken huts, day after day, too, but none of the new cures was known then (later we thankfully used them and saved many), and what cholera can be no one can begin to understand who has not fought it alone, without a doctor and without modern weapons. When permanganate of potash was first prescribed, we found it valuable in prevention; we used to persuade a group of families, from grandparents to babies, to drink quantities of what they called "red medicine" (weak Condy's fluid). They took to it (the color helped, I think), and by this simple means numbers were protected.

Year after year cholera prowls round us, but it has never been allowed to enter our gates. During an epidemic we are constantly among the people, and in the earlier years, when we had no help, we often had to come straight back to our children, stopping only to change our clothes. But all were kept safe, and that year (1906) a work began among us which was like the fall of dew on grass. And soon came the first of these sunset hours that have been so often repeated that the years are starred with them, an hour when the very air and the colors and shapes of the mountains, and the quiet palms, and the birds flying home over the water, seem to be glad with us: a baptism evening by the side of one of the shallow sheets of water that make our countryside so beautiful after rain.

The first evening, early in 1907, saw a little group of six confess their Redeemer, and behind the calm, bright water, more present in a sense than even the hills whose shore that water washed, we saw the striped walls of the temples. There are joys that are unearthly in their power and in their sweetness. None of us who have shared them can talk much about them. Music can express them, words cannot. Is music part of the language of heaven?

But never once have we had such an evening without a

burst of trouble following. After these things—the singers had sung and the trumpeters sounded, the king had rejoiced and the people had kept the feast with gladness—after these things and the establishment thereof, Sennacherib, King of Assyria, came and encamped against the fenced cities and thought to win them for himself; we have learned to prepare beforehand for the coming of Sennacherib. Immediately after that baptism evening, a deadly kind of dysentery broke out in one of the nurseries in Neyyoor. For five days I heard nothing (I was ill, and was ordered home, and had to go to the hills) for Ponnamal's first letter telling of it was lost; it was found later, torn up and thrown on the road. At last her second letter arrived, a short, bewildered note. Sixteen babies were ill, more were sickening. Next day came news of deaths, one following the other so quickly that the little graves were sometimes dug to hold two. Letters took three or four days to reach us. Distance seems immense at such times. Ponnamal wired daily then, to relieve the tension. One seemed to live from telegram to telegram.

The news came from Dohnavur of serious illness there. By this time an English girl who had some training as a nurse had come out, but she was unequal to the strain. And then came the worst news of all. Mr. Walker who, with his wife, was carrying on in Dohnavur, wrote in grief of what appeared to be a triumph of the enemy. The sorrow about the ill and dying babies paled before that: sin is worse than illness and death.

But we were not forsaken. Ponnamal's faith rose through those anxious weeks, and she kept all going quietly in her part of the work, inspiring her fellow-workers with her own beautiful courage. One of the little household was converted, and a servant we had engaged there became so bound to us by grief and love that nothing could ever loosen those bonds. He has been the means of saving many children since then, from the temples and drama, and still continues to seek and save them. "All is windy about us now," Ponnamal wrote from the midst of the trial. "But the wind will not last always. The waves beat into our boat; but when the Lord says, Peace, be still, they will lie down. Let all your prayer for us be that we may rest in the will of God while the wind lasts." And when one very dear child passed on, "My little heart's joy, my own little jewel-of-the-eye has gone. But Jesus stays with me."

If only we had had another Ponnamal or an English woman able to take charge of another nursery, the over-crowding which had led to the rapid spread of infection would have been avoided. But we had not another Ponnamal nor had we anyone else able for so difficult a work. Should we have refused the babies and sent them back to the temples? No; that was unthinkable. Should we have waived the matter of gold, silver, precious stones for a while and, because of the pressure upon us, been contented with something different? But a constraint had been laid upon us. We could not have done that, could not do it now.

In a difficult seaway there may be not only the tall light-house with its great white light, but also the little, low-down (perhaps), colored lights that are fastened to the buoys that mark the one safe way. And so it seems to me that often we are given not only the pure light of revelation, the light which must always be high above all others, but also the smaller lights of the buoys. And these lights are very good gifts. They may be colored by personality, but if they help to show us how to steer our boat, we give thanks for them. And they are often books of the kind that are not mere paper and printers' ink, but force—wind and fire and dew. Such a book came our way just then; it was Arthur Nash's translation of the *Spiritual Letters of Père Didon*.

"The roads are rugged," he wrote, "the precipices are steep; there may be a feeling of dizziness on the heights, gusts of wind, peals of thunder, nights of awful gloom—fear them not. There are also the joys of the sunlight, flowers such as are not in the plain, the purest of air, restful nooks; and the stars smile thence like the eyes of

God." And this came in a letter from a warrior friend at home, "Faith has nothing to do with circumstances. It deals entirely with the word of God. Faith does not feed upon the experiences of others, though these may be a stimulus; its food is the promises of God."

No, we were not asking for too much when we prayed for English women ready, and more than ready—eager, joyfully eager—to do "anything, anywhere, anywhen" for love of their Lord. The future was going to ask for more than we were asking now. There would certainly be incommunicable joy; but there would also be prolonged conflict. Would one whose nature clung to a safe and comfortable walk on the beaten track, the approval of onlookers who disapprove of anything off such tracks, ever survive, much less be happy in our rocky life? *How can she who cannot bear to bathe in tepid water ascend the funeral pyre?* asks the Tamil. "If thou hast run with the footmen and they have wearied thee, then how canst thou contend with horses?" is the Hebrew form of the same question. So Père Didon's *Letters* fitted the time: here was one who understood. "I do not want people who come to me under certain reservations. In battle you want soldiers who fear nothing." He wanted to prove to Christ in this icy-cold age that there are still hearts conquered by His beauty (and did we not want to do that, too?). He asked for all: "Nothing but a burning sanctity will convert this unbelieving generation." Was it strange that such a purpose was challenged? Prison silenced Didon's voice. Were we ready, we were forced to ask ourselves, for whatever was to be the answer to our prayer? And we then began definitely to pray that there might be all possible dissuasions on the home side and every variety of test to those who offered to us. We knew nothing then of the boys in peril, so our thought was only of women, and we prayed that anyone who could be kept back would be kept back. We even found ourselves asking that every belittling story that could shake courage or desire might be told to such a one—

anything rather than to have one who was not meant for us.

The Neyyoor epidemic did not end the batterings of the months; for sharpness of distress what now befell us has been equaled (and surpassed) only once since. Some whom we trusted snapped, and the staff we had leaned upon splintered and pierced our hand. A band of evil men (Christians in name, and therefore the more deceptive) all but wrecked everything by trying to injure the young convert girls who were helping Ponnamal. In Dohnavur a bright young woman, herself snatched like a brand from the fire, was involved in a coil of trouble and, though clear of wrong, she became disheartened and useless in the Kingdom of God; and when there are few, each one counts. Then a willing and unselfish English girl, the first who came to help us, became engaged to a fellow-missionary, who had won her affections on board ship. "It feels as though it should cost more than an anna to take this letter" (the letter written to him), she said as she weighed it in her hand before posting it. It felt like that to me too. Another girl for whom we had waited hopefully drew back when she understood how unromantic our life really was.

Were we surprised at the form in which the answer to so many prayers had come? I hardly know. But I do know that stronger far than the depression of an enveloping and almost conquering physical weariness, which about this time did seriously threaten to undo us, came the sense of a spiritual uplift; we cannot be vanquished if the Lord of Hosts be with us. We follow an undefeated Leader; with cause this truth sustained us then, has often sustained us since.* So, "standing fast in one spirit, with one soul joining for the combat" (as Rotherham renders Phil. 1:27), we went on.

---

* Reminiscent of a passage in *Samson Agonistes* continually with us through those months:
> "This only hope relieves me, that the strife
> With me hath end; all the contest is now
> 'Twixt God and Dagon;—
> Dagon must stoop." . . .

"With cause this hope relieves thee."

That word covers those first six years. That wonderful knitting of spirit which makes of several people one single soul had been given to us from the first. So we were joined for the combat. There is joy in such combat, though there is horror too.

There was horror—stark horror—many a time. What we were learning was new to us, though it was old as time. Students of history know it, and have told of it. We had not read, or if we had read we had not understood what they said. Now we understood. We knew that many a man returned from his worship in some noted temple a more debased man than he was when he went, and we knew that for many a woman that high, carved door was the open door to hell. Once a girl entangled against her will escaped. She found her way to a woman with a feeling heart, who sheltered her. She told what she had seen, but she was half maddened by it all, and she never recovered her sanity. No Hindu husband who is careful of the purity of his wife's mind will suffer her even to know what may happen within those walls.

To touch all this was to touch Sin in the raw. It was to touch something alive, responsive, resentful. We were caused to feel that resentment. Once, on a day of tragic failure to save a child, we found immense comfort in Samson's

> Dagon hath presumed
> Me overthrown, to enter lists with God.

Me overthrown; we were not the first who had been overthrown. But, as the poem says elsewhere, all wickedness is weakness. Dagon must stoop,

> For God,
> Nothing more certain, will not long defer
> To vindicate the glory of His name
> Against all competition, nor will long
> Endure it doubtful whether God be Lord
> Or Dagon.

What great words they are, kindling like the sight of old banners in a church or the sound of marching music. And they are needed still, for Dagon is still upon his throne. The Power that planned these labyrinthine corridors and halls, the Power these great structures represent, fought then, and still fights every inch of the ground with us.

Subterranean attempts to wreck the work became more and more deadly about that time; there were alarms and perplexities, now left far behind, and no way of getting advice, for there was no precedent to follow: no one had been this way before—we had crossed an invisible frontier into an unknown land.

But in that land we met our Lord and learned to know Him. "Thou hast dealt well with Thy servant, O Lord, according to Thy word"—that old glad affirmation covers all those years. He never let us lose our way, He filled our cup with sweetness, and for the handful of dust that we offered Him He poured the very gold of heaven into our hearts.

There were little, private, tender refreshings too, infantile things that would have been nothing to the great and strong, but which to us were like a mother's reassuring touch. "Many there be which say of my soul, there is no help for him in God"; there was a day when some did say so, for they saw nothing but folly in what we were attempting—"But Thou, O Lord, art a shield for me," was our comfort then, and "I laid me down and slept." And that night there was a thunderstorm, and, wakening suddenly, or in the moment before wakening, one who was but a child at heart saw like a picture this: a tossed sky, black clouds flying wildly, chased by racing winds; and then the appearance of a hand that seemed to come from among the inky clouds, and in the hand a wild bird's nest, and in the nest three blue eggs. With the swiftness of a dream it came and was gone. But it did not fade like a dream.

"My flesh and my heart faileth"—let them fail. For "God is the strength of my heart and my portion for ever." Has anyone ever been able to tell what our glorious Lord can be to man, woman, or little child whom He is training to wait upon Him only?

No one has ever been able to tell it. I search for words like jewels, or stars, or flowers, but I cannot find them. I wish I could, for this book may fall into the hands of someone who has been hindered from caring to know Him by the dull and formal trapping which our dull and formal thoughts have laid upon Him—strange disguise for such a radiance. How can I commend my Master? I have not seen Him yet, but I have caught glimpses. Human soul meets human soul, exploring feelers move out cautiously, albeit unconsciously, perhaps to draw back uncertain; it is better that there should be a little film of distance held between. But sometimes it is not like that. The warning instinct is not there. Instead there is a lovely freedom. Each is at home in the other's rooms. There is a joy in that sense of sureness, in understanding and in being understood. There is joy in the recognition of that which makes it safe to trust to the utmost of the utmost. What makes it so? It is the golden quality of love perfected in strength. That gold is Christ. Or some sharp test takes that friend unawares. You see the life reel under shattering blows; perhaps you see it broken. And you look almost in fear. Thus suddenly discovered, what will appear? And no base metal shows, not even the lesser silver, but only veins and veins of gold. That gold is Christ.

Without Him, Lover of all lovers, life is dust. With Him it is like the rivers that run among the hills, fulfilled with perpetual surprises. He who knows his Lord as Saviour and King is taken, as old Richard Rolle declares, into a marvelous mirth, so that he as it were sings his prayers without notes. Life is battle—yes, but it is music. It knows the thrill of brave music, the depths and heights of music. It is *life*, not stagnation. Oh, taste and see that the Lord is good. Blessed (happy, very happy) is the man that trusteth in Him.

10.

Hast thou no scar?
No hidden scar on foot, or side, or hand?
I hear thee sung as mighty in the land,
I hear them hail thy bright ascendant star,
Hast thou no scar?

Hast thou no wound?
Yet I was wounded by the archers, spent,
Leaned Me against a tree to die; and rent
By ravening beasts that compassed me, I swooned:
Hast thou no wound?

No wound? No scar?
Yet, as the Master shall the servant be,
And piercèd are the feet that follow Me;
But thine are whole: can he have followed far
Who has nor wound nor scar?

10. Scars in the Rock

On November 15, 1907, Mabel Wade joined us. She was a trained nurse from Yorkshire, and she had about her something of her own moors, with their transparent air and the beauty of heather. "Have I been here for only one day?" she said, as we came back to the house after our first talk together. So have other gifts of God said, after perhaps a short hour or two with us. "It is as if I had found my spirit's home," said one. Unity, like prayer, like life, may be compared to a musical chord, and I think it must be that our God, who knows beforehand whom He has chosen for us, tempers and tunes us the one to the other long before we meet in the flesh. Constantly we are astonished at the lovely commingling of the very various notes that make up our chord. It must be of Him.

And now we built a new nursery, and in 1908 recalled the Neyyoor infants. The nurse instinct in Mabel Wade, accustomed to leave responsibilities to doctors, was tried in those days, when we had only medical books to guide us; for children never do keep inside the pages of a book, and a young convert girl—the Brownie we call her in the story *From the Forest*—died suddenly of heart disease. It was the nurse's first experience of death without a doctor.

It came to her with a sense of shock that we had nothing to
do when a person died but bury her: there were no formalities of any sort. Life was simple then. It is gradually
becoming a little more complex than it was when both
arrivals and departures were effected without official fuss.

By this time Mrs. Walker was back in India, and the
middle-aged babies, who soon began to be called "tedlets"
because they were so comically like teddy-bears, had won
her heart. She and her husband too had been troubled
about the very firm tying of our feet; but upon Mr.
Walker's return he had written to Indian converts who
knew the underworld of India, and after he had read the
ghastly letters that came in reply, he ceased to doubt. It
was more than worthwhile to turn from all else, he felt,
and save the children. And now that the babies were beginning to grow old enough for school, he and we prayed
for a trained Indian teacher, an evangelist at heart, for it is
God's truth that one loving spirit sets others on fire.

And a teacher was offered to us who appeared to be all
that we wanted, and the hardest thing we had to do that
year was to return her to the one who had so kindly sent
her to us. Another came, but we could not use her either,
and we had to close the kindergarten. Looking back, I
think of our apparent ingratitude to the friends who were
so good as to try to help us as quite the most painful part
of the matter: we seemed to be so deplorably fastidious
that we could only wonder they went on being friends
with us, as indeed they did. But it was as though something in the place acted as touchstone and declared what
was, as apart from what seemed to be, in these whom we
would so gladly have used because we needed them so
much. In each case truth was the rock upon which they
foundered. If our children were to grow up truthful they
must be taught by those who had a regard for truth; and
not just a casual regard, a *delicate* regard. On this point we
were adamant.

It was then we began to know that we were committed

to things that we must not expect everyone to understand. It would not be fair to expect it. And we learned that to cling to a creature is to "fall with the sliding creature." Our story may find its way to someone who must do what may seem foolish ("narrow-minded" is the usual adjective). It is well to know that when the devil finds that his fiery darts fall harmless, sometimes he plucks from his quiver the light-feathered arrow of a smile. But the only way of peace is to go on quietly, so we went on, and tried to obey our light.

That light, like the headlights of a car, threw a steady beam far down the road, and showed what lay ahead with an unescapable distinctness. Hardness lay ahead. The child in the family, whether Hindu or Christian, has natural shelters provided. No love of ours could make up for these. So we were forced to be more than ordinarily careful about the foundations of character. And we wanted those foundations to be laid in truth. One day, about that time, a guest who afterwards became a beloved fellow-worker, gathered the children together and told them a fairy story, and then we discovered (I had hardly realized it before) that I had instinctively left those tales, and had begun with the far more magical true fairy stories that were strewn about everywhere just waiting to be told.

And we saw no reason to change. It was good, when the amazed child asked, "Mé thān ā?" (Is it true indeed?), to be able to answer "Mé thān" (True indeed), and those true fairy tales were so wonderful and so beautiful that I do not think our little lovables lost anything of the silvery glamour that should make the first years of childhood like moonlit water to look back upon, or the golden sparkle either, that is sunlight on that same water.

For several years, until better help came, we carried on ourselves in a simple way, not great enough to dignify by the name School. Mabel Wade was immersed in Tamil, and later in nursing, or she would have been a great ally (somehow she managed to make time for singing, and a delightful musical drill) and after a while indoors we used to go out into the garden. It was Wonderland to the children. We never suggested questions and never answered any that they did not ask (we had as much as we could do to find answers to those they did ask) but we, as it were, ran to meet their minds in welcome. It was a merry kind of schooling, and left many gaps, but it had some uses. Color was one of the chief wonders. The dancing, sparkling, chattering things would stand silent before "the pure enchantment of a rose." How did the color come? The microscope showed them why leaves looked green. The view of rolling, emerald balls in oblong, crystal cells was an exciting discovery, though "How they come and how they go, does anybody know?" as their song said.

For songs began to be needed about that time. It had seemed well to teach them English, and we were given English song books full of the prettiest things; but the matter was too foreign for young Indian children, just as the stuff of which our Indian songs were made would have been foreign to English children. So we had to make our own, and they came of themselves, as they were needed.

Games were a great feature. When the children were a little older the delightful rotifer they saw through the microscope whirling his fairy wheels in a drop of water suggested possibilities: there is a large, deep well in the garden, so why not *be* rotifers? Into it, then, they plunged (they had already learned to swim) and, treading water, they circled about waving twinkling fingers above their heads for cilia, patting their little loricas and walking delicately on their toes, supposed to be sticky like the rotifer's.

We had different types, eager and dull, sparkling and dreamy, and the dreamiest one had a nonsense rhyme all to herself, which shall go in here to lighten this rather serious book a little.

Hurry skurry, worry flurry,
Such a fuss and such a hurry.
Down I slid by a private stair
To a room in a forest of maidenhair.

The glistening walls were of mother-of-pearl,
The roof was a moonstone, the delicate twirl
Of a kind of coiled ladder sprang up from
   the floor
Of loveliest opal. The low, swinging door
Had a way of opening silently
To people like you and me.

In the room was a sea-pool made
In a hollow and carven slab of jade.
And coral polyps and corallines spread
Their pink and purple; and sea-things fed
Each in his fashion. The room like a shell
Curved softly and smoothly; for lamp there fell
A great white Indian star from the sky:
And into that room slipped I.

   Hurry skurry, worry flurry,
   "Where's the child? Catch her. Hurry.

Absent-minded again!" My ear
Thought that it heard, but it did not hear
Really and properly, you know,
For I was slipping and sliding so
That I couldn't listen. At last I curled,
Safe in my dear little inside world,
In the cool green forest of maidenhair fern,
While they clawed the outside of me, said,
"Come, learn your Tamil grammar,
   and do your sums";

   But I was away where nobody comes
   But foolish people like you and me,
   Who are far, far, far from what they should be.

It was sometimes strange—it is so still—to enter into all
this abandon of gaiety with Rome burning at our gates.
But life is as various as shells on the seashore or flowers in

the field, and there has been this outcome of those days—
many who played together then have grown up to help to
snatch their helpless little sisters out of the flames. Perhaps it is because Rome is so near, and the heat of the fire
and the smell of the smoke are so much with us, that we
have never been led to go on to higher education. When a
keen girl-student recovering from a long illness began to
learn Greek for recreation, it was that she might be able to
study her New Testament better, and so do more for the
younger ones. We never had time for what (to us) would
have been luxury. And as they grew older, we tried, by
means of traveling on the King's business, and with the
splendid help of books, to enlarge our children's minds so
that they would be always eager to learn more.

And we learned more than we taught. One day we took
the children to see a goldsmith refine gold after the ancient manner of the East. He was sitting beside his little
charcoal-fire. ("He shall sit as a refiner": the gold- or sil-
versmith never leaves his crucible once it is one the fire.)
In the red glow lay a common curved roof-tile; another tile
covered it like a lid. This was the crucible. In it was the
medicine made of salt, tamarind fruit and burnt brick-
dust, and embedded in it was the gold. The medicine does
its appointed work on the gold, "then the fire eats it," and
the goldsmith lifts the gold out with a pair of tongs, lets it
cool, rubs it between his fingers, and if not satisfied puts it
back again in fresh medicine. This time he blows the fire
hotter than it was before, and each time he puts the gold
into the crucible the heat of the fire is increased: "It could
not bear it so hot at first, but it can bear it now; what
would have destroyed it then helps it now." "How do you
know when the gold is purified?" we asked him, and he
answered, "When I can see my face in it [the liquid gold in
the crucible] then it is pure."

All along we were wonderfully helped, though a "Sab-
bath rest" and suchlike phrases seemed to smile a trifle
ironically as they passed us by. We learned to sleep lightly

with one ear open. But often we were given good sleep, and, if danger threatened, the children's angels (we think) were sent to waken us. Once in a nursery about thirty yards from the bungalow a dozen babies were asleep in their hammocks. The hammock, which is the universal South Indian cradle, is a long strip of white cotton knotted to a rope thrown over a beam. To make it safer we sew tapes on either side of the strip of cotton and tie them across to keep the babies from tumbling out. That night a six-months-old had somehow pushed her head through the space between the tapes, and swung round. How she managed it who can tell? But she was strangling and could not cry.

It was then that, as it were, a touch woke me, and, thinking that something must be wrong somewhere, I got up, and was on my way to the nearest nursery when I stopped for a sleepy and hesitating moment under a tamarind tree, whence I could see that nursery verandah. There was no sound, not even of bird or bat in the night. The lantern was burning low; nothing was moving; no child was crying. "It must be a mistake," I said to myself, but somehow could not go back. I hastened on to the nursery, and was just in time to cut the tapes. Little Balana was choking.

There was another. The nurse who was with us then was taking care of Tara, who was ill, and she said that the baby had not called. But there was a call, and again things were so that a few minutes more would have seen a little life gone. And many and many a time our nurse, Mabel Wade, was just in time to save a child from serious accident. We grew to count on the angels. And now that these children have grown up to give that unpurchasable thing, loving and loyal service, we do not wonder that their angels took such care of them. And we are grateful to them. The work committed to us has now grown beyond our powers. But these our first dear children are rising up about us, and those unseen guardians of their childhood must, I think, feel repaid for their vigils by little white hammocks, and for many a walk across to our rooms at night to call us to come. And we, too, have been a thousandfold repaid for anything we ever did. "The dear Master can never be weary again by the side of any well, but we may be weary by the side of many for Him"—this sweet little word from Hudson Taylor comes to mind as we think of those days. How good, how very good, it was to be allowed to sit on that well-side with Him.

Those were years of rigid economies, for though we were never burdened about funds, we thought in terms of pence, not shillings, much less pounds. Receipts for gifts were often gummed on the back of postcards to save stamps and stationery. And everything else was done in that careful spirit. But no one knew that we were at times almost in straits. They only knew that all our needs were supplied, for we told them so, and it was true. The times of shortness were for the proving of faith; the end of almost each year saw us with something over. It had not mattered that people did not know. Unto Thee, O God, do we give thanks, unto Thee do we give thanks: for that Thy name is near Thy wondrous works declare.

Those years were happy, for many a little wounded life was lifted up into happiness and health, and the desire accomplished is sweet to the soul:

> Look, the bud is on the bough;
> Look, 'tis green where thou didst plough;
> Listen, tramp of little feet,
> Call of little lambs that bleat,
> Hark to it, oh verily
> Nothing is too good to be.

And at times, when we were threatened in various ways by the fatigues and cumbrance of the flesh, these words came and reinforced us: "If the Spirit of Him that raised up Jesus from the dead dwell in you, He that raised up Christ from the dead shall also quicken your mortal bodies by His Spirit that dwelleth in you." We asked for that as a present experience, and I believe received in some measure a life that was quickened and sustained for the sake of the children. For the word is eternally true: "In the day when I cried Thou answeredst me, and strengthenedst me with strength in my soul."

Looking back at the work as it shaped, with its unaccountable refusals and withdrawals, its lessons of reliance upon the Invisible alone, we see it like the mountainside that is familiar to many of us now, for it stands above our Forest House. There is apparent change in that mountain. The colors of the grass and the trees vary with every swift lightening and shadowing of sky and air. Mists in the clefts and hollows, torrents tearing down the face of the rocks, the sweep of the seasons—change is in each of these. But there are scars in the rock, and there is something changeless about a scar in rock.

The ways of our work may change, the colors, the apparent shapes. New conditions will call for new decisions; but the elemental things, the convictions which are part of its creation, these will remain. Stuff up the scars with brushwood, soften their firm lines, try to make them just a little more decorative, and the mountain will not be the mountain that you know.

But we know that it is not enough to have scars in the rock. "The work" will never go deeper than we have gone ourselves. "I bear in my body the marks—I bear branded on my body the scars of Jesus as my Master." How often then, and since, we have been shamed by this word: how often we have pondered the paragraph beginning, *In stripes and imprisonments, in tumults and labors*—and felt unworthy to be called followers of the Crucified.

> Can he have followed far
> Who has nor wound nor scar?

11.

O Saviour Christ, who could forget
    The crown of thorns—the tortured hours?
But on Thy brow there shall be set
    A crown of fadeless flowers.

And may we bring our flowers to crown
    The love that won at Calvary?
Down in the grass they grow, low down,
    The least of flowers that be.

Immortal Love, Thy sun and showers
    Have swept our field, oh take Thine own,
Thy little flowers, Thy love's own flowers,
    Dear Lord, to make Thy crown.

Psalm 132:18. On Himself shall His crown flourish (ever inflorescent, as a flower).—Kay.

11. How We Grew

We grew up from the first very simply, like a family. We were always, as it were, parts of one another.* In the ideal Indian family each member lives for the good of the household, and we worked together in this way, and never as employer and employees. The children called their sisters *Accal* (older sister); English women when they came *Sittie* (mother's younger sister); and later, brothers, Indian and English, *Annāchie*; the word connotes a chivalrous thought of brotherly protection. We found, as we went on, that our way of life was like a transparent shield about us. People came to us thinking it would be pleasant to join us. We could not discern their motives. But they looked awhile and, if they were not in sympathy, they went away. Long afterwards, when our Father's purpose was revealed, we thanked Him for leading us so. "I lean upon no broken reed, nor trust an untried guide"—the words were often with us then, will be with us to the end.

There are pitfalls in this particular pathway. We who walk there know them well. Things are sure to happen which will drain the heart of human hope, but the hallmark of

---

* Ephesians 4:25.—Weymouth.

the true missionary (the good Lord make it ours) is refusal to be weakened or hardened or soured or made hopeless by disappointment. "His only absorbing passion was to press on," Gairdner of Cairo wrote of his friend Douglas Thornton. "Now the God of hope fill you with all joy and peace in believing, that ye may abound in hope, through the power of the Holy Ghost"—the great prayer shines like a lamp in moments of windy confusion and the murky air of uncertainty. At the end of the day grieving things slip out of sight, one forgets the pricking thorn and remembers only the dewy rose. And, going on with Him, we find that in Him is the secret of continuance, and the secret of recovery too, after any disappointment, after any defeat.

At first we built nurseries of sun-dried bricks, with earthen floors and thatched roofs. But we found that too much time had to be spent in keeping the termites out of the walls; the weekly treatment required by earthen floors also took more time than we had to give; and thatched roofs were unsafe, for the conversion of anyone from among the caste people may, in these parts, be countered by the flinging of a lighted rag on the thatched roof of the offender. So, when money came to enable us to do it, we used burnt brick and tiles. But the rooms are Indian, unfurnished save for cupboards, brass vessels and, according to the nice upper-class habit of the South, grass mats for beds; and the red-tiled floors are kept shiny by constant washing. Later on we found shells on the beach at Cape Comorin and waterworn wood like carved work by the river in the forest; and the children learned to dress their rooms with this inexpensive loveliness.

Before the children came, we were continually camping in tents, mud huts, or tumble-down old bungalows, and we never stopped to grow even a flower; but after they came, we had to make home for them, so things were different. And because we know that beautiful things are dear to God (look deep into beauty and you see Him there), and that ugly, vulgar, coarse things are a jar, like a false note in music, we chose, when we had the choice, the beautiful, not the ugly. Someone (the angels perhaps) had planted trees up and down the field for us. We cherished those trees. And flowers began to grow where only scrub had been, and gradually the place became sweet and green, almost as though it offered coolness. And the bare, red blot on the bare, hot plain changed to something pleasant to the eye and beloved, at least to ourselves.

From the first the children did the work of the compound; we teach them to keep their little world orderly because of the cloud of witnesses.*

We had always much singing, and silence counted with us too. We found that the children could learn to understand silence. We had a minute's silence before beginning our worship together, and often a pause somewhere in the middle. It could never be long, because there were so many who were very small. The day from 5 a.m. until 10 p.m. was divided among us, each taking certain hours for prayer—not the whole hour, but whatever space could be given, and a prayer-bell—a disc of metal hung under a tree—was struck hour by hour. From the first we found that even very little children used the bell with a sweet and simple confidence.

As we went on continually asking that the ways of prayer might be opened to us, we learned that the kind of

---

* A friend, writing of Bishop Westcott, says this beautiful thing about him: "In the presence of the unseen he met all life, and you could not surprise him out of it. In this atmosphere he worked and breathed. Not only God Himself, but the cloud of witnesses, the communion of the unseen body of Christ, were more real to him than the things seen."

And the same friend tells a story of how the Bishop's chaplain, finding him struggling late and minutely one night over the draft of a service for a humble country church, reminded him that the congregation would not be critical. "They are accustomed to anything," he said. With a gentle, surprised smile, such as Elisha's might have been in Dothan, the Bishop looked up from his desk and said, "You forget: *who* are 'the congregation'? *We* are only an infinitesimal part of it."

intercession that is like a musical chord, every note in harmony with every other, and all seeking to be tuned perfectly to the keynote (the will of our great Intercessor) is something worth guarding at any cost. There is an uplifting influence in such prayer together—Uplifting, it is the perfect word: "His faith exerted upon me an uplifting influence like that of tides lifting ships."*

We found prayer choruses uplifting too. Years afterwards, we sent a few of these out in a small book called *Wings*, but they could only be a few, and the music which wings the words could not always be given. We grew into a kind of prayer that is, for us at least, very helpful. We ask to be led by the Holy Spirit from point to point, each prayer leading on from the preceding prayer till the particular subject laid on our hearts has been dealt with and we have the assurance that "the Lord will complete all," as Kay translates Psalm 138:8.

This way of prayer is just the opposite to the kaleidoscope kind, which darts hither and thither all over the earth or over a number of scattered interests (often within the limits of a single long prayer) leaving the mind which has tried to follow perhaps dazzled, perhaps tired. It is a much simpler thing. Such prayer is often brief; it is often silent, or it may take the form of song, and we are lifted up as with wings to our Lord's feet. It is possible only when all who are praying together do thoroughly understand one another, are, indeed, as one instrument under the control of the Spirit of God, who moves on each severally as He will, or unites all in silence or in song. Such prayer asks for something not easily defined. Darby's translation of Exodus 23:21, "Be careful in His Presence," comes to mind as a word that expresses its quietness and awe, and the jubilant psalms show its joy.

The habit of having a settled prayer day once a month was a great help. It led to something which we could not

---

* J.R. Mott about Douglas Thornton, quoted in *Temple Gairdner of Cairo*, by C.E. Padwick.

do without now—occasional extra days when we plan, so that the many whirling wheels of our busy world shall run down as much as possible, and we be set free to give ourselves to prayer. "Do not be so busy with work for Christ that you have no strength left for praying," said Hudson Taylor once. "True prayer requires strength." To secure even half a day's quiet in a large family like ours needs careful planning beforehand, but it is worth that. Again and again things have happened after such a day that nothing we could have done could have effected, for prayer is truly force. So when the constraint is upon us we yield to it, believing it to be of God. Sometimes to one or another privately this compulsion comes, and we have a quiet room set apart for this purpose; no one goes there except for quietness. When it comes to all, then, after we have had some time alone, we meet as on our usual prayer day, and this way of being together in prayer is a strand in our gold cord.*

It was not long before we began to understand the reality of the authority often exercised, especially at night, by the evil one, our enemy, upon the minds of these lately delivered from his prison-house. So far as we knew, the babies were not affected, but older children and converts

---

* Others have felt the same necessity. "When any Sister's life of prayer has been seriously broken in upon, as when a Nurse-Sister has had a succession of bad cases, arrangements are made for counteracting the effect of this when the special time of strain is over.

"The time that is thus set apart for quiet and prayer may seem to some to be excessive. But it is to be remembered that the Sisters in India have to face a heathen world, and to work in an atmosphere which is, whether they are conscious of it or not, full of deadly evil influences; and that this, when it is combined with hard work in a very enervating climate, tends greatly to wear them out, and makes it very necessary for them to be in direct and habitual contact with Him who is the Source of Life."—Oxford Mission to Calcutta.

"Christ knew how the holiest service, preaching and healing, can exhaust the spirit, how too much intercourse with men can cloud the fellowship with God, how time, full time, is needed, if the spirit is to rest and root in Him, how no pressure of duty among men can free from the absolute need of much prayer."—Andrew Murray.

were. If strong threads of affection bound the heart to
anyone in the old life, then there would be at times distress, apprehension of trouble there, perhaps a vivid
dream revealing it in tangible form. The immaterial became material, or the material appearing in the immaterial
stuff of dreams disturbed, and sometimes seriously injured, the life of the one thus strained. Often we heard
afterwards of what had been happening just at that time
hundreds of miles away (miles matter nothing where spirit
forces play) and were able to trace the influence to its
source. Tuesdays and Fridays, the nights given up to demon worship for thousands of square miles in the South,
seemed to ask for special guarding by prayer, for the throb
of tom-toms which filled the air and the weird cries of the
worshipers were sometimes reminiscent, and sounds, like
scents, have extraordinary recalling power. But any night
might hold a need.

For all such conditions we found just one sure anti-
dote—the peace of God. Let the will close down the door
on the old life with its allures, its pictured memories, let
the last thoughts before falling asleep be set on Him, the
Eternal Keeper who neither slumbers nor sleeps, let some
hymn or psalm or calming promise or assurance fill the
last conscious moments, and the spell will be broken. An
old prayer (Sir Thomas Browne's) is as sure of an answer
in an Indian room tonight as it was in an English home
three hundred years ago:

> While I do rest, my soul advance,
> Make me to sleep a holy trance
> That I may, my rest being wrought,
> Awake into some holy thought.

And now and here, as always everywhere, there is One
whom the winds and waves obey, and He draws near to the
frightened soul and says, "It is I; be not afraid." And when
He is as near as that, the weakest of His little children sleeps
peacefully, and is almost sure to waken into some holy thought.

Were they ever naughty? "You know, dear children, you are in a beautiful garden, but the serpent entered the garden of Eden," remarked an excellent friend one day, in the course of a Sunday address, and he thought that he was giving them information. There was, I fear, an impious chuckle in more than one small soul, though, to our relief, the upturned faces were suitably demure. Did they not know that? Why, of course. Snakes love gardens. And as for the serpent who "entered the garden of Eden," they know him only too well. But, even so, the garden helped. A carelessly disobedient child would be sent to find a disobedient plant, one whose leaves ought to grow alternately or opposite or in whorls, and which disobeyed its law; a destructive one would be told to stick on the leaf it had plucked off from pure wantonness—a deplorable habit, too common here. For punishments were various. A quarrelsome child had a deer's horn tied round her neck, or, if very small, was put in a barrel out of which she could not climb, and in which she soon tired of her own company. And sometimes persistent offenders were given switches and told to go and fight it out—this always ended in laughter.

Two fables often came to mind in those first days. When we were perplexed by diverse advisers (for we found that both books and people differed considerably about the proper way to bring up children), then we thought of Æsop's old man and his donkey. And when we hardly dared to do anything for fear of doing wrong, the mother-bear story (found in Rosa Barrett's life of Ellice Hopkins) was delightfully in point: "Shall I," said the bear's cub to his mother, "move my right paw first or my left, or my two front paws together, or the two hind ones, or all four at once, or how?" "Leave off thinking, and walk," grunted the old bear. So in a great simplicity we tried to let the children grow as the green things about them grew, not too closely regarded, not pulled up at frequent intervals to see how they were getting on. And there was always the hope that they would be part of the crown of flowers that our Lord would wear one day.

12.

Rock of my heart and my fortress tower,
    Dear are Thy thoughts to me,
Like the unfolding of some fair flower,
    Opening silently.
And on the edge of these Thy ways,
    Standing in awe as heretofore,
Thee do I worship, Thee do I praise,
    And adore.

Rock of my heart and my fortress tower,
    Dear is Thy love to me,
Search I the world for a word of power,
    Find it at Calvary.
O deeps of love that rise and flow
    Round about me and all things mine,
Love of all loves, in Thee I know
    Love divine.

12. Give Them Time to Root

Often then, much more often than now, we had to take risks. What soldier does not? It was second nature to hazard anything to save a child. We tried to walk wisely and lawfully too, but at a time when the only adoption the law recognized in the case of a girl was that of a temple-woman, it was impossible to be always on the safe side. To have a missionary in jail would not have been comfortable for the Society with which we (Mabel Wade and I) were at that time connected, so we arranged with the Secretary on the field that if one of us were imprisoned, that one should drop out. Both he and the Secretary at home were dauntless in their private friendship, and we think of them gratefully. It cannot have been easy for them to stand by such unorthodox ways as ours had to be. And fellow-missionaries, even those who could not quite see with us in other matters, stood by us valiantly in our greater battles. Once, the word was caused to run quietly through South India that should a little girl for whom we were known to be fighting a losing fight in the courts appear at any mission station, she should be protected and passed on safely. And this was done. How often we have thanked God for fellow-missionaries.

The token for good by which our Lord first gave us the assurance that this dangerous work was not of our own devising, but that He was truly with us, was very comforting. It was in 1904, and, except for two Indian sisters to whom all was new and rather startling, I was alone. We had been staying in a Hindu town under the hills when we came upon a tragic little tale. A child of eight was about to be dedicated to the god of one of the great temples of the South. Her father had married out of caste. This had caused trouble, so he had killed his wife and was about to marry again. In a case like that, the child, if there be one, is usually dedicated and the family starts afresh. We tried to save the child, but could not. Now, a month or so later, the Indian friend in whose house we had been staying had found that if certain expenses could be met she might be redeemed. One hundred rupees was the sum required. Would we send it or not? The answer had to be given at once.

It was the first time such a decision had had to be made. The life of a child was at stake. We sent the hundred rupees.

Then doubts arose. *Nor Scrip* tells of these, and of how they were set at rest. But Ponnamal (Golden) and Pearl, the two faithful Indian sisters who shared this matter with me, were unhappy, though their loyal hearts trusted me. It was such an unheard-of thing to pay money for the redemption of a child. Was it strange that they felt apprehensive? I asked then if I might pray for a token that could not be mistaken, to show whether or not we were in the will of our God. And to that the answer, I thought, was *Yes*. What may I ask, Lord? *You may ask for one hundred rupees*. We had never up to that time had a gift of a hundred rupees.

And it came. A fellow-missionary who knew nothing of this (no one knew outside the house) was caused to think of us, and to feel that she should send us something. She was about to write a check for a different sum, so she told us afterwards, but she felt constrained to make it just one hundred rupees. We laid the check on the floor like a little new Gideon's fleece, and, kneeling round it, we thanked our heavenly Father.*

The child—Firefly was her nursery name: she was such a darling, quick, bright little thing—grew up to be a fellow-worker, loving and loyal. She refused to leave us for married life: "No, I will stay and take care of the children." And with all her ardent heart she served the Lord who had redeemed her.

For twenty years we had her. Then a violently painful disease attacked her. "Play the joy-bells for me," she said just before she passed on, the sound of glory ringing in her ears.

At that time Dr. Pugh, to whom we as a family owe so much, and Dr. Somervell, the mountaineer, were working together in Neyyoor Hospital in South Travancore. We had written asking for something to relieve Firefly's pain, and expected it by mail. But who can measure the kindness of medicals? The joy-bells were being played for Firefly when the hooting of a car, then an almost unknown sound in Dohnavur, called us out. It was Dr. Somervell with the medicine.

So we went to our little funeral festival together that same evening; the children carried their colored lanterns, and we sang all the happiest things that we knew. We had even cymbals. And a friendship began that night which has been strength and joy ever since.

---

* Chapter 16 of *Nor Scrip* tells of how, at the beginning of the new work for boys in 1918, we felt constrained to ask for one hundred pounds to come by the next mail. It relates what happened on that mail day. And a later chapter in this book will tell how in 1929 the sum one of us was moved to ask was not one hundred rupees, nor one hundred pounds, but one thousand. We have learned that, though our Lord disciplines His servants by deprivations, mysterious disappointments and many lacks, He does at times cause them to ask and to receive of His abundance, and we have learned also that when the need is in shillings, He gives in shillings, when in pounds, then He gives in pounds. But it is never a light thing to pray in this way. The Lord save us from lightness.

But to go back to those earlier years, in the chapter called "He Took a Towel" we have told how we asked the pastors if they knew of anyone whom we might use, and of their disappointing answer. We also asked those of our missionary friends who were in sympathy with us, and one, to whom we are for ever grateful, found Pappamal.

She was a young girl, fragile, delicate with an inherited delicacy. Both her parents and her older sister, a young saint of the order of Elizabeth of Hungary, had died of tuberculosis, and I do not think that Pappamal had ever thought of herself as intended for the strenuous life of a soldier on service. But she had heard the call to serve, and her heart had responded.

Soon after that, one hot Sunday afternoon, she wanted something to read, and she turned to a little book that had somehow reached the house. It was written by Walker of Tinnevelly and was called *Custom and Liberty*. No one would publish that booklet, for with a firm touch it dealt with matters that are usually left unmentioned because they are too thorny to be comfortably handled, so we printed it ourselves.

Pappamal read it with rising displeasure, and presently, as something in it probed her more sharply than she liked, she tossed the little book aside. She had been wondering if Dohnavur could be the place for her. She knew now that it was not! "Dohnavur." Odious name! Who would go to Dohnavur, that place outside the camp of respectable Christianity? Who would go so far as even to wish to be

> Dead to the world and its applause,
> To all the customs, fashions, laws,
> Of those who hate the humbling Cross?

How extremely unnecessary!

But the hand of the Lord was upon that heart, and the day came when Pappamal set forth upon what to her was a great adventure. Till then, no girl of her station had offered for such work. It was a thing unknown.

And year by year as she went on with God she grew in valor of spirit, till her Lord could trust her to do anything for Him, and she became head of that part of the work which takes the little boys from the nurseries and trains young girls to care for them—a most responsible trust, as mothers will understand. We had at one time among us a girl who believed herself called to join us, and we, too, had believed her to be called, and had welcomed her with joy. But hidden in her nature was the canker of spiritual pride, and this inward thing, covered from us at first, and perhaps from herself, gradually appeared. She was a heavy burden upon Pappamal's heart, and one day when she was trying to help this warped soul to straightness the girl turned on her with, "It is easy for *you* to talk." And Pappamal understood. She had a small inheritance, not riches, but yielding more than sufficient for her needs. She had often wanted to give "all her living" in one gift to the work, but we had hesitated to accept it. She came now, her eyes shining with that lovely light seen only in the eyes of the Lord's blessed givers, and she would not be refused. If that pile of silver could be used to stumble the feet of this girl, Pappamal would have none of it! For His sake who gave all, she must give all. And she did. And a joy that is not of earth was her portion in that hour, a sweetness of joy untasted before. The girl with the canker in her heart went on unmoved, and finally, as her influence was injuring the observant young children in her charge, and as the word still stands, "Be ye clean who bear the vessels of the Lord," we had to part. To what purpose, then, was this waste? Is the precious ointment poured on the feet of the Master ever waste? Eternity will answer that question.

But not in one stream or in two does a life whose springs are in the holy hills flow out in blessing, and this Indian sister, and another also whose special service lies in the training of younger ones, are used in many ways far beyond our borders. For who can stay the flowing of the water of life?

And there are others, so few that it is still true to say that the gift is very rare, but still, thank God, some. There is one, whose name means Perfection, who is now in charge of over a hundred girls of school age, with, under her, young teaching sisters, each with her own little group of small girls. Perfection was at the time of this chapter only a young girl herself, gifted in many ways like her mother Ponnamal, and, like all the girls who are the strength of our Indian fellowship, she was sought in marriage by many. To test her vocation we sent Perfection on a long visit to her relatives—graduates, in good positions in the city of Madras. She returned from that visit sure of her call, and in the steadiness of a purpose that the Lord formed and guards she has gone on ever since.

Sometimes in strange ways the call comes that compels. Often in India, as in older days in Palestine, the Lord speaks to His simple children in dreams. We do not explain this or defend, we only know that it is so. There was one, hardly to be called a child of the household, though she had been baptized, who sat on the floor day after day with her hair streaming round her shoulders and her eyes pouring out tears—for she was a widow.

She must stay in that dimly-lighted room. She must sit there and mourn. So said her mother-in-law, also a baptized Hindu rather than a genuine Christian. So she sat and wept loudly, as custom ordained, and lamented according to custom, and because she had a very bad temper, and her mother-in-law's was still worse, that house, though wealthy, could hardly be called happy.

After some troubled months, the widow had a dream. One whom she did not recognize, dressed in a long white robe, came to her and said, "I will send you to a place where they all love one another." He vanished with the word, and she woke. "If this comes to pass within seven days I shall know that it is certainly the doing of the Supreme," she said to herself. Within a week a festival was held in the church nearby. The bishop came to it. The missionary took him to see the old mother-in-law and her daughter-in-law, as being the noted converts of the place. He stood silently in the doorway and looked at the widow. Then slowly he said something in English. The missionary translated. The words were the same that she had heard. How it was effected she does not know, but a few days later she and her little son arrived in Dohnavur.

At first nothing seemed more unlikely than that we had been given good gifts. A tempestuous Hindu woman, and a spoiled little boy, what was there of help in that? Today that woman is our Indian housekeeper; buyer of supplies; seller of unconsidered trifles that would, but for vigilant eyes, disappear unprofitably (by-products of grain, tins, bottles, and so on). And the boy, grown up and married to a Lotus Bud, is a member of our Fellowship from whom we can never ask too much.

But such transformations require years. As children grew older they did what they could in the nurseries, and the pressure there, though always heavy, lightened; but still we had no one to take charge of the children's education. And what of the future if they were not educated?

Visitors to the place—and even in those days there were many—pressed this upon us. Money came to build a school. "Is it impossible to make the idea of entire consecration the foundation of education?" was Andrew Murray's question when he was founding his Huguenot Schools two or three generations ago. We had not heard that question then, but the same thought was deep within us as we built our school in faith that teachers would be given to us. Pappamal, who was now one of us, and Arulai and Perfection helped as much as they were able, and so did the little growing-up sisters, and we carried on as best we could; though we knew our best was not much. Sometimes the admonitory voices were so unanimous about our folly in not using the kind of teacher easily obtained that we felt curiously alone. Who were we to set up our ideas against those of everybody else?

But at such a time something always happened to rein-
force our convictions and give us certainty which nothing
could shake. Once it was a conversation at the breakfast
table. Missionaries from different parts of India were in
Dohnavur that day. All were one in lamenting that the
type of Christian we turned out from our various institutions was so lacking in certain qualities which make for
character. I could not help wondering, as I listened to the
talk of these seniors, how a new type could be expected to
evolve from an old mold. It could not be that the plastic
stuff poured into the mold was incapable of receiving a
finer impression. Everything in me refused that explanation. It was too easy to be true. "Open your ears to what
Walker Iyer says to you about spiritual things [things
theological], but close them if he speaks of other things
[things practical]" was the advice given to his convert lads
by their schoolmaster in the mission school. This was the
mold. How expect a new type from it? We knew that we
could not use that mold. We could not expose our children
to such influences till New Testament convictions and the
New Testament attitude towards life in general had become part of them, something that could not be torn out or
laughed out of them. "The raft the current carries where it
will" is the Tamil synonym for the life swayed by the
surrounding usual. Those rafts were everywhere.

In our mountain ravine, just above our swimming pool,
a small tree grows on the rock in midstream. When the
river is in flood and a roaring torrent pours over the little
tree, whipping off its every leaf, it stands unmoved. Its
roots grip the rock. We wanted the children to be like that.
"Give them time to root," we used to say to our advisers.
"We are training them for storms and floods."

13.

So many questions lie ahead concerning the work, and a great comforting came this morning in the chapter in Job (Job 28) about "the way" of wisdom and "the place thereof" (verse 23). It tells how God finds the way for the wind and the water and the lightning, and it came with a blessed power what those ways are. The way for the wind is the region of the greatest emptiness, the way for the water is to the place of the lowest depth, the way for the lightning, as science proves, is along the line of the greatest weakness. "If any man lack." There is God's condition for His inflow of the spiritual understanding. Praise be to His Name.— I. Lilias Trotter.

(From a private diary.)

13. What Are You Going to Do With Them?

But fears came up perpetually and danced before our eyes like wearisome, mischievous goblins; we found that we could only go on if we leaned all our weight on the promises. Yet there was always a sense, even then, that something good lay ahead and that we were being shaped for that good thing, though we did not know what it was. Their Redeemer would not waste the children. If only they had the sovereign quality of truth, somehow the way would open. So we tried to bring them up to be truthful and faithful, ready for any sort of hard work, not slackers. And though, when we could not answer the frequent, "And what are you going to do with them?" with a clear-cut plan, and must have appeared unpractical and foolish, we were not cast down. "Thou knowest, Lord; Thou hast not shown us yet, but Thou knowest," we used to say to Him, and found it comforting. "Only teach us how to train them in honesty and thoroughness, in detachment from the spirit of the world and in a pure indifference to all its tinsel allurements. Give us some to help us who will understand about the gold and silver and precious stones.

Let us not be disappointed of our hope." And He answered with a word of strong consolation; for He Himself knew what He would do.

One day a group of caste men gathered on our verandah. They besought us to heal a very sick man whom they had brought in a cart from Holy Town, three miles away. They could not be persuaded to take him to the nearest hospital, which was a day's journey distant by cart—the shaky cart would be too much for him. He had almost died on the way to us, and one of the relatives, frantic and in tears, flung himself at our feet, and, stretched full length on the ground, cried imploringly, "Oh, be persuaded: a child, his wife, beseeches you."

And as we talked, in a house in Holy Town a girl sat waiting. "He" was her husband. If he died, the people would say that a snake had proceeded from her and devoured his life. She would be treated as though this were true. She had seen other children treated so. She had heard the jeers and scoldings, seen the averted faces, for it is unlucky to meet a widow. She knew all about the long penance of semi-starvation, had seen many a girl slowly harden under the strain of daily revilings. How could she bear it? She cried aloud to Heaven in her fear, but Heaven did not seem to hear. She vowed vows, she laid all she had to offer before the family god, she fell at his feet and besought him to have mercy. And in the room where the sick man lay people came and went and did not heed her. Nobody heeded her. She cried herself sick, but nobody knew.

At last a gleam of hope had lightened her sorrowful heart. They were going to take her lord to the white people. Were not his three pulses, called wind, fire and water, all talking together, indicating approaching convulsions? Not only powdered silver and gold, but tiger's claw, elephant's tooth, and stag's horn had been ground up, in combination with the usual mixture of herbs and arsenic, and administered in great and nauseous doses, but in vain. All having failed, and death being imminent, it was time to turn to the white people. That they were not doctors did not matter. They ought to know what to do. Had not white people many wise books? Anyhow, it was the last hope, and so four anxious relatives carefully hoisted the sick man into the cart and set forth. But, to the grief of the white people, who knew the long misery that threatened the girl (of whom the men spoke now, suddenly remembering her existence and hoping that the thought of her would move their hearts), they could only say, "We can do nothing."

But thou, O Lord, art a God full of compassion. Thou knowest to the utmost what human pain can be. Wilt Thou not give us a doctor to help these poor people? We found our way to that prayer as the little procession turned and moved slowly and dejectedly down the road. And like a little white cloud that melts into the blue almost before it is clearly seen, a thought came, and a hope. And the years passed, and then the little white cloud-thought took shape again.

About this time people wanted a book to tell more about the children and what we had been able to discover of the temple traffic. So in odd corners of time *Lotus Buds* had to be written. It owed much to a lifelong friend of the work, Mr. Willoughby Legh, of the Indian Civil Service. He read it through in typescript. We had put the stories last, as of least importance. "No, put them first," he said, "then people will be drawn to go on." So we turned the book upside down, and some did go on. And more than one who went on was led out to India. The first of these was Frances Beath, who joined us in 1910. She was indeed a Godsend in those early days, for she was of the company of the willing-hearted, loving and beloved.

When a new missionary arrives, her first work is the language, and her first trial is to see so much all round her which needs her help, and to be unable to give it. Frances Beath was in the midst of this when an epidemic of smallpox complicated life, and on a day which still laughs across the years to us a guest arrived.

We did not know that she was coming. For we had done the thing that is not done (missionaries have a code of their own about this): we had mentioned the difficulties of a visit at the time—smallpox being chief. But it is hard for anyone touring India to understand how thronged a missionary day may be, and in the middle of the morning work the unexpected bandy trundled up. I can see it now, and feel the 'What *shall* I do?' feeling of the moment; for Mabel Wade was out of reach, busy with babies, Frances Beath was at Tamil, and I was testing and measuring milk at one end of the verandah (surrounded by a crowd of milk-sellers who were in a hurry to go), with a batch of suspected smallpoxes waiting for inspection huddled up at the other end. We had only one guest room, and it was occupied.

Mercifully the guest was one who could come to the rescue, and she piloted our adventurous visitor (who declared that she did not in the least mind smallpox) through that complicated day. It seemed most discourteous not to make time to see more of her ourselves, for that visit had cost her eighteen hours of rough traveling, and yet time is a curiously difficult thing to make. You can only make it if you have it, and if you have not got it how can you get it? We had no isolation room then, and had dug out an old tent and filled it with smallpox cases, and put a hedge of thorns around it, and hoped for the best. But no Indian fears infection, and the guard we had set had slumbered. When we returned after a short absence we found a jovial group outside the hedge passing a sucked sweet across to the convalescing patients, who gratefully sucked it and returned it. It was not well to be off duty. But, "I think missionaries require bracing up" was the cheery remark that greeted us as we met at breakfast, very hot and limp, after some strenuous hours. "Let us sing, 'Praise, my soul, the King of Heaven'—that is a hymn missionaries ought to

sing often. It is so bracing!" And we felt too thoroughly
rebuked to say that we very often did sing it.

But our visitor was brave, the journey across country in
a bullock cart had presented serious possibilities to her.
When we saw her off she showed us a long hatpin. "If the
carter gives me any trouble, I have *this*," she said signifi-
cantly. And as the meek old carter, who would not have
thought of giving trouble to a cockroach, received her
admonitions, translated carefully by us, the humor of that
hatpin piled up suddenly on top of the humors of the
whole day. The next moment we collapsed in helpless
laughter. Is it not a mercy that missionaries can laugh?

14.

O merry love, strong, ravishing, burning, willful, stalwart, unslakened, that brings all my soul to Thy service, and suffers it to think of nothing but Thee. Thou challengest for Thyself all that we live; all that we savor; all that we are.

Thus therefore let Christ be the beginning of our love, whom we love for Himself. And so we love whatever is to be loved ordinately for Him that is the Well of love, and in whose hands we put all that we love and are loved by. . . .

O love undeparted! O love singular! . . .

We praise Thee, we preach Thee, by the which we overcome the world; by whom we joy and ascend the heavenly ladder. In Thy sweetness glide into me: and I commend me and mine unto Thee without end.—Richard Rolle (1290-1349), *The Fire of Love, and The Mending of Life.*

14. A Whiplash and a Bright Unearthly Joy

All through those years of beginnings we had lived with a menace in our ears. It was like living within sound of the growls and rumblings of an approaching storm.

At last, in 1910 and 1911, the storm broke upon us and we were plunged into a welter of troubles in the law courts. It was then that for the first time we understood the seventy-seventh psalm—with one exception, it seems to me, the most poignant in the whole Psalter. "Will the Lord cast off for ever? And will He be favorable no more? Is His mercy clean gone for ever? Doth His promise fail for evermore? Hath God forgotten to be gracious? Hath He in anger shut up His tender mercies? And I said, This is my infirmity: but I will remember the years of the right hand of the most High."

But still, though we did remember, those awful questions pierced us, for the child for whom we had fought so hard was alone in her desolation, snatched from us by powers too strong for us, and she had clung to us with all her might. The thought of her was like the probing of a spear, and a cruel voice cried aloud in our ears, turning the spearpoint in the wound: "Hath God forgotten to be gracious?"

It was then that a scale was given to us by which to measure all that could ever be again. Never more could ordinary trials and trifling rubs appear worth the energy of agitation that is so often spent on them; and we have never yielded to the temptation to make much of them without a feeling of shame. For that long series of lawsuits was a long, single hunt; the hunters were very evil men, and the hunted was a child who had trusted us to save her.

Her name was Jewel, and she was a young, pure-spirited girl to whom we had given a promise that no power on earth could make us break, that we would never give her up to her iniquitous mother. When we gave her that promise we did not know how impossible, from the human point of view, it was going to be to keep it. After anxious months and a miracle of deliverance, Jewel had been given to us in open court. Her mother and her responsible relatives had signed a *yādāst* (a document handing her over to us). But they went back on their word, and filed a suit against us, accusing us of breaking the child's caste, which, according to the terms of the *yādāst*, we were bound to keep inviolate. The judge at that time was Sir Charles Spencer, afterwards of the High Court, Madras; when it was known that he would try the case, the false witnesses fled. Not for silver nor for gold would they face the keen eyes of that sahib, they said. The case was dismissed, and with thanksgiving we brought our Jewel home. But the relatives bided their time. They waited till a new judge came, then they moved again on a new charge.

The matter created a stir all over South India. Missionaries of every name, and Government officials who knew about the notorious mother, openly stood by us, and all the better Hindus and Muslims of the countryside, for once united, were with us in sympathy. We had what everyone thought was a good case; but, to the general astonishment, the court ordered us to return Jewel to her mother. The Courts of Heaven intervened then. While we were away fighting for her, a courageous friend, a guest who was staying in Dohnavur, helped the child, disguised as a Muhammadan boy, to escape. And she was passed from hand to hand till Handley Bird, the Great-heart of South India, risked everything and carried her off to China, where she was sheltered for six years. Of this we knew nothing for a long time, for our friends who acted for us carefully kept the knowledge from us. An anonymous postcard, "For the eyes of the Lord run to and fro throughout the whole earth, to show Himself strong in the behalf of them whose heart is perfect toward Him," greatly comforted us; but many felt that, should Jewel be found and brought back, the only way to save her would be to broadcast her story, so we wrote it and held it ready. A page from it now (for we had not to use it) may show the supreme hour of that long fight, the hour of utmost defeat, when for the first time we tasted public shame and scorn, and knew how little we had drunk as yet of the cup of our Saviour's agony for souls. But that hour of our humiliation in the sight of men was the hour that shone as no other hour in our lives had ever shone, and it shines in our memory still like a great star in a moonless night. This is the page:

The hours between sunset and midnight of that last night [the night before we went to court for the last time] were sacred to Jewel. As we lay close together on the cane cot on the verandah we fell into silence; but our last talk was of John the Baptist and of faith that nothing can offend. And before I left her I took her hands in mine and looked down into her upturned face, "Promise me, whatever happens, by His grace, you will never be offended in Him." And she repeated, "I promise by His grace, I will never be offended in Him." For a moment we stood so in the starlight, looking into each other's eyes. Then we looked up together to Him, our Beloved, "Lord, dear Lord, whatever happens, by Thy grace we will never be offended in Thee." Then we parted. The child stayed in Dohnavur, and we started for our night's journey by bullock cart. And on the way the open oval of the cart framed the Southern Cross.

Next morning at eleven o'clock the court opened. For ten minutes or so we stood straining our ears to catch the words of the judgment read by the judge. But he read inaudibly, and our pleader told us that we must ask to be allowed to read it ourselves, which we did. It was handed down to us, and we went to the court library, where the clerk read it to us. We were as those smitten in the place of dragons.

But we were not forsaken. We were sitting round the table, the clerk was floundering slowly through the bulky manuscript, some thirty or forty pages of foolscap, glancing at us every now and then to see how we bore it, his drone occasionally jumping into a metallic staccato as an encouraging grunt from the mother's pleader roused him, when suddenly I saw through the open door a paradise flycatcher, a dear bird that had cheered us before. It alighted on a branch of the mango tree near the door and looked in as if giving a message to someone; and then it flew in among the dark-green shadows, its long, white tail-feathers streaming like little pennons of victory.

The heavy, hot hour wore on: we had reached the last long minute of it, when a word stung like a whiplash. The clerk was wide awake now. The cruel face across the table tightened up. The mother's pleader shot forth his hand and snatched the paper from the clerk. "Costs! Has she to pay them? For the whole suit?" He had never dreamed of that.

Then suddenly, all unbidden, unprayed for, came a strange triumphant joy utterly unknown before. We might have been the victors, it was such a victorious joy. It welled up like the springing of a fountain. It was so new, so pure, that I did not recognize it for my own. Was it the sudden shining of His face? Was it the joy of those who departed from the presence of the council rejoicing that they were counted worthy to suffer shame for His Name? Was it that sacred joy?

I do not know. But I do know that all that went before and all that had to follow, when the time came for paying the price in hours emptied of all conscious illumination, was as nothing in comparison with one moment of that joy.

15.

Here lies a lover who has died for his Beloved, and for love; who has loved his Beloved with a love that is good, great and enduring; who has battled bravely for love's sake, who has striven against false love and false lovers; a lover ever humble, patient, loyal, ardent, liberal, prudent, holy and full of all good things, inspiring many lovers to honor and serve his Beloved.—Raymond Lull.

O Lord of love and Lord of pain,
    Who, by the bitter Cross,
Dost teach us how to measure gain,
    And how to measure loss—
Whom, seeing not, our hearts adore,
    We bring our love to Thee;
And where Thou art, Lord, evermore
    Would we Thy servants be.

15. In Acceptance Lieth Peace

That court case was the beginning of a long period of keen anxiety, or what would have been anxiety but for the presence of our Shield and our Defense. "The shields of the earth belong unto the Lord" is a word that we have often proved. We were advised by an English Christian barrister to "disappear the children and lose their traces." For precedent is everything in India, and there were many evil men who, encouraged by that unexpected order of the court, were ready to go to law to claim children to whom they were not related; false witnesses who would swear to relationship were, of course, only a matter of rupees. But we could not possibly "disappear the children," so we went on from day to day depending upon the God of our mercy, and when threats muttered more like low thunder than ever, we gathered the children round us and looked up, and again and again were delivered from all our fears. But the story of these deliverances would fill a book. When we meet the gallant friends whose prayers and deeds stood round us and wrought for us through those days, will the unwritten stories shine for them like pictures? Will they see, rather than read or hear, what they were used to do in this faraway corner of India by the mighty means of prayer?

On the home side good help had before this been given to us. Our kindergarten, so sadly closed, had been re-opened; a friend who broke down in the University Settlement, Bombay, had come to us, and she stayed with us till ill-health forced her home. Before that had to be, the answer to our years of prayer had come—strangely enough, through the loss that, more than any other in those early days, cast us upon our God.

On August 24, 1912, Walker of Tinnevelly was with Christ. His wife was in England, ill; she cabled in answer to our cable, "The Lord gave and the Lord hath taken away, Blessed be the name of the Lord." A sentence in a letter from Bishop Moule when bereft of wife and daughter shows life as we slowly, painfully, learned to live it: "I am learning the lesson set to the weaned child: I am learning to do without." We had to learn to "do without." Did our friend see from the other side the answer to the prayer that we had so often prayed together about the children's education?

Fifteen years before that date, Agnes Naish of Westfield had come to a South Indian college with one purpose: to teach and train Indian girls to be winners of souls among their own people. She was now with her elder sister, Edith, evangelizing in the villages. Her heart had been deeply moved about the children who are in peril all over South India, and through the delirium of a severe illness she had been haunted by the thought of them. When Mr. Walker left us, she and her sister offered to come and help us through the pressure of the time. In the following year they joined our Fellowship, and Agnes Naish took charge of our school. Frances Nosworthy, a trained kinder-gartener, came a year later, and after two years, Helen Bradshaw, also trained; and so our prayer was answered. Years afterwards, when the work had grown beyond our expectations (for is it not the glorious tale of all who know our Master that His ways with us pass not only our asking but even our thinking?), two young sisters, Alice and Joan

Roberts, were given, and nineteen-year-old Joan just lapped up the language, as someone said, and acclimatized so beautifully that her parents' faith was justified in the eyes of many who had looked on doubtfully when one so young came out. Then an older one, Ella Colville, joined the school side too, to its great gain, so that though its needs are growing, as the needs of all living things must, we have proved that it is a very safe thing to trust the Lord our God.

It is a safe thing too to trust Him to fulfill the desire which He creates, and "when the desire cometh it is a tree of life." Those who were given us then, these who are with us now and are in charge of the varied parts of the work, or in our Muslim or Hindu outposts of which later chapters tell, are all of the kind in whom the heart doth safely trust; and if the heart can safely trust in its companions in service, it knows what peace can be, and peace in the tumult of battle is a wonderful thing. I shall not name those who were given to us in order of their coming, for a list of names means little except to those to whom each several name is dear. But I would put all I can into this single paragraph anticipating the joys of many years, the golden joy of seeing our Lord Jesus Christ made manifest, made luminous in loving human lives. There is nothing to compare with it for pure delight. "Now I know what He is like." When this is the involuntary word of the heart as it learns to know a fellow-worker, that heart has tasted heaven.

Soon after Agnes Naish took charge of the children's education, our principles were tested. A friend of an influential official in the educational world came to stay with us. She told her friend of what we were doing. He was interested, and the end of that was the offer of a grant if we would come in, even only partially, under the general scheme. We were to have large concessions, but, of course, would have to prepare our children for the usual examinations. This would have bound us to use as teachers some who could not build in gold, silver, precious stones, and sometimes (to mention one matter only) to use as readers books which we did not believe could do anything towards forming the character we wanted.* We had no freedom of spirit to consent. To be outside the running of the official machine was certain to handicap us in many ways in the future, but we could not touch money that must sooner or later lead to compromise. It was a thing forbidden.

Twenty years later, when the choice of literature to be used in the schools was in the hands of educational experts who could not be expected to see with us in such matters, books were chosen which here and there troubled the conscience of Christian parents and schoolmasters; but they could do nothing effective to change things. We thanked God then that, in days less inimical to what we care for most, we were guided so clearly that we could not doubt what His will was for us as a family.

The year 1912 was one of proving our strength in many ways. We were building a wall around the compound at the time. Once a tiger from the foothills wandered through the place, walking softly close to the rooms where the children lay asleep on the verandahs and past the cows (for at that time we had no farm) tethered close to the kitchen. He hurt no one. But there were other tigers abroad of a much more dangerous kind—men who would have rejoiced to injure us, and so our Father gave us a wall. We

---

* See *The Republic* of Plato (Golden Treasury Series, page 15 of Analysis). (The passage takes point from the fact that our one purpose was to prepare children for war.)

"But war implies soldiers, and soldiers must be carefully trained to their profession.

"They must be strong, swift, and brave; high-spirited, but gentle.

"But how must they be educated?—In the first place we must be very scrupulous about the *substance* of the stories which they are taught in their childhood. . . . Truth, courage, and self-control must be inculcated by all the stories that are employed in their education."

were getting on with it when a lawyer's letter came saying that part of the land that we were enclosing was not legally ours, and his client required us to cease our building and tear up by the roots a nursery already half built on that land. He had waited till Mr. Walker's death left us, as he thought, defenseless, almost desolate, and sure to be easily cowed by threats of court trouble.

We were reading Psalm 48 that Sunday morning at the time when the letter came, and we went on reading. Before we had finished the psalm we had a quiet assurance that we, too, would be able to say, *As we have heard, so have we seen,* for our God is not a God far off or of yesterday only, and the things He did of old He does still. And so it was. We went on building the wall and the nursery, and that lawyer's letter was the last we heard of the matter.

But we were never, then or since, left without being made subject to forces that work like the backwash of a river in flood. There is a place in a river in the mountain forest behind Dohnavur where the stream after heavy rain on the heights dashes down a face of rock and then curls swiftly into a cave by the pool below. It sweeps then with irresistible force through every little secret crevice of that cave. When the floods have passed, and the river once more sings its pleasant song, we swim in it and look down, and see a floor of rock, clear and glistening, and see a polished cleanliness. Not one shred of rotten wood, decaying root, fragment of dead fish or other defilement lies in any cell or on any shelf upon the fretted walls. God grant that we may be like that cave when the searching forces of life have had their way with us.

The searching forces of bereavement were close upon us now. Ponnamal (Golden), with whom the earliest journeys on behalf of the children had been undertaken, she who had cared so faithfully for the little nursery in Neyyoor, gradually failed, and soon became very ill.

We had no liberty of spirit to "claim healing"; we hardly understand the use of that phrase; we know too little to "claim" where temporal blessings are concerned. But we felt free to have a solemn service of Prayer and Anointing and Committal. It was led by a friend of many years, Dr. Stewart of Madras, and as we laid palms about our dear Ponnamal we knew that, however the answer came, there would be victory, there would be peace.

And as the days passed we were kept in the same mind. We knew our Father. There was no need for persuasion. Would not His Fatherliness be longing to give us our hearts' desire (if I may put it so)? How could we press Him as though He were not our own most loving Father? In that understanding with Him we lived through the next two years:

> And shall I pray, Oh, change Thy will, my Father,
>   Until it be according unto mine?
> Ah no, Lord, no, that never could be, rather
>   I pray Thee, Blend my human will with Thine.
>
> And work in me to will and do Thy pleasure,
>   Let all within me, peaceful, reconciled,
> Tarry content my Well-Belovèd's leisure
>   At last, at last, even as a weaned child.

Can one pass that for peace and deep heart's ease?

It was soon evident that healing as by the touch of His hand was not to be. Our Lord often uses His human healers now, so we took Ponnamal to hospital.

Our Neyyoor friends were away at the time, but the Salvation Army hospital at Nagercoil in Travancore was good to us. In the dawn after our night together in the bullock cart, as it trundled slowly along the road leading between the hills into Travancore territory, she and I wondered what the end of that journey would be. Would it be relief? Neither of us had assurance about that. Then what new valley of sorrow was opening before us? These strange valleys which cross the plain of life are not unknown ways to any of the Father's children, but at the entrance the soul trembles just for a moment—then it enters unafraid, "For Thou art with me, Thy rod and Thy staff they comfort me." And so began the walk through the valley which was to prove a valley not of shadow only, but far more of illumination, of springs of water and of cornfields, and at the end, for Ponnamal, the light of her Lord's face.

We were three months in Nagercoil: "Do Thou so make my bed in all my sickness that, being used to Thy hand, I may be content with any bed of Thy making" was our prayer then. While we were there a wave of malaria, not usual in our neighborhood, swept over a Muslim town near Dohnavur, and seventy of our children were ill at once, with temperatures often above 106, and there was no doctor.

Sometimes groups of them, after having recovered (for none died), had various ailments impossible for lay people to understand. And Arulai, who had to take charge then, had the heavy care of arranging for journeys for the more seriously ill children, whom she sent to us in Nagercoil. Out of the midst of the stress and strain came a letter from her: "Are you tasting the sweetness of this time? I am."

Ponnamal suffered long. We need not recall what she has forgotten, and what can be shown to the greater glory of God has been told in the book called, *Ponnamal, Her Story*. But it was not all storm and rain: there were sunny spaces. I cannot show them more tenderly than in the melodious words of the old tale: "And behold, at a great distance he saw a most pleasant mountainous country, beautiful with woods, vineyards, fruits of all sorts, flowers also, with springs and fountains, very delectable to behold. Then he asked the name of the country: they said it was Immanuel's Land." On August 26, 1915, Ponnamal was received into the Celestial City, and to us again was set the hard lesson, to learn how to do without.

We missed her at every turn. We were too few to be able to protect every part of a compound whose wall was nearly

a mile long. Ponnamal's vigilance had been a continual
help, and now that it was removed the evil one had his
chance. Anxiety upon anxiety followed. "No one is indispensable. You will be given another Ponnamal," said some
easily. Mistaken words, and vain. They did nothing to
help us through.

No, it is not by giving us back what He has taken that
our God teaches us His deepest lessons, but by patiently
waiting beside us till we can say: I accept the will of my
God as good and acceptable and perfect, for loss or for
gain. This, word for word, spelled out by Ponnamal's
deathbed, was the lesson set to us to learn:

> He said, "I will forget the dying faces;
> The empty places—
> They shall be filled again;
> O voices mourning deep within me, cease."
> *Vain, vain the word; vain, vain:*
> *Not in forgetting lieth peace.*
>
> He said, "I will crowd action upon action,
> The strife of faction
> Shall stir me and sustain;
> O tears that drown the fire of manhood, cease."
> *Vain, vain the word; vain, vain:*
> *Not in endeavor lieth peace.*
>
> He said, "I will withdraw me and be quiet,
> Why meddle in life's riot?
> Shut be my door to pain.
> Desire, thou dost befool me, thou shalt cease."
> *Vain, vain the word; vain, vain:*
> *Not in aloofness lieth peace.*
>
> He said, "I will submit; I am defeated;
> God hath depleted
> My life of its rich gain.
> O futile murmurings; why will ye not cease?"
> *Vain, vain the word; vain, vain:*
> *Not in submission lieth peace.*

He said, "I will accept the breaking sorrow
Which God tomorrow
Will to His son explain."
Then did the turmoil deep within him cease.
Not vain the word, not vain;
For in acceptance lieth peace.

16

But indeed through it all God does make known to us wonderful resources of His Mercy. *He does help us, beyond all that we can ask or think, by the kindness and gentleness that He teaches others to show us,* and by the Light that changes the look of all things, and by the uplifting power of His Grace, and by showing us our task in life, and by setting us to help and think for others: so in all these ways He bears us on from day to day. And it is just from day to day that we have to hold on; not looking into or puzzling about the further distances of this life, but doing our best each day, with each day's task and each day's duty, trusting God to give us the strength and light which for each day we need.—*Francis Paget, Bishop of Oxford. His "Life,"* by Stephen Paget and J.M.C. Crum.

> An angel touched me and he said to me,
> The journey, pilgrim, is too great for thee;
> But rise and eat and drink,
> Thy food is ready here,
> Thy Bread of life,
> Thy cruse of Water clear,
> Drawn from the Brook, that doth as yesterday
> Flow in the way.
>
> *O Cake of Bread baken on coals of fire,*
> *Sharp fires of Love, O Water turned to Wine,*
> *And can it be such food is daily mine?*
> *Then never, never can the journey be*
> *Too great for me.*
>
> And I shall go in strength of that pure food,
> Made mine by virtue of the sacred Rood,
> Unto the Mount of God
> Where my Lord's face
> Shall shine on me,
> On me in my low place,
> Down at His feet, who was my Strength and Stay
> Through all the way.
>
> *O Cake of Bread baken on coals of fire,*
> *Sharp fires of Love, O Water turned to Wine,*
> *The word is true, this food is daily mine.*
> *Then never, never can the journey be*
> *Too great for me.*

16. Let Me Be "Buthil"

Shortly before Ponnamal left us, a letter came from the city where a little girl called Cuckoo had been saved from destruction. The letter said that her guardians demanded her back. If we did not send her back they would charge us with kidnapping. We had no sufficient defense, for though we knew that their purpose was bad, we could not prove it; and we had not the signed statement that would have shattered a kidnapping case.

But we could not give the child to perdition. As with Jewel, so with Cuckoo, there was a compelling *must*. Cost what it might, we must save her. We had learned that the best way to protect such a child was to put her in some safe place pending the decision of the court. We could not always depend on a brave guest or on the cooperation of fellow-missionaries. So the only thing to do was to put Cuckoo where she could not be found, and, if things went against us, to say that we had done so and take the consequences—seven years' imprisonment.

But Ponnamal lay dying. We had been with her through months of suffering, and she had counted on us to be with her to the end. How could we leave her? "But do not think of me," she said to that. In the gathering up of the love of the years she said it, "Do not think of me."

It was impossible for any English person to travel unobserved with an Indian child. We had no Indian women who could do it. But there was one who could do it—Arul Dasan, he who had narrowly escaped having his eyes filled with pepper because he would not turn from his Lord Jesus. He was a young man now, and he was with us. He listened as we told him what it might cost if things went wrong. We did not know how the law would regard his share in the matter. It might be impossible to shield him even though we declared ourselves responsible.

Opposite to us as we talked, hanging upon the wall, was a picture, "The Vigil." I took it down and gave it to him. "Keep your vigil," I said, and he took the picture with him. That night he kept his vigil, and received his sword and buckler, the empowerment from on high.

And yet it was in fear and in much weakness that he started, and it was a worn and weary Arul Dasan who returned six days later. He told us that on the second day, in a houseboat on the backwaters of Travancore, as he sat with the little Cuckoo nestling close to him, a group of men stood talking in the stern. "Look at that child," said one of them, and spoke of the criminal case about to come on in Madras. The two men dropped their voices and went on talking, glancing round again and again at him. The loss of little Cuckoo—prison; Arul Dasan faced both in that hour.

And the accals, the Indian sisters, how show the temper of their steel? After Arul Dasan had started on his journey, we gathered them together and told them everything. They were all young, inexperienced, timid by nature, and terribly afraid of the very word "prison." There was a breathless silence as they listened; consternation was on every face. It was to them an unutterable thing that this might be appointed to the one they counted mother. It could not be. But it might be. It might be within a week.

It did not appear to help them much to be reminded that

in olden days prison was usual. The martyr stories, they seemed to think, belonged altogether to another order of life. It shamed me that they could feel so. We seem to have wandered far from the place where suffering for our Lord's sake was accepted as a matter of course. I had been a poor leader to the girls if they failed now and were not willing to let me go.

At last someone spoke. "Will it not be possible to have a *buthil*?" (Buthil means one who does something instead of another.) And from all round the group came that one word, "Will it not be possible?" Then, more earnestly still, "Oh, let *me* be buthil!" Yes, up to seven years' imprisonment, "Let *me* be buthil." I looked round the group— Arulai, our Star child through so many nights; Pappamal, fragile as a flower; Rukma, in her young brightness; Lola and Leela, those fast friends; the little Elf, now grown up. And Ponnamal's daughter—she was there; to her, too, that mother would have said, "Do not think of me." "He had asked of him the ultimate service, as a friend should," is one of John Buchan's unforgettable sentences. Here was an ultimate service we would never have asked. It was offered. It was even pressed upon us. But never was I so thankful that the law does not accept a buthil. Next day a telegram came—"Criminal case dismissed."

Why is the tiniest incident attending the silver shock of joy photographed forever upon the memory? I can see the servants washing up on the back verandah where the telegram was handed in, hear the clatter of cups and plates, see the coolie waiting unconcerned for his pay: how inadequate the sixpence we gave him appeared, how little he knew what he had brought. Then up from everywhere raced dancing waves of blessed glad relief. Gone were the anxieties about how the other children would be protected; gone was the fear of having to lay too heavy a burden upon willing fellow-workers (for a conviction in court would have meant prison, and prison would have meant just that for them); gone that other nightmare fear of seeing Arul Dasan disgraced before the world; gone the dread of detestable publicity. Gone was everything that had pressed so heavily for weeks.

And yet we knew that we must not relax. For a while we did not know how things would be. Surely the two stories of Dothan were written for such times. Mountains full of horses and chariots of fire for Elisha, empty blue sky for Joseph, and bare hillside. How could we know which of these was to be in His answer to us? So we had asked for a heart prepared for either, and knew that He would understand the human in us that hoped our Dothan would be Elisha's. And it was. "He has been so kind about other things that we have no doubt but that He will care for this too," said a loving servant of His once. The word would have been fulfilled either way, but it was with profound relief that we all welcomed the wonder that met us now. The guardians did not appeal to the civil court, as the magistrate who dismissed the criminal case had advised them to do. His advice appeared to have fallen on deaf ears. Who deafened those ears? Who opened the eyes of the young man that he saw? "Among the gods there is none like Thee, O God; there is not one that can do as Thou doest."

When we were sure that all was safe, the friends who had sheltered Cuckoo sent her back to us. We met her at a big junction in the midst of the usual crush and clamor of a railway station. When first she caught sight of us among the crowd there was a whoop, a wild leap into our arms, and a joyful jumble up of hugs with all four limbs at once. When we had liberty and leisure to look round, we saw a crowd of smiles.

Blessed forever be the cord that binds those who yield to its mighty bonds one to another. "Do not think of me"— "Let *me* be buthil." The love in such words is eternal. This is a thread of our gold cord.

17.

In answering the questions of the Christian as to the failure of science to throw light on the nature of God, Sir Arthur Eddington says, "I doubt whether there is any assurance to be obtained except through the religious experience itself; but I bid him hold fast to his own intimate knowledge of the nature of that experience. . . . We may embark on the venture of spiritual life uncharted though it be. It is sufficient that we carry a compass."

The writing which is written in the king's name, and sealed with the king's ring, may no man reverse.

I hold that the line of thought which offers by far the least difficulty, not to faith only, but to reason, is that which relies absolutely on His affirmation, wherever He is pleased actually to affirm.—Bishop Moule.

17. The Finances of the Odd Sparrow

Those who know the Dohnavur Fellowship know that it could not be at all if it had any doubt about the truth of the Scriptures (for this position we "see reasons and reasons"). So all through our story certain things are taken for granted, and from year to year we prove them to be true (for "what begins as an experiment ends as an experience," though experiment is hardly the word for action based on a promise, if we accept that promise as given by God). But the books of the world come to us, and we know what this present age is saying, and now and then find a grain of gold in the heap of words. Sir James Jeans' *The Mysterious Universe* gave us this grain: "The universe can be best pictured, though still very imperfectly and inadequately, as consisting of pure thought, the thought of what we must describe as a mathematical thinker." So far does Science take us, and it is a long way; but who can describe the wonder of the leap across what seems to be a void and to find on the other side the Mathematical Thinker indeed, but with a new name now, Abba, Father? and to find oneself like a child who has trusted its father's word and leaped into that father's arms and found itself safe?

I have told nothing, so far, of how supplies have come so that we could continue from year to year, because any who care to know about that will find it written in three little books, *Nor Scrip*, *Tables in the Wilderness*, and *Meal in a Barrel*. But there may be some who would like to know, before they read further, something of how we were taught to take such words as our Lord's about the lilies and the ravens and the sparrows quite simply (perhaps "the odd sparrow," the fifth thrown in as an extra by the birdseller, is as good a description as we could find for our Fellowship—the odd sparrow that is not forgotten). So I will copy a few paragraphs from the first of these records. They belong to our earliest days, and to a time of temptation to fear.

Then, as never again for fifteen years, I was allowed to taste of the cup which would be poured out for me if the money did not come. Allan Gardiner, for some hidden good purpose, was allowed to starve to death. Therefore such an issue could not be regarded as impossible. The children—I need not trace in writing the end of that thought. But I did that day tread every foot of it in imagination, and came to this: Suppose the children die, and we all (of course) die with them, and the Christian world cries shame on the one responsible, what will it matter, after all? The children will be in heaven, and is that not better than the temple? (Years later I read of a similar temptation assailing Hudson Taylor by the sea at Brighton. Apparently the adversary sometimes repeats himself.) Later another question came:

I thought of dear younger ones who had been given as fellow-workers. What if suddenly this burden is laid upon them? None of them has had the previous experience in this particular way of the Lord which prepares the soul for its peculiar disciplines. What if quite suddenly they are left to face a situation for which they are not responsible before they have had time to learn how to walk by faith? If we are fed as it were from meal to meal, and something intercepts the coming of the next meal, and they are alone?

Perhaps it was a faithless thought; but we have a tender Master. He did not rebuke, but took me to the same chapter and the same story which had spoken to my soul when first the work began.

"Philip answered Him, Two hundred pennyworth of bread is not sufficient for them, that every one of them may take a little.

" . . . And Jesus took the loaves; and when He had given thanks, He distributed to the disciples, and the disciples to them that were set down; and likewise of the fishes, as much as they would.

"When they were filled, He said unto His disciples, Gather up the fragments that remain, that nothing be lost.

"Therefore they gathered them together and filled twelve baskets with the fragments of the five barley loaves, which remained over and above unto them that had eaten."

And, as I believed, the promise was given to me then that there should be baskets over and above our daily supplies, and that, just as those men and women and their children were free to use the pieces of the loaves left over from that great meal if they needed them before they reached home, so we would be free to use ours, should need arise before we too reached Home, we and our children.

Remember the word unto Thy servant upon which Thou hast caused me to hope—if the prayer is repeated in these pages it is because it was so often repeated in our hearts—And now: Thou hast dealt well with Thy servant, O Lord, according unto Thy word. For the first five years before that day of prayer and promise, enough had come to meet the expenses of the work. But after that time something happened which we could not help connecting with the word about the baskets. More than was needed began to come, and continued to come until the year 1912, so that we had money in hand, and when the War years brought expansion in the work, which made building necessary, and when the value of the pound began to fall, until in 1919 it reached less than half its pre-War value, and many expected to see the work collapse, the baskets were ready, and we drew from them. Our heavenly Financier is not like the financiers of earth—past, present and future flow before Him in one wide stream. We have been taught that this is true by the things that He has done. We have seen it most clearly in the preparation of the members of our

Fellowship; we have seen it with awe: "There is not one that can do as Thou doest." But we are now thinking of the finances of the odd sparrow, and, standing on sure ground, can affirm just this: we have never lacked one good thing; and during the years of the War, people in the towns and villages began to say, "God is there"; for they could not account for what they saw except by saying that. And, later on, when we were able to do more outside work, we found that true thoughts about His love had already been spread abroad, because of what He had done. We have never had to labor to prove that He hears and answers prayer; the fact of our existence witnesses that it is so.

There were days of tension, days when it cost fifteen times more to bring a child from the nearest station than it had cost before the War, because of the fall in value of the pound and the rise in the price of rice, which sent exchange fares soaring as they had never soared before. And yet we were enabled to go on.

A note in an old Bible on Jeremiah 17: 6–8 recalls a day when our mail brought us letters that took it for granted that we must retrench: "If we look to man and limit our expectations and consider retrenchment as a way of meeting the difficulties of the time, then we shall be like the heath in the desert, and Dohnavur will be a parched place, a salt land. But if we truly trust the Lord we shall not even 'see' when heat cometh. Why should we see if our roots are spread out by the river? All through the heat our leaf will be green and we shall not be careful in the year of drought as though God were not responsible for us; neither will we cease from yielding fruit. We shall not retrench." And another day beside those comfortable words, "Now, therefore, fear ye not: I will nourish you, and your little ones," we found much help in writing as a little child might have written: *Our Joseph never dies.*

It is true that we were sometimes brought very low; as the graphs and the sketch of the sacks of rice in *Nor Scrip* show. But never once was a child left unsaved or unfed because we had not money or feared that we would not have enough in the future; nor was a bill ever left unpaid. Soon after the War, when the pound had fallen in value till it appeared to be about to dwindle away altogether, there was a night when I walked up and down the verandah in the moonlight, thinking of the children. For once the unearthly beauty failed to rest me, and I found myself saying aloud, "But, Lord, the children cannot live in moonlight." *Nor Scrip* tells how quickly and how lovingly He succored us. We closed down nothing. "Beat me a retreat," said Napoleon to his drummer-boy. "Sire, I know not how. Desaix never taught me that." Nor were we taught that. We had for our unfailing strength the mighty promises; we also had the records of those who had proved them before. The brave books sent out by the China Inland Mission especially were meat and drink to us. So were such marrowy words as Jeremy Taylor's "He that believes dares trust God for the morrow, and is not more solicitous for the next year than he is for that which is past." And still older words came with their music: "Thou feddest thine own people with angels' food, and didst send them from heaven bread prepared without their labor, able to content every man's delight, and agreeing to every taste. For Thy sustenance declared Thy sweetness unto Thy children." We knew that we should prove that His sustenance would content our delight and declare His sweetness to us His children. On September 4, 1914, we paid an advance for land on which to build nurseries. The note for the day says, "The beginning of the new walk on the water. Lord, if it be Thou, bid me come . . . and he said 'Come.'" And He Himself came to meet us on the water.

So in our darkest times he came, He who is the Light of the morning came to us. He is faithful that promised. He quickens the dead and calls the things that are not, as though they were.

We say, then, to anyone who is under trial, give Him time to steep the soul in His eternal truth. Go into the open air, look up into the depths of the sky, or out upon the wideness of the sea, or on the strength of the hills that is His also; or, if bound in the body, go forth in the spirit; spirit is not bound. Give Him time and, as surely as dawn follows night, there will break upon the heart a sense of certainty that cannot be shaken. These hundreds of pounds (or thousands for that matter), they will come. For the work that He has commanded they must come. Only, O God of heaven and earth, God of all the gold mines of the earth, keep us from going one foot beyond the way of Thy commandment.

What the Tamil calls the sap of the matter lies in that last sentence, and at the risk of repetition we underline it here. *No master is responsible for uncommanded work.* We find it necessary constantly to ask for a spirit of wisdom and penetration through an intimate knowledge of Him, so that, the eyes of our understanding being enlightened, we may know what we ought to do, and never, through carelessness in waiting upon Him, pledge Him to do what He did not intend should be done. "Depend upon it, God's work, done in God's way, will never lack God's supplies," said Hudson Taylor, and in our much smaller undertakings we have proved it so too.

But lest any should think of us more highly than they ought to think, I will tell of something that once befell us. Enough was coming in for daily needs, but we were looking forward to advance. Nothing came for advance. For a little while we went on, thinking it was only, as it had been sometimes before, delayed answer to prayer, and so by other and more painful discipline we were caused to retrace our steps, for we had taken a wrong turning. Long after we had returned to the way appointed for our feet, an auditor, knowing nothing of these matters, going through our accounts, noticed and pointed out to us a certain dip in the ascending line and, later, a quick ascent, so quick indeed, that the line for the year shows only the ascent. And we understood.

There are questions that we cannot answer. We had not acted without prayer, and we had believed that all was well. But we should have been more careful, walked more softly. This book is not written to explain mysteries, but only to bear witness to what actually is, and to tell, if it can, what we have been taught about giving time to be sure that we have the mind of our Master. And most of all in this matter we want to bear witness to the great kindness of our Lord Jesus Christ, with whom is forgiveness, and longsuffering, and mercy.

So we cannot fear for the future, however uncertain the prospect may be, or however apparently unsafe. "He stretcheth out the north over the empty place, and hangeth the earth upon nothing" is a sustaining word in times of faintheartedness. Tomorrow's sea is as uncharted as was yesterday's. "It is sufficient that we carry a compass."

18

God of the golden dust of stars
　　Scattered in space,
God of the starry blessings that light
　　Our happy place,
God of the little things,
　　We adore Thee,
　　Come before Thee,
Grateful in loving thanksgiving.

God of the blue of glancing wing,
　　Song of the bird,
God of the friendly comfort of smiles,
　　Cheer of a word,
God of the little things,
　　We adore Thee,
　　Come before Thee,
Grateful in loving thanksgiving.

God of the fairy pollen ball,
　　Frail flowery bell,
Touches of tenderness that would seem
　　Nothing to tell,
God of the little things,
　　We adore Thee,
　　Come before Thee,
Grateful in loving thanksgiving.

18. Three Tender Mercies

We have all known the gentle solace of human love. There has been a trouble, and we have braced ourselves to live through the day without letting anyone know. And then there was just a touch of a hand, or a word, or a penciled note—such a trifle; but that trifling thing was so unexpected, so undeserved, so brimful of what our beautiful old English calls tender mercies, that the heart melted before it, all the hurt gone. And there was a sense of something more. "Lord Jesus, what was it?" "My child, it was I; it is I."

Or we were about to enter into some cloud of tribulation, and He who goes before us turned back, as it were, to prepare us for the approaching trial. We had found it so, for example, before the passing of our friend, Walker of Tinnevelly, who would have been such a stay through the years of the War. The child of this chapter was the last one with whom he had played, just before he left Dohnavur to take a mission in the Telugu country, where he died. She was in perfect health then. But she outran him in the quick race home, and was standing on the doorstep to welcome him when, a few days later, he was there. It was what we saw before she left us that helped us so much that we think of it as a tender mercy.

Her name was Lulla. She was five years old, a Brahman child of much promise. She had sickened suddenly with an illness which we knew from the first must be dangerous. We could not ask a medical missionary to leave his hospital, a day and a half distant, for the sake of one child, but we did the best we could. We sent an urgent message to a medical evangelist trained at Neyyoor, who lived nearer, and he came at once. He arrived an hour too late.

But before he came we had seen this. It was in that chilly hour between night and morning. A lantern burned dimly in the room where Lulla lay; there was nothing in that darkened room to account for what we saw. The child was in pain, struggling for breath, turning to us for what we could not give. I left her with Mabel Wade and Ponnamal, and, going to a side room, cried to our Father to take her quickly.

I was not more than a minute away, but when I returned she was radiant. Her little lovely face was lighted with amazement and happiness. She was looking up and clapping her hands as delighted children do. When she saw me she stretched out her arms and flung them round my neck, as though saying good-bye, in a hurry to be gone; then she turned to the others in the same eager way, and then again, holding out her arms to Someone whom we could not see, she clapped her hands.

Had only one of us seen this thing, we might have doubted. But we all three saw it. There was no trace of pain in her face. She was never to taste of pain again. We saw nothing in that dear child's face but unimaginable delight.

We looked where she was looking, almost thinking that we would see what she saw. What must the fountain of joy be if the spray from the edge of the pool can be like that? When we turned the next bend of the road, and the sorrow that waited there met us, we were comforted, words cannot tell how tenderly, by this that we had seen when we followed the child almost to the border of the Land of Joy.

And before the War there was another look through to the Unseen, for it was as though a hand drew back a corner of the curtain that hangs between our world and that other where forces move to direct our tangled and painful affairs.

There may be some who still remember the tragedy of Portugal, the great meeting led by Adeline, Duchess of Bedford, the rousing articles by Sir Arthur Gibb, the courage of *The Times* and the *Spectator* * and other papers, and the final victory, when the prisons opened and the political prisoners were set free from their living death.

We in India had followed the fight. We, too, were working for the liberation of captives. We wondered what lay within; for always there is a spiritual secret at the heart of a great battle for righteousness. And now came a letter from her who had led that fight, warrior and lover of God.

> I have had a beautiful confirmation of the victory of faith, over quite insuperable obstacles, in the recent amnesty given to the Portuguese political prisoners. When I went out to Lisbon this time last year, there was no hope for them, speaking humanly. I went to as many as I could and told them God would open a way of escape, and one sailor boy slipped a letter into my hand, unknown to the jailers, who were very cruel; it was a statement of his case, and the cover was addressed in Portuguese, "To the care of God." He had written it in hope; and one day the cell door opened, and a stranger came in, and he took his chance. I held a public meeting in London, and showed the writing, and said that justice would be done and they would be free. Everyone was kind and helped me, but a few *believed*, and so it has come at last. This is just to tell you what you know, that there is a performance of those things that are spoken of the Lord.

That letter was with us through all the years of the War: its glorious assurance succored us many a time. But, even

---

* Then a gallant paper edited by St. Loe Strachey.

so, there was a day after the War was over when we could
see nothing but the vanishing pound. And now I hesitate.
For this third loving-kindness belongs in spirit to the last
chapter, and it is so very small that I do not like to tell it at
all. Set beside that noble battle, it is mere anticlimax. But,
after all, life is just that—a jumble of great things and little
things.

Exchange had done its worst: a pound sent from home
meant less than ten shillings here, when, for the first and
last time in our history, we had not enough (we thought)
for our many guests. It had, of course, always been our
pleasure to care for the guest room ourselves; but now it
seemed that whatever we had of our own should be kept
for the children. And with grief and burning of heart, we
forced ourselves to put a card in the guest room saying
what the day's food cost.

The card had not been there long when Dr. Inwood
came from England and stayed with us. We could not bear
that such a card should be his welcome, so we took it away
and filled the room with roses. They would be his welcome. We told him nothing. Like others, he thought that
someone or something was behind us. But one day, as he
stood under the big tamarind tree near the school and
watched the children swarming in and out, he said suddenly, "His compassions fail not, they are new every
morning, and that means this," and he put his hand into
his pocket and drew out a bundle of notes.

Never shall I forget the inrush of the sense of the love of
our Father that flooded my heart then, or the sudden
sweetness after the misery of writing that wretched little
card. The rebuke was so gentle that it seemed a caress. It
was the very comfort of God.

We never told Dr. Inwood about the card. But we did
tell him about the provision of the years, and he asked us
to share it with others. And so *Nor Scrip* came to be written, and two years later *Tables in the Wilderness*, and after
six more years, *Meal in a Barrel*.

That minute by Lulla's cot when we saw the bright reflection of unseen things, that letter telling of the hidden working of the powers of the world to come, and this drink of the love of our Lord—how can we tell what they were to us? We cannot tell it, but this we know:

> He who has felt that Face of beauty,
>   Which wakes the world's great hymn,
> For one unutterable moment
>   Bent in love o'er him,
> In that look finds earth, heaven, men and angels
>   Grow nearer through Him.

In that look such a thing as the card over which we had grieved so foolishly became unthinkable. Earth, heaven, men and angels were nearer now. The card was torn up and, with a great sigh of relief, dropped into the wastepaper basket; and never again has anything like that been done anywhere within the borders of our Fellowship.

19.

Lord Jesus, Intercessor,
  Oh, teach us how to pray:
Not wave-like, rising, falling,
  In fitful clouds of spray.
The mighty tides of ocean
  A deeper secret know,
Their currents undefeated move
  Whatever winds may blow.

Lord Jesus, Intercessor,
  Creator of the sea,
Teach us the tides' great secret
  Of quiet urgency.
Spindrift of words we ask not,
  But, Lord, we seek to know
The conquering patience of the tides
  Whatever winds may blow.

19. Our Friends

In the early years before we knew of the temple-children, when the first convert girl came out of her Hindu home to confess Christ in baptism, there was a great commotion in the district. We were pelted with handfuls of refuse, shouted down and hooted out of the streets of all the towns and villages within a day's journey of her home. We did then what the early China Inland pioneers did on the Sian plain—we fled in a circle. We turned westward, used as headquarters for a year the empty and disabled mission-house at Dohnavur, and returned to the eastern village near Great Lake, as we have told in Chapter 4.

While the furor over the girl's conversion was at its height, the house of the schoolmaster in Great Lake was burned down. He sent to the mission a list of his damaged property. The list showed much more than had been lost in the fire.

It was the ordinary thing to do. No one who knew him was surprised that he did it. They would have been surprised if he had not done it; the people in his immediate world would have thought that he had lost an opportunity unlikely to recur; so we had not the help of public opinion. We have no idea how much we owe to public opinion till we find ourselves in a place where, in our sense of the word, there is none. In writing to a friend I told her of this, not knowing that she had supported him for years and had thought of him as her own evangelist. Naturally she felt aggrieved.

This incident was like a jerk on the reins pulling me up before I had seen anything to avoid, and when the children came, and people wrote affectionately offering to support this one and that, with a view to having their "own missionary" in the future, I remembered it. How could we honestly promise an own missionary to anyone? "Mine the mighty ordination of the pierced Hands" is a line that belongs to the Indian evangelist as much as to us, and that should give pause to promise. There was another thought at the back of our minds. "I am your humble Supporter," wrote a schoolboy to the missionary who paid his fees. He meant *supported*, of course, and what that boy expected when he coined his new noun was that he could be supported up to B.A. or F.B.A. (Failed B.A., quite a decent degree here), and if he had been asked to do anything with his two hands towards his own support, his feelings would have been badly hurt. We did not want even the whisper of such feelings. Also, and chiefly, we did not want any child to lose the kind of prayer that it would perhaps desperately need, from lack of knowledge on the part of its friends at home. And, because we are human, it is easy to glide down that so gradually graded incline that leads eventually to giving people what they naturally like best to hear—nice things, encouraging things, rather than the less pleasing truth. So we did not enter into temptation. We settled it then and there that we would have no supporters as such. We would offer the friend who cared enough to accept the gift (which is a burden too) a child, to be hers or his for prayer. The bond would be one of prayer only. Anything the friend was moved to give would be used for the good of the family, not earmarked for an individual child.

Some did not care for this; so we suggested places where the usual plan was followed, and they found themselves at home there. But many understood, and we counted on them; we have never regretted our confidence. Some have even asked for our most perverse children, for those who would be generally called "hopeless." Again and again we have seen their faith rewarded.

So gratefully we put prayer-friends—men, women and children all over the world—to the front of our scheme of life. Their faithfulness is part of the gold cord.

So is the comradeship of fellow-missionaries whose hearts and consciences have been touched on behalf of the defenseless children. All over India we have such friends, Indian and foreign, medical missionaries, evangelists, teachers in mission schools—we cannot name them all; the Lord remembers them. The cord is made of many golden threads.

And men and women in the great Services of India have been our friends. Little do their detractors know them. Here and there we come upon an exception, but no one who has lived out among the people and seen these men's lives can question that, far oftener than not, something money could not buy has been given. It will be missed when it is gone. It is being missed now in many a little village far off the road, which in old days knew itself fathered and now feels fatherless. But our business is to tell of what some of these Servants of India have done for us. Some have saved children or have quietly stood by us and made it possible for us to save them. And this meant that those men were not afraid of being known to be on the side of the angels.

In various countries we have friends whom we call secretaries. Our first came to us, as we say in our ignorant speech, by accident. One day—it was February 20, 1909—without notice, a bullock cart arrived, and out sprang two girls. Their letter proposing a day's visit had been delayed. "And I can remember nearly every hour of it," wrote, twenty-one years later, the dearest friend that a work like this could ever have. "The picture I shall never forget is of you, with Tara in a wee blue *cumusu* and with an armful of crimson hibiscus flowers, coming to put them in our room after we had been there about an hour; she was the first child I saw." And when our new friend had to go: "Tendrils were torn as of a plant; and life could never be the same as before."

For it was she who, a few months afterwards, became Mrs. Streeter, and in 1913 our Home Secretary. There was a lightened day when a cable came whose two words told us all we wanted to hear: "Satisfied, Hallelujah."

We had not known of any hunger when first we met. We had seen only an ardent love that longed to serve to the uttermost. There had been no hint of husks, and waste places, and a consuming thirst, nor sign that we were not one regarding the Bible. But afterwards we came to know, and now He who satisfieth the longing soul and filleth the hungry soul with goodness had filled and satisfied her, and, in the gift of Himself in this new fullness, He had given her Bible back to her, a new book now.

Then others helped us, sometimes the mothers and sisters of different members of our Fellowship—Mabel Beath of Victoria, Australia, Mrs. Waller of Dublin, Mrs. Roberts of Edinburgh. Each was pledged not to ask for anything for us but prayer. And even where prayer is concerned, we may not "importune."

For it is the Master of the field, not we, who must appoint workers by prayer. The field is the world. Who can pray for anything so large except in a vague general way? To each, then, is his or her part of the field. The call to work there in spirit is, or may be, as definite as the call to the missionary to go there in body. But when, constrained by a great love, we look over the hedge of our own plot to the wide acres beyond, we may, thank God, work there too. The spirit has powers denied to the flesh. It can fly over hedges. And yet somehow it always flies back like a homing bird to the place appointed for its special ministry.

Out here mountains of difficulty have often appeared to melt into air. Impossible, we have said; and seen the thing done, we hardly knew how. Then we have known that someone was in prayer. Or a change, gradual or sudden, has come over a dangerously difficult child or man or woman. The wonder of this is described by George MacDonald in a sentence that at first seems rather obscure. It repays a second reading: "So long as evil comes to the front, it appears an interminable, unconquerable thing; but all the time there may be a change, positive as inexplicable, at the very door. How is it that a child begins to be good? Upon what fulcrum rests the knife-edge of alteration? As indistinguishable is the moment in which the turn takes place; equally perplexing to keenest investigation the part of being in which the renovation commences. Who shall analyze repentance, as a force, or as a phenomenon? *You cannot see it coming. Before you know, there it is and the man is no more what he was; his life is upon other lines. The wind hath blown.*"

Lord of the field, Lord of the wind, Christ Jesus, Intercessor, teach us to pray.

That blessed wind blew through our life late in 1912, when R.T. Archibald, of the Children's Special Service Mission, came to Dohnavur. The first sign of that invisible presence was when a little girl put her fingers into her ears in her Bible class. The story of the day was about Achan, and for some reason she did not wish to listen. The reason appeared later. She had found a discarded doll on whose minute garment a morsel of lace had attracted her. She wanted that inch of lace for her doll's pocket-handkerchief. So she ripped off the other doll's garment and took possession. No thought of self-excuse came to relieve her awakened conscience—that the doll was nobody's in particular did not help her; she was Achan. It was intolerable to listen to his story just then, so she put her fingers in her ears. But there was no relief in this and, greatly worried, she took the offending handkerchief and buried it in a remote corner of the garden, feeling more Achan-like than ever.

It was then that the Wind of God blew through us as a family, and one night, by the light of a lantern, that Achan treasure was dug up, and the whole tale came out.

I think that incident shows more than anything else I could tell just what that mission did for us. There was a true conviction of sin, a true repentance, honest confession and a change of life that lasted. Not one child then converted went back. Some are mothers of families now, and some are our fellow-workers here. There can be few communities of children in India who do not owe much to R.T.A., and gratefully we count ourselves among the number.

Sometimes, by means not to be explained except by believing that the Spirit of God directs prayer, people who care for us are moved to intercession in a way which they do not themselves understand. I recall a letter from America which asked if on a certain day, which the writer named, we had been in danger of fire? On that day she had been stirred to prayer by a sense as it were of fire, in connection with us. It had perplexed her, but she had yielded to the sense of urgency. Could we tell her if there had been a cause? But we had not been in any such danger. It was years since our last fire. All our buildings were now tiled, not thatched. Wondering what could be meant, I turned to the log book, on the chance that an entry there would explain it, and found that in truth that day was full of trouble, burning trouble. Within three days it had wholly passed—so passed, indeed, that the very date had been forgotten.

During all the earlier years we were constantly travelling on behalf of the children, and often this protective prayer turned what might have been peril to safety and opportunity. There was a difficult journey in a Native

State when Pearl (she who with Ponnamal had stood by us from the first) and a younger Indian sister found themselves at night on a deserted road with only their carter, who did not know the language, and a very evil man (as they knew afterwards) as guide.

The man was evidently bent on mischief, and the elder woman was anxious about the younger. From what far corner of the earth was prayer rising then? They, too, were praying as they sat in the dark in the cart as it moved slowly along the dark road. And as they prayed, the guide's intention seemed to change—he spoke in a new tone, and presently led them to a big, lonely, but safe farmhouse set among its fields, where the family welcomed them almost as though they had been old friends, and they had a wonderful opportunity to speak of the things of God.

And after the household had retired for the night a little sorrowful widow, thirsty for comfort, crept out of her corner and went to them. It was the strange sweetness of their happiness that drew her. She knew that they were very tired, and yet they were glad and peaceful. "Tell me more, tell me more," she said wistfully over and over again; and they talked together far into the night.

20

Father, hear us, we are praying,
Hear the words our heart are saying,
We are praying for our children.

Keep them from the powers of evil,
From the secret, hidden peril,
Father, hear us for our children.

From the whirlpool that would suck them,
From the treacherous quicksand, pluck them,
Father, hear us for our children.

From the worldling's hollow gladness,
From the sting of faithless sadness,
Father, Father, keep our children.

Through life's troubled waters steer them,
Through life's bitter battle cheer them,
Father, Father, be Thou near them.

Read the language of our longing,
Read the wordless pleadings thronging,
Holy Father, for our children.

And wherever they may bide,
Lead them Home at eventide.

20. The Children

This is not a book of flowers; it is more like a steady walk through a wood. But our Indian forests sometimes open on a sunny slope—"I know a bank whereon the wild thyme grows"—that kind of place. For on either side of the path, however straitly it presses on, there are ferny hollows and little flowery patches. And there are other forest ways, tiny and winding. When one comes upon them it is impossible not to wonder whence they come and whither they go. There is always a kind of mystery about an untracked path. So here, with the children, we are among paths, and we want to follow them all. To what loving little nest among the grass does this path lead?

Moonflower, three and a half years old, was in trouble one day over a bee. It had stung her and then dashed into the flame of a lantern. "Dead, and it never prayed to be forgiven," she said solemnly. Or this, so full of quick humor: "The hippopotamus brought up the little girl"— Sunflower's explanation to her Sittie of her drawing of a large hippopotamus beside what was meant to represent a very little girl. It must have suddenly occurred to her that it looked like an unsafe arrangement.

Perhaps the dearest of all, like banks of woodland flowers, are the stories of our children's children. "Don't throw that nail down like that!" And the little daughter of Vineetha, one of the first of the Lotus Buds, remembering her Good Friday story, took the nail that a carpenter had dropped and another child had used as a plaything; and she kissed it.

Or this, Bala's sweet Lotus to her mother (the flower has at least thirty different names, so there is no confusion in Tamil, though so many of our children are called Lotus): "Take the bag off my thumb, please. I will not suck it any more," followed some hours later, when she felt her baby resolution failing her, "Now please put the bag on again."

Or this, which is about the children of Jullanie, our first surviving baby, the only Christian woman in a hard Hindu village. One day Delight, then very small, heard the bell in the idol temple near their home ring in the early morning, and she shut her eyes and covered her face as she had seen others do here where, hour by hour, the prayer-bell rings.

"What were you doing?" asked her mother.

"I was praying," said Delight, who had never been distinguished for special sanctity.

"For whom did you pray?" asked her mother gently. And Delight, who could not talk plainly, signified somehow that her prayer was for the people of the village who do not know our Lord Jesus.

So it has become the custom of the children (Sunshine who is five, Pearl-boy, four, and Delight), every time when the idol bell rings, to pray for the people of that Hindu village.

Moonflower, the little one who mourned the impenitent bee, has a story that, even if it were the only one of its kind, would make the work worthwhile.

She was born in a country village, in a small house belonging to her grandmother. The old lady pottered about and saw to the day's cooking, and the girl-mother lay in her corner, the darkest and stuffiest in the dark and stuffy house, thinking of the husband who had gone away somewhere and had not returned, and pondering a plan that was to lead to finding him if he still lived.

Life was hard on her then. Who would be responsible for the children's marriage expenses if indeed he had died? Her own people were poor, as caste-folk often are. And fears lay heavy on the mother's heart as she thought of the future. The only glimmer of light was a poor hope of perhaps being able by pilgrimage to many shrines to win help for him if he were ill or in trouble. One day seductive whispers like little winds began to blow about her: "The mother of a servant of the gods is favored of the gods," they said. "Much merit is hers. No marriage expenses oppress her. Her child can never be a deserted wife, or a widow." But the mother knew what lay behind the glitter of temple service. "That shall never be," she said. And as soon as she could drag herself from her corner she was up, and, with the old grannie and her two children, she set off on her long journey, tired in spirit, tired in body, but brave as an Indian woman can be. Day after day, week after week, they wandered on, till the young mother's strength failed and the baby was slowly starving in her arms.

Then they came to a town. In the heart of it was set a great temple sacred to Siva, the third in the Hindu triad. Round about stood the Brahman streets.

Through the huge gates and portals they passed with their offerings of fruit and flowers and what silver coins they could spare. They prostrated themselves before the shrine, with hands outstretched they worshiped, and turned away, worn out, almost penniless, uncomforted. Nearby were temple-women's houses. A widow or a deserted wife, if she be of good caste and has pretty children, is always sure of a welcome in such houses. The old grannie knew this, the young mother knew it too; but they never considered going there; they went on to the Government hospital, for the mother was too ill to walk farther.

The baby, too, was ill. The mother, true to her training, thought first of her husband. The pilgrimage could not be interrupted, and there were still more shrines to visit. But the baby would die if she took it with her. Then the nurse offered to take it and care for it as her own. And the mother, seeing in this offer the only chance for its life, consented. But she did all she knew. On a thin slip of palm leaf she had a statement written with an iron style, and the scored words were rubbed over with saffron to make them indelible. The little one was to be properly cared for, educated, and never given to the temple or any other evil.

There is no record of what that mother felt. But we, who have seen one like her compelled, by the hard unwritten laws of her land, to choose between two evils and know no other choice—we who have seen her raise her hands to heaven in one last mute protest, one dumb plea—we know how it must have been with that mother as she turned her back on the hospital and slowly walked down the long street, with the other child clinging to her sari and the old grannie, mournfully mumbling prayers, following wearily.

The nurse watched the three forlorn figures as they faded out of sight, and then she broke her promise. And the cold gods looked on with their cold stone eyes as the little living child was made theirs.

But there is a God in heaven. That mother's cry had entered into His ears. Within a week that little child was safe in Dohnavur.

And now she is Moonflower. And as you watch her, with her diminutive garment of washed-out blue carefully tucked up, carrying, with another elfin creature's help, a bucket of water for the flowers, or sweeping withered leaves from the path with a grass broom, or down on her knees scrubbing the red tiles of her nursery floor, you think of that mother and of her prayer to the Unknown God, and everything in you is glad that He is not far from any one of us.

He was not far from the sorrowful child who stood alone in a room whose only door was shut and locked.

There was no window in the room, so it was quite dark. But Pink Lotus was not so much afraid of darkness as of light. With the opening of that door her father would come into the room and command her to do what she could not do. No, she would die first. She had promised the mother, who had been carried out of that room only a week before, that she would be good. This that her father commanded was bad. But one day he might force her to go to the hated temple. There was only one way of escape. In the court-yard of the house was a deep well; she had often looked into its black depths. Deep, deep down there was a little sparkle of light in the blackness. Better the well than the temple.

At last, tired out with longings for her mother and fear of her father, Pink Lotus fell into a troubled sleep.

But she was soon wakened. The door creaked on its hinges. The light that she dreaded pricked her shut eyes; she sprang up and stood before her father trembling.

"Pink Lotus!" he said, raising his arm threateningly, "The priest demands thee. Thou must obey." And when she refused he struck her down.

This was repeated; day after day there was the question, the refusal, the blow, till one day instead of the blow came a young man with a pleasant face. Pink Lotus hardly dared to raise her eyes to him, nor was it required that she should. "I have found a bridegroom for thee," said her father. "Thou shalt be free from that other. This is what is written in thy forehead." And gratefully she accepted so blessed an alternative. The marriage was duly performed, no ceremony of importance was omitted. Content, un-speakably happy and quite unsuspicious, even though the wedding had been singular in quietness and quickness, Pink Lotus went to her new home.

But there was something strange about that home. It was not as other homes. There was no mother-in-law, no relative appeared, no one came near her but an old woman who cooked for her. And Rama, her husband, was often away—business called him, he said. They lived in a city, and its ways were unknown to her. Business doubtless did call husbands away. Sometimes this kind husband took his bride for a drive in his car, and he gave her beautiful jewels. She had all that she could wish, except just a little more of her husband whom she soon learned to love dearly.

But one day he dropped something when he left her. It was a letter. Pink Lotus had learned to read. She had never been taught that she should not read the letters of another, and innocently she read that letter through, at first without clear understanding. Then soon its full meaning flashed on her mind. It was from her husband's wife, his real wife. She was not his wife, not even his legal second wife: her wedding had been a mockery.

What that loving girl endured during the two or three days that passed before Rama returned, we can only gather because of what we know she endured afterwards.

When he next came, she took off her tali—the gold marriage token that she wore round her neck. She gave it to him. "It is not mine," she said simply. "You are wronging her, your real wife." But the words must have torn her heart.

He fell on his knees, imploring her to keep it. He had been married against his will. This, his marriage to her, was his true marriage. She only was his beloved. But nothing could move that resolute will. She knew of no God to whom to pray, for the god whom she had been taught to worship was he who had demanded a far more evil thing than this, or so she believed, for so she had been told. She prayed no prayer in words; she dared not frame a prayer. But her heart cried out for help. There is a word in our Scriptures about the widow and fatherless child: "If thou afflict them in any wise and they cry at all unto Me, I will surely hear their cry." Pink Lotus, motherless, was more bereft than if she had been fatherless. She did not know how to cry in the great way of prayer. "But if they cry at all"—surely love could go no further—O Power of the unseen world, how tender You are! Already help was commanded. In that great city of many sins and griefs was an American woman, wise and pitiful. She heard of this poor little Pink Lotus and worked for her salvation.

A few weeks later a letter came to Dohnavur asking if we would take a lotus bud, trodden into the mire but pure of spirit. We do not as a rule take any but little children, but who could refuse a story like this? So she was brought to us, a lovely thing in jewels and soft, pink-colored garments, and when we saw her for the first time by the clear waters of a mountain river (for we were with the children on the hills near Dohnavur at the time) we could only think of the flower whose name we have given her here— the lotus of our temple pools. She had never seen running water and, as she delicately stepped in and followed the little blue-clad girls who were wading and splashing joyfully, we did not wonder that a butterfly mistook her for a flower and lighted on her hair. Water with golden lights upon it, the dancing blue, the great crimson-and-black butterfly fluttering over that radiant pink lotus, and all around the green of the forest—could there have been a brighter or a more serene beginning?

But soon she began to suffer keenly. Terrible waves can roll up and sweep over such a soul when the first relief of safety has had time to pass. Like a bird with a broken wing, like any desolate thing that heart can imagine, she lived for many months among us, turning on her new world great sad eyes. Then illness came to make life harder, and sometimes she all but gave way. But in the end there was deliverance and peace, and now the pent-up energies of love have been set free in the service of the sick and sorrowful who come to Dohnavur; for Pink Lotus is one of our nurse-evangelists.

21

God seems sometimes to confound our prayers, by putting off deliverance to such a point that it seems removed to a distance from which it cannot reach us. He does not often deal thus with us, because He is merciful, but He does it sometimes, for the very same reasons.—Adolphe Monod.

The Lord seems to come steadily to us in every individual case we meet—"Believest thou that I am able to do this?" Whether it be a case of demon possession, bodily upset, mental twist, backsliding, indifference, difference of nationality and thought—the challenge is to me. Do I know my risen Lord? Do I know the power of His indwelling Spirit? Am I wise enough in God's sight to bank on what Jesus told me? Am I foolish enough according to the wisdom of the world to do it? Or am I abandoning the supernatural position, which is the only one for a missionary, of boundless confidence in Jesus?—Oswald Chambers.

Lord, art Thou wrapped in cloud,
    That prayer should not pass through?
But heart that knows Thee sings aloud,
    Beyond the grey, the blue.
Look up, look up to the hills afar,
    And see in clearness, the Evening Star.

Should misty weather try
    The temper of the soul,
Come, Lord, and purge and purify,
    And let Thy hands make whole,
Till we look up to the hills afar
    And see in clearness the Evening Star.

Oh, never twilight dim
    But candles bright are lit,
And then the heavenly vesper hymn—
    The peace of God in it,
And we look up to the hills afar,
    And see in clearness the Evening Star.

21. The Care That Cometh

I have told in Chapter 15 how *acceptance* became one of our pivot words. As we went on, it became the warp and woof of the fabric of life. As each child came we welcomed her with hope and expectation of the best. Nothing is more fatal than to cease to expect and to hope. And yet we knew that we might have a long way to go before we could draw breath and lean back, and feel that all was well where that child was concerned. For some we had to accept "the care that cometh daily" as our daily bread.

When our first little girl, Pearleyes, had been with us for a few months, a friend sent her by mail a picture of our Lord Jesus Christ. We never use pictures of our Saviour. We ask the Holy Spirit to show Him to our children; for who but the Divine can show the Divine, and who but one that has seen can show unimaginable beauty? So this picture was the first of its kind that Pearleyes had seen. She opened the parcel eagerly. It was a photograph of a noted painting, a thing of reverence. "Who is it? Our Lord Jesus?" She gazed at it for a moment dismayed, then burst into tears. "I thought He was far more beautiful than that," she said.

To such a child, so responsive by nature, came very

keen assaults, and perhaps the attacks were the keener
because her coming had led to the unlocking of so many
prison doors.

We have no matron here, nor ever have had one. We
have no one between the children and ourselves, so
Pearleyes brought all her childish naughtinesses to us direct, and sometimes they were serious. But we wrestled
through together, again and again bringing her to Him
who had redeemed her, and waiting for the full surrender
which was so long delayed.

After several arduous years, just when we were beginning to dare to hope that we were through the worst, a
little child of three, in whose ears were set the golden
jewels that marked her dedication to the gods, came to
Dohnavur, and Pearleyes eagerly asked to be allowed to
take care of little Blueflower. Often when a child is saved
something disastrous immediately happens. It is as though
the dragon, balked of his prey, swings the scaly horror of
his folded tail in the little one's direction and lays her low.
Be that as it may, Pearleyes had hardly begun to take care
of Blueflower when an accident occured. Blueflower's leg
was broken.

Pearleyes rushed to me. "I did it," she sobbed, for she
was always honest. "I was impatient with her, and put her
down suddenly." How so slight a thing could have done it
no one could tell. But it seemed providential that a medical student passing through the village had called to see
us that day, and he set it. It was wrongly set. Blueflower
had to be taken to Neyyoor, where the leg was broken
again and reset.

As the little procession left the compound (Mabel Wade
in charge of the child, who had to be carried those thirty-
nine miles in a hammock and, entirely undisciplined, was
crying vehemently) I noticed Pearleyes slip out through
the gate and set off by herself. She was desperate with
grief, remorse and wounded pride, and was "going away."

Bonds of love, divine and human, held her from that;

but months of spiritual vigil followed. Blueflower returned from Neyyoor, and not even Pearleyes could find anything wrong with her. And yet, "Yes, she can walk, but she will not be able to run." Blueflower ran. "She will not be able to swim." It sounded like a senseless perversion, an obsession, but Pearleyes was in earnest, she was acutely wretched, and she could not see that she herself was creating her own miseries.

It is never safe for a convert, or for a child who is practically a convert, to be unhappy for long. Behind him or her is a darkness. Phantoms haunt that darkness, and memories, like hands, are ever pulling, pulling, pulling. As soon as we could we went to the forest near Dohnavur, taking with us, among others, Pearleyes and Blueflower. If Blueflower could learn to swim, Pearleyes would know that her prayer had been heard and that she was not rejected. If not—she did not finish the sentence; but we knew how another would finish it for her, and he was near, even there in the beautiful forest by a pool whose waters are so clear that one wonders how he dare approach them. Intently, day by day, Pearleyes watched the first few strokes, as Blueflower learned them; and when at last for the first time the little one crossed the pool, amid jubilant shouts from the children, those watchful dark eyes lightened. "There is no flaw in the stroke," said Pearleyes, and turned and walked into the wood in a quietness that we did not disturb.

Only our prayer followed her on little loving wings, and we drew a deep breath of relief. "We have turned the corner at last," we said.

But round the corner was that other who had slipped away baffled at the pool, and over the borders of that troubled soul the shadow crept again, moving in a stealthy way like a thing alive. But was it not alive? The powers of the darkness live. Alone, and together, in earnest prayer we brought her to Calvary:

By Thy Cross and Passion,
Precious blood out-poured,
Plead we now, "Command deliverance,
Blessed Lord."

That was the burden of our prayer. And we looked for an instant answer.

It did not come. We probed ourselves for a cause, we asked for the searchlights to be turned on all our ways: "Try me, O God, and seek the ground of my heart." For eighteen months, in tension of spirit, we waited; but such a time is timeless; it might as well have been eighteen years. And we learned to accept the mystery of a delayed answer to our prayers, even to such an urgent prayer as this had been. "Oh, if I could adore Him in His hidden ways, when there is darkness under His feet, and darkness in His pavilion and clouds are about His throne!" wrote Samuel Rutherford in 1659. To learn to do that was the lesson assigned us then. And in the end, not gradually as it had crept over her, but suddenly as at a word of command, the gloom passed. And that dear child, fully delivered, became our fellow-soldier in the battles of the Lord.

The lesson that had been assigned us was the willing acceptance of daily, nightly perplexity and disappointment without explanation. In the Gospels such a matter was always dealt with instantly, and we had seen instant salvation and had read of the same in books. Here was delay. And we were not told why, and have not yet been told. We learned to accept the silence of our God.

In such days we prove each other. For the demands are greatest then. And to find that nothing is too much to ask of one another is to know what our gold cord can be, a golden thing right through.

22.

Strength of my heart, I need not fail,
    Not mine to fear but to obey,
With such a Leader who could quail?
    Thou art as Thou wert yesterday.
Strength of my heart, I rest in Thee,
    Fulfill Thy purposes through me.

Hope of my heart, though suns burn low,
    And fades the green from all the earth,
Thy quenchless hope would fervent glow,
    From barren waste would spring to birth.
Hope of my heart, oh, cause to be
    Renewals of Thy hope in me.

Love of my heart, my streams run dry.
    O Fountain of the heavenly hills,
Love, blessed love, to Thee I cry,
    Flood all my secret hidden rills.
Waters of love, oh, pour through me;
    I must have love, I must have Thee.

Lord, give me love, then I have all,
    For love casts out tormenting fear,
And love sounds forth a trumpet call
    To valiant hope; and sweet and clear
The birds of joy sing in my tree,
    Love of my heart, when I have Thee.

22. A New Thread in Our Gold Cord

There was a day, near the close of 1916, while the depression of the War was heavy upon us all, when the future of the work rose up and frightened me. My heart sank. I knew that I must ask for something to brace the slack fibers, and when a call for a new decision of faith came and I could not rise to it, the deadly truth had me in its grip: I was afraid. Of what use is a frightened soldier in a battle?

But God hath not given the spirit of fear, but of power and of love and of discipline. *Discipline*—the word was like the sting of cold rain in the face. This flabbiness was not faith. How recover? How be renewed in the spirit of the mind? Lord, do something, do anything. Bid me come to Thee from any boat on any water, only teach me how to walk on the sea. There was no answer that I heard for a while. Then, suddenly, and with complete unexpectedness, came a word in the ear.

It is not necessary to write that word; to each apart is his discipline. And lest "he yield to some enchantment and liquefy and waste away till the spirit is melted out of him and the sinews of his soul are extirpated and he is made a feeble wielder of the lance," the wise Captain of souls Himself chooses His soldier's discipline to the end that he may be "not brittle and useless, but tempered like steel."*

This page is being written in the early morning, before the life of the day begins, and just now the chimes of dawn come floating over the quiet spaces as one of the children beats out note by note on the bells:

> God is my strong salvation,
>> What foe have I to fear?
> In darkness and temptation
>> My light, my help is near.

It is so now. It was so then. When Peter was come down out of the ship, he walked on the water to go to Jesus. But when he saw the wind boisterous, he was afraid; and, beginning to sink, he cried, saying, Lord, save me. And immediately Jesus stretched forth His hand, and caught him, and said unto him, O thou of little faith, wherefore didst thou doubt? Not, Wherefore didst thou come? He never asks that question. But, Wherefore didst thou doubt?

How good, how happy, how safe it was, when that hand was stretched out. One hardly realized what had happened till a soft and gentle gladness came, like a bird coming home to its nest.

But before this, in the little interval between the coming of that beginning-to-sink feeling and the stretching forth of that loving hand, a new thread was added to our gold cord. I cannot doubt that this which I have told bears directly on that. Something had to be done which would be difficult because it was new here, and we of the South are conservative; also it would be greatly attacked by the enemy of souls. And just at the hour appointed, the mail

---

* Plato, *The Republic*, Book III, 411.

brought a little paper-backed book, *When God Came.** Love burned along its pages. It was a book aflame.

We had at that time seven Indian girls who were seeking to live a life of unreserved devotion, a life without fences. "From poor content with less than all, my soul is called to go"—each in her own way said it. Something was required to unite and fortify them. Jonathan, Saul's son, arose and went to David in the wood and strengthened his hands in God. We needed to meet one another in Jonathan's wood. We did meet there; we shaped ourselves into a group, and called ourselves "Sisters of the Common Life"; and immediately trouble chased the heels of trouble, and we learned that our enemy is more aware than we are of the spiritual possibilities that depend upon obedience. We should never be surprised that he seeks by assault and, if that fails, by undermining our defenses, to compel us to give way.

The name "Sisters of the Common Life" came from the Brotherhood of Common Life, founded by Gerard Grote of Holland. The Brothers worked with their hands and gave themselves to the training of "such as sought, apart from the evil about them, a pure and godly life." Communion with God and laborious work filled their days. They lived the common life, but they lived it with God for men. Our thought in taking the name was that the line so often drawn between spiritual and secular has no place with us if we follow Him who not only withdrew to the mountain but also went about doing good. As the earlier part of this story tells, we wanted to rub out that line. He took a towel. We were still learning how to take our towel; and when we found the translation, "Put on the apron of humility to serve one another" (1 Peter 5:5), we wondered if the apostle as he wrote thought of that day when the Lord of lords took a towel and fastened it on like an apron. The teaching of the usual pulpit and poem is (we believe)

---

* By Bishop Bardsley, then Secretary of the C.M.S.

all wrong about Martha and Mary. The Lord rebuked not service, but fuss. And so when we built our House of Prayer we set on its highest roof not one needle, as the Tamil calls the little pointed shaft that ends a gabled roof, but two. The spirit can sit at the Master's feet while the hands are filled with work for others. "Come unto Me and rest—take My yoke upon you." We have it again in the inexhaustible words, "Abide in Me and I in you. As the branch cannot bear fruit of itself, except it abide in the vine; no more can ye, except ye abide in Me. I am the vine, ye are the branches: he that abideth in Me, and I in him, the same bringeth forth much fruit: for without Me ye can do nothing."

Our meetings were mainly in English. Except our Bible and the *Pilgrim's Progress*, there were no books in Tamil that offered just what these girls began to want. Rolle and Suso and Tersteegen, on whom the still dews fell in the century of turmoil that we think of as Tamerlane's, and Bishop Moule and Josephine Butler of our own time, and Thomas à Kempis, pupil of Grote and Brother of Common Life, Samuel Rutherford and Père Didon, brothers in spirit though divided by the letter of the law, and the brave and burning souls of every age, these had left torches.

This group of girls has grown steadily year by year as one and another, drawn by the irresistible cords of love, have come asking to join it. It is still assailed, but chiefly from within. It is as though the adversary could never get accustomed to this little company of Indian women (and of later years, others) whose one purpose is to be spiritually ready to go all lengths with their Lord.

They have meant much to the Fellowship, whose ministry includes the care of and dealing with many different characters. Some of the children are from the best stock of India, but some have everything against them (and the underpull of heredity can tell hardly on a child). There are various races in our family, and there are many castes. Nothing but the love of God can control and fuse into happy unity such diversity as this, and not all have yielded to the love of God. The unyielding can greatly exercise the patience of those who have to do with them; they send us again and again to the God of hope for renewals in hope.

But perhaps only one who has had to guide a work which is continuous (that is, without free spaces such as school and college offer) and which is always demanding more and more spiritual energy, can fully appreciate what it is to have such fellow-workers as these in the center of things. Is there something to be done from which the flesh shrinks? "Ask her, she is a Sister of the Common Life. She will do it." And about matters where one of two ways is open, there is an instinctive soldierly choice. And there is the kindling example to the younger ones: promotion does not mean more honor in the usual sense of the word. It means more work, harder work, the trust of the hardest.

We soon gathered much lovely stardust such as Raymond Lull's well-known saying about the Moorish battlefield: "It appears to me that victory can be won in no other way than Thou, O Lord Christ, with Thy apostles didst seek to win it, by love and prayer, by shedding of tears and blood, by self-sacrifice, by spiritual not by carnal weapons." And Rutherford's from his prison in Aberdeen: "Why should I start at the plough of my Lord, that maketh deep furrows on my soul? He purposeth a crop." And Thomas à Kempis' calm word from his cell: "Blessed are the single-hearted; for they shall enjoy much peace."

"This sacred work demands, not lukewarm, selfish, slack souls, but hearts more finely tempered than steel, wills purer and harder than the diamond." Père Didon gave us that, and Bishop Bardsley this: "When a soul sets out to find God it does not know whither it will come and by what path it will be led; but those who catch the vision are ready to follow the Lamb whithersoever He goeth, regardless of what that following may involve for them. And it is as they follow, obedient to what they have seen, in this spirit of joyful adventure, that their path becomes

clear before them, and they are given the power to fulfill
their high calling. They are those who have the courage to
break through conventionalities, who care not at all what
the world thinks of them, because they are entirely taken
up with the tremendous realities of the soul and God."

"The Cross is the attraction." This was one of our words
from the first. For "the symbol of the Christian Church is
not a burning bush nor a dove, nor an open book, nor a
halo round a submissive head, nor a crown of splendid
honor. It is a Cross."*

These and other true things we read together and then
very simply wrote:

My Vow.
Whatsoever Thou sayest unto me, by Thy grace I will do
it.
My Constraint.
Thy love, O Christ, my Lord.
My Confidence.
Thou art able to keep that which I have committed unto
Thee.
My Joy.
To do Thy will, O God.
My Discipline.
That which I would not choose, but which Thy love
appoints.
My Prayer.
Conform my will to Thine.
My Motto.
Love to live: Live to love.
My Portion.
The Lord is the portion of mine inheritance.

Teach us, good Lord, to serve Thee more faithfully; to
give and not to count the cost; to fight and not to heed the
wounds; to toil and not to seek for rest; to labor and not to

---

* C.M. Clow.

ask for any reward, save that of knowing that we do Thy will, O Lord our God.

Between twenty and thirty girls have signed this confession of love since that first evening, March 18, 1916. Of these, several have married, for it is always understood that obedience to their Lord's "whatsoever" may lead to that. Some are out in the villages, some are here. The greater number of those who have not married are with us, serving in various parts of the work. I would like to name each name, for such names are dear; but the first seven may stand for all.

Arulai, she who, hearing for the first time the mighty message of a Saviour who could change dispositions, immediately believed and went all the way from that first hour in her allegiance to her Lord;* Pappamal, of whom we have told before, who broke her alabaster box of very precious ointment for love of her Redeemer; Purripuranum (Perfection), who was bequeathed to us by her mother, Ponnamal, as her last gift; Rukma (Radiance), another young convert and like her name; Preena, whose name means Beloved, also known as Pearleyes; Latha, the bright little Firefly, for whom we were to ring the joy-bells; and Manoharum (Heart's joy), Pappamal's cousin, whose brave soul lodges in a fragile vase. These, and the others who, blessed by their example, have given themselves to the service, are our comrades and companions in this Fellowship.

---

* *Ploughed Under*, the story of of this flame of love that Love divine has kindled, is as revealing of the ways of our wonderful God as that of her sister Mimosa has been.

23.

Home of our hearts, lest we forget
    What our redemption meant to Thee,
Let our most reverent thoughts be set
    Upon Thy Calvary.

We, when we suffer, turn and toss
    And seek for ease, and seek again;
But Thou upon Thy bitter cross
    Wast firmly fixed in pain.

And in our night star-clusters shine,
    Flowers comfort us, and joy of song;
No star, no flower, no song was Thine,
    But darkness three hours long.

We in our lesser mystery,
    Of lingering ill, and wingèd death,
Would fain see clear; but could we see,
    What need would be for faith?

O Lord beloved, Thy Calvary
    Stills all our questions. Come, oh come,
Where children wandering wearily
    Have not yet found their home.

23. And a Light Shined in the Cell

How good it would be to leave it at that, and tell no more. But truth is sacred. There is a Tamil word for insincerity which means literally *showing brass for gold.* (Shishak, King of Egypt, took away the shields of gold which Solomon had made. Instead of these, Rehoboam made shields of brass—the story illustrates that Tamil word.) The Lord save this book from anything of that sort.

Sometimes those in whom we place a perfect confidence crash at the moment of utmost need, and the hopes of years and the work of years appear to be swept away like a straw before a flood.

And we have had both men and women, who, after running well, took the turning in the road that leads to compromise and entanglement. We have seen an upright Hindu hindered by one who should have helped him, till any desire he might have had to consider the heavenly Master of such a servant vanished, and he said in effect, Better to be a Hindu than that sort of a Christian. And yet that Christian man had once been a witness and a winner of souls.

We have seen some, on whom all that love can offer had been poured, shrink at the first touch of the offense of the Cross and, in common with all who know what such wounds can be, we have learned to feel them first as His whose love still follows these who deny Him.

But—truly and exultantly we can say it—we have seen what love can do. These in whom we can have perfect confidence, in whom the slightest flaw in truth is inconceivable, these who set no limits, saying, This far and no farther will I follow my Lord Crucified—they are our joy and crown.

There are days in this work when it is as though black seas swept over us. There are evil things which are so common in this land that no one is shocked by them. The reaction is not shame, but a smile. An older person will refer to detestable sins using a casual word which may mean *play*. Many a child is born into a heritage which must be harder to triumph over than we can imagine. Certainly it is so with some whom we have known. Given ancestors who belonged to one of the secret phallic cults (cults old as the East), must not there be a terrible hellward pull day by day, night by night? Education is utterly impotent before that pull. Nothing is strong enough to counter it but the powers of Calvary. We have seen those mighty powers triumph. Once, in a very dark hour, when an uprush of these black seas appalled us, such a horror of sin as seen by the Holy God was wrought in the convicted soul of one who had sinned that it was almost more than could be borne. Several were sharing the matter in prayer, of whom one had lately joined us (the date is later than this chapter, but dates are of no account in the things of the spirit), and, much concerned (for who could see unmoved a tall white flower bent down on its stalk till it touches very slime?), we asked, "Are you sorry you came?" There was no answer then, only a smile, but an hour later the answer was given on half a sheet of notepaper. We have sung it many times on our knees since that night:

O God of peace, strong is the enemy,
    But Thou art nigh,
And he must fall beneath our feet, because
    Of Calvary.

Give us calm confidence of victory,
    Lord of the fight,
And when the enemy comes like a flood,
    Put him to flight.

Mighty the weapons of our warfare are
    Through Thee alone;
Oh, lead us to the battle, captain us,
    Most mighty One.

And the God of peace did captain us. The Lord wrought a great victory that day, and the captive for whom that fight was fought with the powers of darkness was set free to become a force for good among us. For Thou, O God, hast a mighty arm: strong is Thy hand and high is Thy right hand, and Thou art the glory of our strength.

All who understand spiritual conflict such as this, and what it means to hold a long line on the edge of the enemy's country, will know what the loss of even one in that thin line can be. There was one among our Indian Sisters who was able, because of certain gifts of insight and character and knowledge of Hindu ways of thought, to succor souls caught in these black seas. In her Bible I find this: "The man who has no experience in the dark has no secret to communicate in the light." Perhaps these words will show to the discerning what Arulai had to give, and why we all felt that she was indeed impossible to spare. She had never been strong, and, shortly before the Sisters of the Common Life came into being, to give her the best chance of health that we could, we sent her in the hot weather to friends in the hills. She returned home far advanced in nephritis.

There came a day (it was our Prayer Day, but every day was a prayer day then) when, as I left her for an hour's wrestle with the fear that was now overshadowing us, a desperate kind of comfort came in the thought that she at least would never have to drink of this cup. The endurance of this pang (the rending of flesh from flesh) would never be asked of her, and somehow that did help. But we had to go further than that.

All that day she had been delirious, and she was still unconscious when I returned to the little side room where one or other of us was with her night and day. And that night, when all was quiet, and when all human hope had fled, He to whom belong the issues from death came into the house, and took her by the hand, and called saying, "Maid, arise."

But before this happened there had been time for a question and an answer. And again one instinctively turns to familiar words, because they tell so much better than mine could what I want to show: "And behold there stood a man over against him with his sword drawn in his hand, and Joshua went unto him, and said unto him, Art thou for us, or for our adversaries?" (Lord, if Thou dost take her, how can the work go on? Drive that question back to its root and how does it differ from Joshua's?) "And he said, Nay; but as captain of the host of the Lord am I now come. And Joshua fell on his face to the earth, and did worship, and said unto him, What saith my Lord unto his servant?

"And the captain of the Lord's host said unto Joshua, Loose thy shoe from off thy foot; for the place whereon thou standest is holy." And he did so. And we did so too.

Such an experience does not leave any who share it just where they were before. They may not be able to put their gains into words, but something has been gained; the precious things put forth by the moon, the chief things of the ancient mountains are theirs, and they can never lose them. But sometimes words can be found that sum up

these gains, and for us there are three which will be forever bright because of that darkness. These words are,
Good, acceptable, perfect—"That ye may prove what is that
good and acceptable and perfect will of God"—that was
the piercing word. And, in Tamil, "Acceptable" is ren-
dered by a word meaning *lovable*. This word leads on
through the acceptance which is peace to something else,
to somewhere else:

> Things temporal
> Are transparent in that air,
> But the things that are eternal
> Are manifest there.

In ways like this, in dealings which again and again
touched the key people of our work, those precious ones
who could never be replaced, we were taught that the
disposal of His forces is wholly in the hands of our Com-
mander-in-Chief. And it was in times like this that our
nights became light about us.

Years later, in an hour of need, the Everlasting Comforter came through the Septuagint version of Psalm
105:18, "His soul [Joseph's] entered into iron." It was not
that others put him in irons (though they did, they hurt his
feet with fetters), it was that he himself acquiesced in,
willingly walked into the unexplained trial of his God's
dealings with him. "His soul entered, whole and entire in
its resolve to obey God, into the cruel torture," is Kay's
note on that great matter; but what fathomless depths it
must have held for our Lord Jesus when He set His face
steadfastly to go to Jerusalem, Gethsemane, Calvary, and
certain it is that whatever way of pain may open before
any one of us, we find as we walk in it the marks of our
dear Lord's footsteps leading on. He walked alone on that
road so that we need never walk alone. No star, no flower,
no song was Thine, but darkness three hours long.

He was hard on Himself, but there is no hardness in His
ways with us, and the dimmest pages in our story shine as

we look back on them. We saw this once in parable. Some of us had gone to the coast to try to get rid of a persistent fever, and one night we bathed deliciously in a little bay between dark rocks. The night was moonless and starless, and the sea, except where it broke in ripples or waves, was as dark as sea can ever be. But when we came out of that water we were covered from head to foot in phosphorescent light, and when we sat down on the wet sand and dug our hands into it, diamonds ran between our fingers.

There are lights that watch for an occasion to appear. Such are the lights of strong consolation that have come when all was dark, whether because of some black trouble like the black seas of sin or because of threatened harm or loss to that which is so much dearer to us than ourselves. For truly the love of the Lord whose brightness is as the light, who is Himself light, passeth all things for illumination, and if I say, Surely the darkness shall cover me, even the night shall be light about me.

Light—there is something in the word that is not of earth. On a day when it brought us the very tenderness of God, a cable came from Australia: *And a light shined in the cell*. The words turned to song, such simple song that it would not be written here if it were not that so often very simple, almost infantile things carry little cups of comfort:

> And a light shined in the cell,
> And there was not any wall,
> And there was no dark at all;
> Only Thou, Immanuel.
>
> Light of Love shined in the cell,
> Turned to gold the iron bars,
> Opened windows to the stars;
> Peace stood there as sentinel.
>
> Dearest Lord, how can it be
> That Thou art so kind to me?
> Love is shining in my cell,
> Jesus, my Immanuel.

24

O Star, whose sweet untroubled song
    Floats tranquil down the moonlit blue,
Do you not see the ages' wrong?
    Nor hear the cry, "How long, how long,
      Till all things be made new?"

The wounded silence aches with prayer,
    Do broken prayers not rise so high?
A sound of tears disturbs the air,
    Does it not beat upon you there,
      Nor pain of human cry?

'Tis Dawn has lit his beacon fire;
    The Conqueror rides in His car;
He comes, He comes; yea, nigher, nigher,
    The nations' hope, the world's desire,
      The bright and morning Star.

He hath looked down from His sanctuary . . . that He might hear the mournings of such as are in captivity and deliver the children appointed unto death.—Psalm 102:19–20, P.B.V.

I will seek that which was lost, and bring again that which was driven away, and will bind up that which was broken, and will strengthen that which was sick.—Ezek. 34:16.

24. Not Found Yet

But though in truth we have seen what the mighty arm of the Lord can do, and our nights have been light about us, we know what it is to be defeated. Shattering things can happen. We stand dumb before them. There are times when the pain of the poor animals, like the pain of little children and of simple, harmless people, can crush. But the question that cuts like a knife striking down to the ground of the soul is not, Why do the innocent suffer? It is, Why do the innocent sin? Why this triumphant evil in a world created by the Holy One, supreme in love as in power? That, not the other, is the mystery of life. We think of the children of all lands who never had a chance to be good:

"I found my lamb," he said,
"But when I found it, my lost lamb was dead."

That is what breaks us. But we know only in part: All souls are Thine, not the foeman's, conquering Christ. And "lost" means "not found yet."

One of these who is not found yet, and for whom we still watch, is Rungie. When we first saw her she was a little girl of nine.

A guest of the time, Dorothy Waller, had come with us to a temple festival in the town where Rungie lived. The child had run into the house where we were and, sitting down on the floor beside us, had presently begun to sing.

After that we made friends, and she invited us to come home with her, so we followed her down the street that flanks the temple wall till we came to a quiet little house. She took us upstairs. A feeling of something wrong with the place came over us. There were pictures on the walls, and an air in the rooms that oppressed us. But even then we did not know, for a temple-house is like any other in the street, and the people of the house were at the festival—till to some chance word the child's laughter rang out, and she told us that she was going to be a servant of the gods.

We were sitting close together. The child's hands were in ours, her brown eyes fixed on us filled with surprise, then compassion. "Tears?" she exclaimed. "Tears? Oh, why? Am I not going to be just what you are? Are not you also servants of God?"

This passed tears. We sat speechless, looking into those puzzled, compassionate eyes. How could we make her understand? How snatch from the terrible this his innocent prey?

We talked awhile, opening things to her, but she was too bewildered at first to understand. Then, as gradually it broke upon her that this which she had been taught to look upon as an honor was a thing of shame, her hands caught ours with a clasp that would hardly let go. We had to leave her then. We would have given all we possessed to carry her off that night.

Soon afterwards the child was writhing in convulsions. She had never been so before. Our visit was the cause, the people said. The god was angry, he was punishing her. The house was ceremonially cleansed with the five products of the cow and the god was placated with offerings. Then Rungie recovered.

We prayed for her unceasingly. Forty pounds had been spent by her adopted mother on her dancing lessons, and a friend at home, hearing of this, sent that sum to redeem her. The foster-mother laughed. Then the child, understanding better now, tried to escape to us. She was overtaken, caught, dragged home, beaten, shut up and watched day and night. Gradually desire faded, the temple gathered her into its shadows. But that child's need was the call of God to Dorothy Waller to give her life for the temple-children of India.

Eleven years later, she saw Rungie again. She wrote of that piteous meeting:

> There were a brass band and singing, and a crowd watched as two great figures like gigantic dolls, which were carried by men inside them, bowed and danced their way along the street. They must have been likenesses of a god and goddess, and there was something unspeakably vile in their loathsome expressions as they turned to each other and to the crowd.
>
> The temple elephant was resplendent in magenta and gold trappings. Behind him, and immediately in front of the palanquin containing the god, walked Brahman men. The procession was followed by a number of Brahman women. There were no women in the procession itself except two, and as they passed in front of our house and stopped to read the texts painted in red letters on zinc sheets which were hung in the verandah, I recognized one—it was Rungie.

* * * * *

> One evening Mimosa and I found her sitting on the inner verandah of the house of the temple-woman who lives next door. She looked thin and tired, and her somewhat receding forehead, plastered with a black ointment, threw into prominence the great dark eyes which never left my face as she listened with the thirst of barren years to the story of Calvary. "Go on, tell me more, I do understand," she said, with almost impatient eagerness, when I stopped to find out how much she had taken in. When I had finished, Mimosa talked to her, beginning by speaking

of temptations which must come. "Temptations, yes, I know them," she remarked, and settled herself to listen. She interrupted with many questions, as to how it was possible to live alone among the heathen. Mimosa then turned to the elderly temple-woman, who was also listening, and I had a talk with Rungie. She edged nearer and nearer, all thought of caste defilement forgotten. As it came home to her that the salvation we told her of was really for her, that she, too, might have with her always the same protecting One who kept Mimosa safe in every danger, it seemed to dawn on her that the One she had as a child wished to serve had not forgotten her, would never forsake her if she put her trust in Him. The time before, the first time we had visited her, Jasmine was with me, and Rungie had been too sad to speak much, but now it seemed as though hope had begun to dawn, in the assurance that the Saviour had indeed come for sinners such as she.

Then were the powers of evil aroused in all their fury, and when Arulai and I visited her later we realized that her house is indeed as the way of hell going down to the chambers of death and, as we shrank from contact with such a place of wickedness, feeling ourselves defiled, we entered a very little into what it cost the Holy One when He trod the winepress alone and with His own arm brought salvation.

25.

O God, forasmuch as without Thee we are not able to please Thee, mercifully grant that Thy Holy Spirit may in all things direct and rule our hearts; through Jesus Christ our Lord.—Gelasian Sacramentary, A.D. 494.

Yesterday—got hopelessly confused, and Professor Milligan amused me by quoting a Scotch minister's reply to a neighbor who came into the kirk while another (young man) was preaching. "What's his grund?" was the question of the perplexed hearer who could not follow. *"He's nae grund, he's sooming"* (swimming). I am afraid we often "swim" in sermons and elsewhere.—*Life of Bishop Westcott.*

Thou that dwellest in the gardens, the companions hearken to thy voice: cause me to hear it.

> Cause me to hear, for it is life to me;
> I perish when I am away from Thee,
> Love of my love,
> Tell me, where walkest Thou?
> I would be with Thee now.
>
> Let me be Thy companion, even I,
> For whom Thou once didst in a garden lie;
> Love of my love,
> Than all my dear more dear,
> Tell me, may I draw near?
>
> I may, I may. Thou callest me to come;
> O Dweller in the gardens, this is home.
> Love of my love,
> Dear Lord, what would I more
> But listen, serve, adore?

25. In All Things Direct and Rule

Until 1925 the first two of us who were together here belonged to the C.E.Z.M.S., and committees are usually responsible for the guidance of their missionaries. But, without knowing it or meaning it, we soon passed the place where we could look to any for counsel except the One who was near enough to us to tell us what to do from hour to hour. It was His word which had caused the work to begin, and only He (we write reverently) knew what we should do. And then, too, we always had the feeling that there was more in each apparently small decision than we could understand. We dared not move in anything without a sure direction. Our friends at home were very kind. Sometimes they inquired though, through their Secretary on the field, what our plans were, and how much bigger we proposed to grow, and what our financial liabilities would be. But we could not tell them, for we ourselves did not know. We could only assure then that those "financial liabilities" would never be theirs to meet, for that responsibility belonged (again we write with reverence) to our Lord and Master, our Unseen Leader.

So we went on looking to Him to tell us clearly what we were to do. I do not mean by that anything mystical, but something as practical as possible. We did not live in the clouds—we have never lived there: our way is in the dust of the ordinary road. But it is not presumption to count upon a promise being fulfilled. It is not "sooming" to lay hold on such words as these: "If any of you lack wisdom, let him ask of God, who giveth to all men liberally and upbraideth not; and it shall be given him." "What man is he that feareth the Lord, him shall He teach in the way that He shall choose." "O Lord, I know that the way of man is not in himself; it is not in man that walketh to direct his steps." London was too far away to direct our steps, but our Lord Jesus was "very easy to find,"* so we came to learn that the greatest aid we could ask from our friends was not advice but the much more effective help of prayer.

There can be nothing *new* to write about this happy subject, and so why write? And another thought holds me back. We all know what it is to shrink from hearing too-defining words used about some holy thing (the Lord's Supper, for example), words that seem, like clumsy fingers, to pull the petals from the lily. I do not want to write such words about this intimate thing—the leading of our Lord. But something must be said, for to say nothing would be to drop a thread of the golden cord that binds us together.

"When was this written?" asked Jasmine, the Brahman pilgrim, about one of the psalms. "The words of this song are all about me." And she could hardly be persuaded that words which described her affairs so exactly were written a long time ago.

It was like that recently when we read the Acts with the Sisters of the Common Life, using Weymouth's translation. We found there guidance under God being given by circumstances, sometimes disturbing, sometimes helpful. Also guidance after thinking things over ("He who sighs for a particular inspiration, or direction in common mat-

---

* "Dieu est notre retraite, notre force, et notre secours dans les détresses, et forte aise à trouver."—Psalm 46:1.

ters, which his own reason and judgment can determine, is liable to deception," Madame Guyon said. The words are beacons, warning off shoals). And we found guidance given after prayer and fasting through the general feeling made known by a show of hands, a unanimous decision after hearing all the facts. ("Having become unanimous," implying diversity of opinion at first and serious discussion, is Weymouth's note.) And there was the strong lead of an impelling sense of duty; and help was given by a word of the Lord, remembered and quoted when the perplexed Peter said, "Then I remembered the Lord's words, how He used to say. . . ." The Lord quicken our memories, and our inward ear too, so that we may not be deaf to the Comforter when He comes to bring familiar words to our remembrance.

Sometimes the Spirit of Jesus gave a direct command: "The Holy Spirit said." Sometimes an angel was sent, sometimes a vision. (The difficult passage of apparently confused guidance in Acts 21:4 is clear if we may take Rotherham's translation: "The dissuading friends began to say through the Spirit, that Paul would gain no footing in Jerusalem." Even so, Paul having received his Lord's leading, went on.) We have not seen the angels who companion us, but, with countless of our Master's servants, we have known His guidance in all the other ways mentioned in the Acts.

Often, as an earlier chapter told, while all was new, we were allowed to ask for some sure token which even our ignorance could not mistake. There is a simplicity about this that is comforting to inexperience, and we gratefully remember the wet fleece and the dry, and the dovetailing of events, like the dreamer's telling his dream to his fellow just when Gideon and his servant crept softly to the edge of the camp. But though this is only the alphabet of the matter, like the first easy lesson given to the children of Israel at the Red Sea when the waters were divided, even now, when there is neither inward assurance nor the vis-

ible opening of circumstances, and yet a decision must be
made, we find ourselves asking for this kind of leading.
And we are not refused.

But as we continue with our Lord we often find ourselves by the further waters known to so many of His
followers—the waters of the Jordan when it overflows its
banks. The feet of the priests had to be wet in the flood, the
people had to begin to do the impossible, before they saw
how it could be made possible. There must be a word
which cannot be mistaken before that can be done.

Obedience here can be costly; there are some in the
mission fields of the world who know how costly. When
the word of the Lord "that doth in a way known to Himself twine and bind the heart which way He pleaseth"
comes to one whose dearest do not hear, cannot understand, then there is room for pain:

> He heard a voice they could not hear
> That would not let him stay;
> He saw a hand they could not see
> That beckoned him away.

Say unto the children of Israel that they go forward.
How did that word come to the man by the shore of the
shallow sea so very long ago? Was it a voice spoken in the
secret cell of his being or to his outer ear? How good it
would be (has not the heart felt like this often?) if only
others might hear or overhear, so that not to one only but
to all should be the same assurance, the same compelling.

This kind of obedience can never be a light thing to one
who loves. Was it nothing to the Son of Man when the
sword pierced His mother's soul? There is no promise of
ease to the heart that is set on following the Crucified. But
it learns to drink of the brook in the way.

That brook flows through many a pleasant runlet. First,
always first, there is the living water that refreshes us
every day, but there is, too, the constant joy of companionship in spirit with His own of all the ages. How many,

following hard after Him today, will find sweetness in this lovely word of His faithful servant, Madame de la Mothe Guyon: "God has the same right to incline and move the heart as to possess it. When the soul is perfectly yielding, it loses all its own consistency, so to speak, in order to take any moment the shape that God gives it; as water takes all the forms of the vases in which it is put, and all the colors." Sometimes there is a new sparkle on the brook as we find in some new discovery an unexpected illustration of a truth of Scripture. This from *Science and Religion* we set alongside St. John 12:23–29:

> Take the scientific fact to be the wireless message sent out by the broadcasting station, and the intelligence of the scientist to correspond to the receiver. If the receiver cannot be tuned to the proper wavelength, no message is received although it really exists round the apparatus. That would correspond to the case of a mind which cannot grasp certain truths. We all know what that means in trying to teach children. However, this is not quite what I want. Suppose that the wireless receiver is not very sensitive, then it may happen that you only receive some part of the message and yet can make sense of it. Nevertheless that sense is not the full sense of the message sent out, and, although the partial message is still part of the complete message, its meaning in the new context is rather different.

". . . The people that stood by, and heard it, said that it thundered: others said, An angel spoke to Him." But the Son of God heard the voice from heaven saying in answer to His prayer, "Father, glorify Thy name"—"I have both glorified it and will glorify it again."

"If the receiver cannot be tuned to the proper wavelength, no message is received," only a muffled sound is heard—the people said that it thundered. "Suppose that the wireless receiver is not very sensitive"—others said, An angel spoke to Him.

If no message can be received, what is it that hinders? If we are insensitive, why are we so? "A single sin, however

apparently trifling, however hidden in some obscure corner of our consciousness—a sin which we do not intend to
renounce—is enough to render real prayer impracti-
cable."* This brings us to the Cross: The blood of Jesus
Christ His Son cleanseth us from all sin. What should we
do without that healing word? Flow over us, O powers of
Calvary. We are dust of the earth, but Thy dust, Lord. Oh,
turn Thy hand upon us, and purely purge away our dross,
and take away all our tin.

Only for God waits my soul, all hushed. Speak, Lord,
for Thy servant heareth. My Sheep hear My voice, and I
know them, and they follow Me. It was a wise teacher who
said of that quality of quietness that is a gathering up of
the energies of the soul, "We are, to a great degree, unable
to 'wait still upon God': we habitually take refuge in manu-
als when we might, I think, listen with more profit for the
voice of the Spirit."†

"Cause me to hear Thy lovingkindness in the morning;
for in Thee do I trust: cause me to know the way wherein I
should walk; for I lift up my soul unto Thee. . . . Teach me
to do Thy will; for Thou art my God. Thy Spirit is good.
Lead me into the land of uprightness. Quicken me, O
Lord, for Thy name's sake" (Psalm 143:8–11).

We have it all there: Cause me to hear; cause me to
know; teach me to do; quicken me, O Lord.

A thousand miles from Dohnavur, in the land where
peacocks run in the jungle, their gorgeous tail-fathers are
made up into fans and sold for a few pence. Everyone
knows the iridescent greens and blues, the purples melting into brown, set in a soft old gold; but the feather must
be held with a nice care before the eye catches the sheen of

---

* F.P. Cobbe.

† *Westcott, His Life*, Vol. II, p. 285. On John 12:28–29, he says, "Like
all spiritual things, this voice required preparedness in the organ to
which it was addressed. The apprehension of a divine voice depends
upon man's capacity for hearing."

mauve, and not many see it. God, who so richly yet so delicately painted the feathers of this bird, can open our eyes to see what a careless glance would miss. He can quicken us.

After obedience we have found that there may be miles of hard going; but no one who has walked in these ways of our God would go back to the sheltered tameness of the road where never the sharp storm blows that takes the hide off our faces, as Samuel Rutherford (contemporary of Milton and Shakespeare) put it: "It cost Christ and all His followers sharp showers and hot sweats ere they win to the top of the mountain. But still our soft nature would have heaven coming to our bedside when we are sleeping, and lying down with us, that we might go to heaven in warm clothes; but all that came there found wet feet by the way, and sharp storms that did take the hide off their face, and found to's and fro's, and up's and down's, and many enemies by the way."

In the end our God justifies His commands. And often He seems to plan some little special cheer. One evening, on returning from a commanded journey, the traveler found, by way of welcome, these verses on her table (the allusion to the barefoot walking was that obedience just then had meant walking barefoot in the filthy lanes of an Indian city):

> Step by step, Lord, lead me onward,
>   Walking barefoot with my Guide,
> Listening for Thy softest whisper,
>   Saviour, for me crucified.
>
> Lead me on, though flint and brier
>   Wound our feet at every stride;
> Tireless till we find Thy lost one,
>   Saviour, for him crucified.

And we have a very understanding Master: we have noticed that when some specially sharp strain on faith and

hope and patience is to follow, then He draws near beforehand, and with shining wings overshadows us, and there
is a sound of gentle stillness, there is speech. Or there may
be a Showing. (I think this word must be the right one, for
long before I met it in old books it was the only one that
came to express the luminous thing that I mean.) And
through the hours or even years that come after, before
there is fulfillment, the soul that heard, that saw, knows
only to say to itself and to all that confronts it, *I believe God
that it shall be even as it was told me.* What a Lord is ours—
"Many a visit does He make to the interior man, sweet is
His communication with him, delightful is His consolation, great is His peace, and His familiarity exceedingly
amazing."

But the patient years have taught us this tremendous
lesson: God never condones. "From His right hand went a
fiery law for them. Yea, He loved the people." His pure
holiness cannot pass over a deviation from the appointed
course. Thanks be to God for the consuming fire.

We have found it possible to be directed as a company
so that we can move together in a harmony of spirit that is
restful and very sure. A company has to wait longer than
one or two might have to do, but if all be set on doing their
Lord's will and be truly one in loyalty and the New Testament kind of affection that makes each one feel safe with
each other one, if all flow together to the goodness of the
Lord, unanimity is certain. It is not difficult for our Father
to make His children to be of one mind in a house, like the
city of His purpose, "that is at unity in itself"—"Jerusalem
that hath been builded a true city, all joined together in
one." And we have always found that before the ultimate
word must be spoken, divergent thoughts have vanished,
as by some peaceful magic. The interval is sure to be
perplexed by a temptation to the futile fuss of talk. Recognize this for what it is, the influence of the adversary (for
hurry of spirit confuses), and before long the same quiet
word will come to all. If the inmost law of such a company

be holy peace, it must be so.

And of one thing we are certain: if prayer be hindered, and we go on insensitive ("he wist not that the Lord was departed from him") or in cowardice we shrink from whatever it must cost to recover loyal unity, then this Fellowship will perish. For a while, but only for a while, it may continue to seem to be. But to the clear eyes of the spiritual watchers, from that first hour of insincerity it will appear as a vanished thing and its Lord will say of it, "How is the gold become dim. How is the most fine gold changed."

So we must end on our knees: O let me hear Thy lovingkindness early in the morning, for in Thee is my trust; show Thou me the way that I should walk in, for I lift up my soul unto Thee. Teach me to do the thing that pleaseth Thee, for Thou art my God; let Thy loving Spirit lead me forth into the land of righteousness.

26.

Lord, make me part of this green wood
    That I may praise and worship Thee;
All here is beautiful, and good,
    And full of melody.
Lord, make me part of this green wood
    That I may worship Thee.

O sunlight on the ruddy ground,
    O moss, thou covering charity,
O every small thing perfect found,
    Like you I want to be—
Like you I would be perfect found,
    My Father, fashion me.

As moves the wind above the wood
    And sings, rejoicing in each tree,
So fill me with Thine utmost good,
    The bliss of harmony;
O Father, singing through the wood,
    Fill me with harmony.

— B.C.O.

26. Where the Birds Built Their Nests

If this that we have told is a thread of our gold cord, and it is, for nothing is more uniting than prayer about guidance, so is our use of the hottest weeks of the year, when vigorous life is impossible on the plains. In the South we have two such seasons: one in April and May, the other in September and on till the monsoon breaks about the middle of October.

South India is rich in her hill stations, and we all owe much to them and to the welcome of friends there, and to their kindness to us. But from the time of the first converts, to be so far from home was not a simple matter. Our kind hostess could welcome a few, but as they increased it was impossible to take them, and we could not leave them in their loneliness to the devastating temptations that beset converts. Would a mother desert a sorely troubled child just when its need was greatest? And soon there were little ones, too, and Indian sister-workers who required change and rest and refreshment as much as we did. What were we to do? We looked up to the Lord our Leader, and then we looked up to the hills that lay so near

Dohnavur. And the thought came to try these nearer hills. The first trial proved disastrous. "I hear you were carried down on a stretcher." There was more than a hint of "Now you will see that it can't be done." But we did not see. It was not the fault of the hills that we had come to grief. So next year we went again.

We stayed in a little house that belonged to the Forest Department. Elephants haunted those uplands, and bears and tigers, sambur, wild pigs, deer, the ever-fascinating monkey, the huge monitor lizard like a toy crocodile, and countless furred and feathered marvels. Life was all gladness there. Once the children, entranced, saw a tigress at play with her cubs. They rushed down to call me, but the tigress heard their cries of joy and took her cubs elsewhere; and once one of us met a tiger full face, but he, too, politely moved away. Later, we were to meet panthers, wild dogs, bears and other forest people—not every day, but often enough to lend zest to life. And the children, and we with them, scrambled up dizzy rocks to almost inaccessible places, to the amazement of the foresters, who had not seen before, they said, such adventurous children. This was nectar to me. And indeed they were splendid climbers and never knew fear. Cool air, climbs, heavenly views, a mountain river, ferns, flowers, mosses (cushiony moss was a special pleasure, it does not grow on the plains)—what was there left to wish?

A dear little story is connected in my mind with our first visit to that woodland place. We left Dohnavur one evening in the heat of early September, and spent a breathless night in a forest hut under the hills. Next morning, the children set off to walk the three thousand feet to the house, leaving me to follow when the chair-coolies came; but they were late, and I walked on alone, not sorry at first to have the solitude of that hillside path after the crowded months. The way was long, and it was evening when I reached a stream not far from the house and stopped to rest, wishing the ineffectual wish of all such hours, that the others down in the heat could share this coolness and water-beauty, especially the dear two who had been away in April and May and were now holding the fort at Dohnavur. And then from the other side of the stream I heard merry laughter, and shouts of welcome, and the children flew across like a flock of blue forest birds, and there were kisses and embraces so eager and so loving that we might have been parted for weeks. Then in the evening light that filled the air with gold-shine, we all went up to the house, and my tiredness fell from me in the happiness of being with the children again. It was one of those earthly pictures of heavenly things that cannot be forgotten. How many mothers every evening must cross the last stream, and be met by their own dear children who reached Home first.

We had hoped that this pleasant place among the hills would suffice us, but there was no certainty of always being able to rent it and, as the family grew larger and new workers from England joined us, it was clear that we needed to have a house of our own.

Rising to six thousand feet, and only a few hours' walk from us, were those mountains of peace that had so often brought us calm and the sense of eternal strength. Their heads push out from among green woods. Those woods are pierced with ravines, down which swift torrents flow. Below lie the plains, touched with silver where there is water, and bounded by the blue ribbon of the sea.

So we explored our mountains, and found many a lovely place within half a day's climb; but none appeared quite perfect till we came upon a wide ravine opening on a horseshoe valley so folded up among wooded hills that its discovery seemed almost an adventure. And yet it was open to every wind that blew.

There was an old coffee estate of forty acres up there. It was for sale for a hundred pounds. *Nor Scrip* tells the story that is still full of a sweet freshness for us, like the young green of the forest.

We had not thought of buying anything so extensive;
we had thought of a much smaller undertaking. And yet it
was a very desirable place, and there was no other to be
had anywhere near Dohnavur to be compared with it for
convenience or health or beauty. So, after making sure
that we might do so, we asked for a hundred pounds, if
our Father wished us to buy the ravine.

The time of the prayer was about noon, June 11, 1917,
and the place the river that flows through the ravine. In a
quiet half-hour's rest in the shadow of a great rock the
psalms for the day, morning and evening, had been re-
freshing. This word especially smiled up from the page
like a friend: "God showeth me His goodness plente-
ously." It was the first to be painted and put up in our
Forest House. We returned home in the evening to find
that a mail had unexpectedly arrived, and in it was a
hundred pounds. For a moment we thought it was the
sign. Then we saw that it was earmarked, "For a Forest
House." But how could we build a Forest House if we had
no forest? Or was it that we were to be content with the
smaller thought of the previous months and build in the
few acres the Forest Department might let us use? Thus,
being uncertain, we waited. There were temptations to
hurry; for the temple authorities of Four Lakes, a town
near Dohnavur, who were thinking of buying it, were
moving, and with them money is nothing. That particular
temple owns lakhs of rupees and much land. But what of
the hazard of running before the Lord? "It may cost what
thou knowest not to bring thee home from there."*

---

* Thou hast enough to pay thy fare?
    Well, be it so;
  But thou shouldest know, does thy God send thee there,
    Is that it all? To pay thy fare?
  There's many a coin flung lightly down
    Brings back a load of care.
  It may cost what thou knowest not
    To bring thee home from there.

So till August 25th we waited, and on that day in the early morning we set forth with a friend, experienced traveler in many lands, who was staying with us at the time, to look at the place again.

It was a perfect day, the kind of day when the trees of the wood sing out at the presence of the Lord, and our friend was charmed. "If only I had the means, I would buy it at once," he said, and he tried hard to induce the owner, who was living in a cave in the face of a cliff, to let us buy the site that would be perfect for a house. But the old man was firm. He would sell all or none. He knew that he could sell to the temple if we did not buy it, and no one can explain why he did not do so. The only explanation, we think, is that in the purpose of our God the place was meant for us.

We knelt down then among the grey boulders, in whose crevices wild pineapples were growing, their pinky crimson tufts of fruit and spikes of bluish-green leaves showing brightly on the grey; and we prayed for some clear sign, something we could not possibly mistake, to assure us that the whole enchanting ravine, with its uncontaminated water (for the heights above were too steep for commercial uses, and so the water was clean) was to be ours.

It was late when we reached home. Again an early mail was in; but we were tired and went to bed without opening it. In the morning we found again a hundred pounds. And this time it was a gift straight from heaven—a legacy.

But still (does this sound unbelievable?) we feared to run before our Guide and embark on costly follies, for land is the least of forest expenses, as we were soon to find. And yet it did look like an assurance repeated in order that we might go on without a doubt that this was to be. And four days later it was shown that we might take it so. On the 14th of September the place was ours, and the sign was confirmed when a third gift of exactly that sum (one hundred pounds) came, earmarked for its purchase.

To tell it like this makes it seem as though hundreds of pounds had a pleasant habit of dropping upon us; but it is not so. Six months passed before anything approaching so large a gift reached us again. And even then it was a broken sum, and not a complete round hundred.

As soon as we were sure, we began to build a house. And now, had we doubted—which indeed we did not—we could have known that our Lord was in this thing; for there was sharp opposition, and all that man and devil could do to stop that house being built was done. The place had been sacred to a godling called the Demon of the Chain. Its late owner, a Muhammadan, had feared the demon, and had never disturbed the shrine—even the little brass censer and oil cup and bell which stood on the open air altar had been left untouched. We took the idol down. At first none of the prophesied ills occurred; but soon it was as though a thousand invisible malevolent things were plucking at us from all sides at once.

One night, almost in despair, for the clouds were rolling in great white billows down the hillsides—sure sign of imminent rain—and the house, built not of stone in lime but of stone in mud, was not roofed, we suddenly recognized with whom our contest lay. There was only one thing to do. We gathered all the workmen, who were bent on going home to their villages that night (and would not return for a week), and read for our own strength of soul the twenty-seventh psalm, they listening in silence to the mighty words, strong as the mountains round about us, eternal in truth. And in the pause that followed, we told them to go if they chose; we were not afraid—the Lord our God would send us help, yea, even if no other but the angels of heaven would dare to build with us. There was no answer to this, but they looked up astonished, almost as though they expected to see the angels of whom we so confidently spoke descending in the clouds upon the mountains. And I think that if they had gone down, we too would have looked up for the angels, for human help there was none, and truly "where man's help fails God's is near." But the men were turned from their purpose. One by one they shuffled off to their grass huts under the rocks, and the house was saved. Every foot of that house was built with prayer, so we cannot wonder that to many of us it is full of memories as of a Presence shining through a very thin veil. "It is a fragrant room when a bundle of myrrh is the chief thing there," said Robert Murray McCheyne. It is indeed.

Year by year ever since that year (1918) little groups have gone up expecting "glorious discoveries of Christ—and His person, beauty, work and peace," and they have not been disappointed. It was new to some that the Holy Spirit would take of the things of Christ and show them to us, without an interpreter, as it were; and there were joyful times together too (by together I mean with the Indian sisters for whose sake we are here). And yet perhaps the chief gain of the forest was its stillness: "Be still and know that I am God."

But the test of the worth of such times is the staying power afterwards. The forest had done its best. It had given a river and a swimming pool, mountains to climb and pure air flowing up from the sea. But would the effect of all this last? Would there be as much gain as might be expected from the more usual kind of holiday? There was. We who were responsible for the work found that all who had been together there had learned to understand one another in a new way. The young Sitties had grown together with their Indian companions in a new sweet intimacy of spirit. When the difficult days came, that do come at times, they were often able to help one another because of that uniting. And later, when the boys' work began, it was the same with the Indian and English brothers.

After a while we built another and larger house, and here again there was a fight. The battle for the soul of a certain brigand chief (Raj of a later chapter) had begun, and those who claimed that soul for its destruction saw to it that we should be harassed in the rear. The houses of the carpenters were burned down, masons were threatened, coolies were terrorized. Relatives on the plain in mysterious unanimity fell sick, or were married or buried (often quite frequently, so that we kept a careful list of these events). We were often left without anyone, and unseasonable rain fell, greatly adding to the anxieties of building without lime. (To build with lime carried up to such a height would have been very expensive.) But the more such powers contested, the more surely we knew that the Lord of hosts was with us. Satan is too wise a strategist to waste ammunition on vanity. Does he see further than we do? Did he see the part this house was to play in the campaigns of the future? And yet he is strangely circumscribed. He does not seem to have known that the Holy Child was safely sheltered in Egypt when he moved Herod to slay the innocents, nor could he show Elijah's cave to Jezebel (comfort to us sometimes when we had to hide a child from the devouring enemy). So here again he was limited. The house was built and hallowed.

Once a botanist came to our forest. He found plants belonging to higher zones growing freely there. He said that we have an unusual climate. And doctors came up, and they told us the same. We gain more than the height (about three thousand feet) would lead one to expect, and we are not surprised; for He who knew all the ravines on the mountains chose it for us.

This forest life together supplies one of the threads that make the gold cord of this story. There must be a special tie between Moses and Elias, who met their Lord on the hilltop in Palestine and heard Him talk of His passion. And what golden cords must unite Peter and James and John, who, when the others had gone away, saw no man save Jesus only with themselves.

27

The Cross of Christ is the only hope of the world. Our constant danger is that we cry, Behold this new opportunity. Behold our new methods. Behold our human brotherhood. And forget to cry, Behold the Lamb of God!

Dr. Zwemer tells of the Abyssinian representative at the Treaty of Versailles. He was thinking of the future of the world and of how peace could only be through the sacrifice of Christ. "And his Abyssinian mind conceived the idea of representing this in symbolism. He sought out a Paris artist and gave him his ideas. The result is the famous painting of the Crucifixion so weird in its conception, so real in its symbolical significance, strangely attractive and compelling in its message. The Saviour is hanging on a cross which rests between two globes of the eastern and western hemispheres against a cloudy and lurid sky. A halo of coming victory already rests above the thorn-crowned head of the Sufferer who looks down upon two worlds for which He died. Blood-drops from his pierced hands color every continent and island red. It is a vision of the whole world redeemed by the blood of Christ. Underneath the painting one can read in three languages: *For God so loved the world that He gave His only begotten Son that whosoever believeth in Him should not perish but have everlasting Life."*

27. Pilgriming

The arrival of a child is a beginning that asks for a faithful continuance, and, as we have said before, this means a bending of everything we have to give towards a single purpose. But all around us are Hindus and Muslims.

We could not forget them. One day when we were wishing that we could do more for them we were greatly comforted by this word, "I will bring them to you." We were not at Dohnavur when that word came, and when we returned home it was a beautiful thing, but not a surprise, to find someone waiting for us. She was a Brahman widow who had gone on pilgrimage to all the holy places of South India seeking for light; and now she was brought to us who could not go to seek her. Since then we have seldom been without someone brought to us apart from anything that we have done. "I will bring them to you."

And the coming of this dear woman—Jasmine we call her in the *Widow of the Jewels*—was the beginning of a new work for which we coined a new name—Pilgriming.

We had never quite discontinued going to temple festivals, but we could not go often; and the thought of those crowds, as sheep without even the semblance of a shepherd, had never left us. It was in the month of April 1920 that the new leading came. April is one of our hottest months, not the season anyone would choose for that stirring up of the spirit that sometimes must be if prayer is to be effective. "There is none that stirreth up himself to take hold of Thee," cried Isaiah. "None rouses himself to take firm hold on Thee"—the words smite the slothful soul, and heat does somehow tend to sloth. But on a Sunday in that hot month, to those of us who were not in the forest, as we knelt together at noon, the thought of the urgency of our Lord's last command and of His (we hope near) return led to our hearing, as we believed, His word to us about two of our number, "Separate them unto Me for the temple festivals."

The two whose names came before us then were Edith Naish and Jasmine, the Brahman pilgrim. To the one had been given a great love for the people, ability to travel without too much strain and—this counted for much— silver hair. To the other was all that her wonderful background gave her, and with it a deep affection and a rare humility of spirit. Brahman as she was, she never seemed to feel her Brahmanhood, but it opened doors to her that are fast closed to most. To these two the call was confirmed, and just then a gift came from New Zealand, enough to cover the expense of several pilgrimages. It was marked "Maranatha" (The Lord cometh).

From that time on, till for a while the villages claimed them, our pilgrims were perpetually traveling from festival to festival. They were often the only witnesses for their Master among thousands, sometimes among tens of thousands.

Such work is exhausting. The trains are crammed, the heat in third-class compartments is almost unendurable. But just in those packed places lies the opportunity. Then the immense crowds around the temple, the glare, the crush, the pandemonium of sounds, the heat, sap the strength. Often there is no privacy, no quiet. Life must be

Indian in every possible way.

Only the tireless love of the Lord is enough for such fatigue. Ordinary evangelistic energy has a disconcerting way of evaporating. All you want, all your uncomfortable flesh and slack soul want is to get out of the noise and the crush and smells, and be cool and clean again. But He who sat by the well too tired to walk farther, and yet not too tired to speak eternal words to a needy woman, He can teach us how to draw on His immortal tenderness.

After each of these tours, our pilgrims used to come back and tell the children something of what they had seen. Once they described a boy from some northern land, fatherless and motherless, who was traveling from temple to temple—such a lonely child. They had nothing in his language, but he knew a little English, so they gave him a wordless book and explained it to him. And with this single seed in his hand he went on.

28.

What Anatomist knowes the body of man thorowly, or
what Casuist the Soule? What Politician knowes the dis-
temper of the State thorowly; or what Master, the disor-
ders of his owne family?

Hell is darknesses; and the way to it is the cloud of
Ignorance; hell itself is but condemned Ignorance, multiplied Ignorance.—Donne.

One or two terrible facts about the children must be
known and faced; but what would we not bear to save
them?—Ellice Hopkins

From a publisher's advertisement: "A charming story of
the Marian Persecution."—Is "charming," we wonder,
quite the best word?—*Punch.*

28. Not a Big Cow

As far back as 1909 we had known of the sale of a baby boy for wrong uses. The thought of that child had held us in bonds. What did it matter that the little thing was not crying out for aid like a poor little snared rabbit?

> But I cannot tell from where
> He is crying out for aid,
> Crying on the frightened air,
> Making everything afraid.

He did not know enough to cry. He was too young.

Gradually the fact was forced upon us that just as unprotected girls are in danger, so are unprotected boys; and we found that all over the country there are men on the watch for them. The baby boys are sent to foster mothers and, when old enough, are passed on to trainers. Some are taken to temple-houses, and become musicians and teachers of dancing and poetry to the girls. Both the dancing and poetry are debasing; the whole life is vile. Others are adopted by Muslims; this may mean ordinary adoption, but often boys are used for infamous purposes. Many become the property of the various dramatic societies of the South. The drama is wholly unclean.

When the work for girls began I was alone; there could be no question of consulting with others. "Immediately I conferred not with flesh and blood; neither went I up to Jerusalem to them which were apostles before me"—there was something of that about it. But later it was different. There were those alongside with whom it was right to confer, and their advice was, "You have not the workers. There are not enough—not nearly enough—for what has to be done already. This cannot be your responsibility. Let us pray that someone else will take up that special work." As the years passed and no one did, we were very sorely tempted to wonder if we had missed the way. If we had stepped out in faith as we had done before, would miracles have waited for us round the first corner?

It is never good to look back on guidance. A long time afterwards, when the first group of baby boys had become schoolboys, we looked down the breakfast table and asked each of the English brothers who, as later pages will tell, had been sent to us, "Where were you in 1909?" And one answer was, "I wasn't anywhere." It would have been the answer of several of the Indian brothers too. Creation and preparation had to be, before the work that was appointed could begin.

During those years we could only think of the boys whom the years were destroying and everything pleasant was shadowed by the thought, even as the bluest skies had turned black when first we heard the secrets of the temples.

There are times when I covet words with an edge like a razor. "Ignorance is not onely the drousinesse, the sillinesse, but the wickednesse of the soule," said John Donne. This is true. "The cruellest man alive could not sit at his feast unless he sat blindfold." But ought we to sit blindfolded?*

---

* "Only by refusing to think about things as they are can we remain indifferent."—*Baffled to Fight Better*, Oswald Chambers.

"They burn them, don't they?" It was a pleasant, placid lady who asked the question; she was at lunch at the time. Frances Beath of our Fellowship was at home for her first furlough, and she had been trying to bring the children's danger to the hearts of Christian women. This one was interested. "They burn them, don't they?" she asked and, not waiting for an answer, continued tranquilly to lunch.

Far off, sorrowful things are perhaps endurable. It is always possible to disbelieve them. "Do you think I could sit in this chair if I believed that such things could happen?" It was one who sat in high places who said that, and he leaned back in his chair and struck his fist in his open hand with a gesture of frank indignation. Notes that he did not read were on the table before him. They told plainly what was being done in low places quite out of sight of the high. Would they have haunted his nights if he had read them? I think they would, for he was not a cruel man; his very wrath absolved him from that charge. He was only blindfolded. But for some of us there is no merciful distance. We cannot sit blindfolded.

While these pages were being written, the ceremony of purification was being performed for a certain Rajah in a Native State. A young relative of the officiating priest told us about the ceremonies.

First came the familiar: "He ate of the five products of the cow, and he made a golden cow and gave it to our caste and feasted my caste men, thousands of them; then"—and this was said in exactly the same everyday tone—"then there was also a special sacrifice, the sacrifice of a cow."

"But how take life? And of all life, that of a cow?"

"We do not take life," was the calm answer, "the fire takes it. The Rajah must spiritually pass through that cow's holy interior." (I soften his speech a little, it was explicit.) "There is a special hut made, and four of us are chosen to see that all is done correctly. The cow is taken into the place where the fire is lighted. The cow may not be killed, of course. Then the door is shut. What is done after that is not done by man, that would be a cow-killing, which is unlawful. It is done by the fire. . . ."

A rumor of this had reaches us, but we had not believed it. "Burned alive, you mean?"

"So it is said."

"Are you sure? Have you seen it?"

"Yes," the colorless voice replied. "I can say I am sure, but I have not seen. No Brahman could look at such a thing. It would be unlawful and too much unpleasant; so the low caste people are appointed to do it."

"But they kill the cow first, surely?"

"With a knife? That is forbidden. That would be cow-killing. That would be a crime. To slay any animal is a crime. They are not allowed to do that."

"But to burn it alive is horrible. Can nothing be done? Could we not go to the Palace and . . ."

"It has been done for many centuries," was the gentle interruption, and the weak mouth smiled. "What can be done against custom? And who could withstand the Brahmans? In my country they have much power. They have power to curse the son and heir."

Even so, it was incredible. "Perhaps the low caste men carry off the poor beast and deceive the Brahmans."

"Do you think that they dare?" was the sufficient answer. Then patiently, as to a child unduly moved about nothing, "It is not very often, only once at the beginning of a new Rajah's reign. And" (as an oddly happy afterthought) "it is not a big cow, it is only quite a little one."

That was enough. We chanced to be near a blazing wood fire. "Could you put your finger—not your big finger, only your little one—into that fire and keep it there?"

Mechanically, then, he raised a cold and flaccid hand. (Even in that moment I remembered that to shake hands with him was like shaking hands with the tail of a fish.) Then recoiling, "No!"

But there is no way to refuse, no way out of the fire for

the little cow that has been put into it. And there is no way
to refuse and no way out of a life which will consume all
that is good in the little boy who is put into it; and will anyone be greatly comforted by remembering that he is not a
big boy, but quite a little one?

Thy sword was bathed in heaven,
And that great sword
Bathed in clear glory, Lord,
Has conquered me,
And conquering, set me free.

Oh bathe my sword in heaven,
Lest creeping rust,
Or stain of earthly dust,
Dim the bright blade,
Pledged to my Lord's crusade.

Thy sword, bathed in high heaven,
Purged ancient wrongs;
To Thee my sword belongs
For that same fight.
Bathe it, O Lord, in light.

29. Boys of the Temple

Wrote Harriet Meuricoffre to her sister Josephine Butler, "Do you remember that nice Russian lady who used to help the Sisters every morning to dress the wounds of the poor who came to the Convent, and a great lady said to her: 'I really cannot rise early; but will you, dear friend, every morning tend one wounded person to my account, and another to the account of my daughter'?" When that young Brahman said "No," and drew his fingers back from the flame, it was because his torpid imagination had been suddenly quickened. May the Lord quicken ours if we are content to deputize someone else to get up in the morning to wash the wounds of the world.

The god whose priests demanded the burning alive of a little cow is worshiped in a temple town near Dohnavur. The first time we saw small boys as acolytes was at one of the Car festivals there.

We were waiting under the eaves of a house, trying to get shelter from the blazing sun, when, with shoutings and flingings of arms in the air, the brown flood swept past. Every man was stripped to the waist in honor of the god. The flood grew denser, the shouts were frenzied, the car moved round the corner, rocked for a dizzy moment and stopped.

This was inauspicious. If we could have done so, we would have faded out of the picture, but there was no way of fading in that jam. So we stood there quietly, and we watched the car pullers as they strained and sweated at the ropes and cried for levers. Scores rushed off to get them.

Seen thus in the glare of day, and dressed up for festival, the car was a garish thing. Its dark, carved surfaces were covered with colored streamers, and from the scaffolding, tied about it to add to its height, depended strings of tinsel and garlands of withering flowers.

But the clamor was growing frantic; crowds pressed in about the wheels, and policemen, anxious lest a late tragedy should be repeated (for a year or two before a devotee had flung himself under the wheels), pushed in like a wedge and drove the nearer people off. For ten long minutes in blinding white light and smothering white dust we stood, till down a side street came the levers, trunks of young palms, which with frenzied haste were pried under the wheels, dozens of hands grasping above, while dozens more worked feverishly below. There was a mighty warning shout as the trunks were pushed down, and the men below sprang aside. "Pull!" yelled ten thousand throats. Creaking and groaning, the reluctant wheels turned, and in clouds of dust the car rolled off. Behind it roared the rabble; in their wake, stretched naked on the ground and turning over and over, hands extended so as to change the begging bowl from one to the other, rolled, covered with dust and breathing dust, a Saivite ascetic.

But not the car, nor the crowd, nor the ascetic, nor even the lovely vision of peace that had drawn our eyes in wonder when we looked down the street—for a palm, bending over, framed in shining feathery fronds the sweet blue of hills and sky, like a heavenly thought dropping down among us all—not these are most firmly fastened in memory, but this: little boys attendant on the god. One of them sat on the upper tier in front of the altar, a wreath of pink flowers on his bare shoulders. Others hoisted up the baskets of offerings from the people who pressed as near as they might to the car.

Nine years later, a young Englishman on his way to China climbed a hill overlooking one of the famous temples of the South. It was evening, and the beauty of the view, black mountain peak, dark forest, reddening sky, rice fields spread like a green carpet, water falling in white masses into a deep pool—"pool where the moonbeams die"—held him in the silence of worship.

Suddenly the stillness was shattered. Drum and flute and wild clashing of cymbal told of the evening puja beginning in the temple. And a great rush of pity, and more than pity, for the polluted children bore down upon him. And he cried to the Lord about the children. And the Lord spoke to him there—told him the task was hard, told him that He waited—but for whom?

How should he know? He did not know. He was not told then, so he went on to China. He did not dream that it was for him his Lord was waiting; nor did we dream of what was being prepared for us and for the boys.

30.

Who will bring me into the strong city? Who will lead me into Edom? Wilt not Thou, O God?

That they may know that this is Thy hand; that Thou, Lord, hast done it.—Psalms 108:10–11 and 109:27.

It will be: God hath said it.—Samuel Rutherford.

Let the hope of life give way: let the hope of God ascend.—St. Augustine.

30. Boys of the Drama

It was much more difficult than we had expected, to get on the track of little boys. We were continually catching glimpses, but they were vanishing glimpses; the brothers of the Lotus Buds were even more elusive than their sisters had been. But we knew that just out of sight things were happening all the time—soul-destroying things.

One evening, led by an Indian friend who knew the ways of this underworld, I found myself at the door of a long, low house. There was nothing to mark it from other houses in the street. It had barred windows and verandahs, and a heavy, strong door; but so had they. It looked secretive; so did they. Most houses do, if they turn a blind wall to the street and keep their barred windows shuttered. We knocked at the door. It opened an inch or two. An old hag looked out.

"Are the children well?" asked my Indian friend in a kindly, interested voice, after the brief preliminaries etiquette demanded were over.

"What children? There are no children here."

"The boys, O elder sister, the boys who learn here."

"No boys learn here," and the door all but shut.

"Oh, say not so, sister. Do they not learn songs?"

"No boys learn songs here." And the door shut.

Later we tried; but this time the house was evidently empty. "The school has been removed," said the people in the street. The dumb, blind house, its doors and windows fastened up, in the dim light of the evening looked like a long, low rock; "O rock, rock, rock, when wilt thou open to my Lord?"

We tried again, and this time our objective was a travelling theatre. We threaded the tangled lanes of the city, thronged, late at night though it was, till we reached an odorous yard in which the theatre was set. Small boys were thumping a tom-tom, cracking jokes with one another, stopping when they felt inclined to play, but soon resuming their exciting business, tom-tom, *tom*-tom, tom-a-tom, *tom*-tom.

We passed them, bought our tickets, asked when the performance of the night was to begin, found that we had some time to spare, and wondered how should it be spent. "Where do the children live?" The ticket-seller, having no idea of our identity, told us.

Then we ran through a maze of mean streets, our double rickshaw blundering through the crowd like a beetle bent on business through a swarm of ants. At last we stopped before a house whose door was open. Without waiting to give the people within time to consider us, we walked straight in. "We have come to see the children," I said to the first man I met, as if it were the most usual thing in the world for a foreign woman to penetrate into this den. But he did not seem to recognize the foreign. At such times inconspicuous Indian dress is of the greatest help. He let us pass through the central courtyard. What next? How get further?

A boy ran to meet us, holding out eager hands. "Come, Amma," he cried in welcome, as though he had been waiting for us, "Come." Then in English, "Shake hands," and he held out his hand gravely. Just as gravely I shook it, but it was astonishing.

"These are my friends," continued the child, speaking in English and introducing with an easy grace two of the boys, who advanced politely. "Shake hands." We shook hands all around.

"Where are the other boys?"

"Here, I will show." And he took us straight into a room where a number of boys were chanting their parts aloud.

It was a large room, stone-paved, high-walled, with two heavy black doors, one leading to the courtyard, the other opening into the back parts of the house. And it was full of boys. Twenty-five or more immediately surrounded us, lads of all ages between six or seven and seventeen or eighteen, beautiful boys. "Sit down, Amma," said the others, surprised but delightfully polite as they dragged in a chair from somewhere. It felt too amazing to be true. No power on earth could have opened those doors. I could hardly believe I was there, inside, with the boys of whom I had heard so much but whom I had never seen before. And the feeling of strangeness did not lessen as they crowded round, friendly and lovable and keen to make the most of this welcome interruption to an apparently strictly enforced routine.

For twenty wonderful minutes we talked together in Tamil. They told me about their lives, their training, their habits—would have taken me to the back regions to see their oil-bath arrangements had I not feared to lose precious minutes in mere seeing, for there was so much to hear. They were in full flow, and I was learning all I wanted to learn, when the outer door was flung open and an angry man rushed in upon us like a whirlwind.

"Off to your lessons, boys!" and he blew them away with a storm of words through the other door, and turned the key upon them.

We waited till the hurricane had spent itself, then rose and departed with the usual salaam, which he returned, too confounded for speech. But we heard the house door bang behind us, and knew that our adventure could not be repeated. Was it "chance" that had opened that door? Was it "chance" that years before led us through the wood just as a child was being taken to the temple to be married to the god?* Were not forces of prayer unloosed that day that have never lost their power? Had the time come for the unloosing of the doors that shut the boys up in perilous places? Would the new insight, granted now, help towards that? There was a dear boy of six in that house, such a pretty nut-brown child with great solemn eyes, who, as I sat there among them, came nearer and nearer, till his hands were on my knee and he was looking up into my face. Suddenly the big eyes filled with tears. The other boys noticed it. "He has only lately come," they said. He looked like a child who had lately left his mother.

But there was more that we must see, and we found our way back to the great open, iron-roofed shed, called by courtesy a theatre. Nothing more unlike the English idea of such a place could be, except that there were a stage and a curtain and footlights. The rest of the inside structure was frankly Eastern and, as it filled, the roar of voices was like the roar at a large railway station in India, where every man shouts down his fellow as a matter of course. But when, after much agitation, the curtain rolled up and a throne was revealed, on which, robed in a shimmer of pink and gold jewels, sat a little queen, the roar subsided into a murmur like the murmur of waves on the shore.

Spellbound, we too gazed. The child—it was our first friend—was playing an Indian musical instrument, which showed to perfection the delicate sensitive hands. And as he played he turned his little head slowly from side to side and bowed in the approved fashion of beautiful queens. From that point on he held the audience. The roar from some fifteen hundred throats would burst out again between the acts or when others were acting; but let that

---

* *Things as They Are*, Chapter 24.

exquisite child appear, whether as frolicsome boy or dainty queen, and the whole mass of excited humanity gave itself up to gaze. Now I understood why such children are practically priceless. Every seat in the theatre was filled: it was that child who drew the crowd and held it.

His acting was wonderful. As the sordid plot unfolded, he was the central figure. There was a king, a handsome youth gorgeously appareled, excellent in his way; numbers of Court ladies (the boys of our brief friendship); a clever fool ("This is the fool," the little queen boy had said, pushing that bright boy forward); a musician who pattered on a kind of harmonica, his nervous fingers working interminably, whether he was actually playing or not. Every word of song or dialogue was clearly sung or said in perfect Tamil, but only the front seats could have heard much of it, for the railway-station roar prevailed always, except when that child and his attendant children were the chief actors. Once the audience was so much occupied with its conversation that it did not perceive the child, who, after a dull interlude, had come forward again, and for that one moment he stood, his hands stretched out imploringly. Evidently it was very necessary that he should be a success. There was an anxious look in his eyes then. (On another night in another city we watched the chief theatrical trainer who was teaching the boys to recite poetry, and we saw the cane the trainer held in his hand, and understood that boy's anxiety.) But now with a great shout, as he stood there before them, the crowd returned to its allegiance, and the rumble and the roar stopped suddenly. The charm of the child had won.

We left the theatre with hot hearts. But deep in us there was hope, for from the hour we had entered it, behind and below the apparent, it was as though we had seen kneeling in a corner among the stage scenery the figure of a little girl of seven or eight, and through the clamor we could hear her pray aloud, "Lighten our darkness, we beseech Thee, O Lord."

That child had been kidnapped or bought by the dramatic company; she had been carried off to a far city, and the whirl and terror of new sensations, helped possibly by some benumbing drug, had dazed her memory as regards her past. But some things stood out clear. She had somewhere heard of the Lord Jesus Christ. The one who had taught her had spoken in English. All she knew of Him, therefore, was in English, though except for these fragments she knew nothing of our language. She had seen, "at the time of the lighting of the lamps," someone (she could not tell us who it was) kneel down and pray, "Lighten our darkness, we beseech Thee, O Lord; and by Thy great mercy defend us from all perils and dangers of this night; for the love of Thy only Son, our Saviour, Jesus Christ." For fourteen hundred years, from many kinds of darkness, that prayer has found its way to God from countless human hearts, and this little girl in her desolation, alone among strangers, prayed in these same words. And then God moved. The theatre people who wanted to make her a violin player found that she could not learn. An Indian friend who was on the watch for us heard of her. A month later she was safe in Dohnavur. She is now a loving and eager seeker of others out in the dark.

> God! Fight we not within a cursèd world
> Whose very air teems thick with leaguèd fiends—

But the leaguèd fiends are doomed. "Theseus whispered to his companions, 'Have hope, for the monster is not immortal.'" And a Greater than Theseus is here.

There is a path which no fowl knoweth,
 Nor vulture's eye hath seen;
A path beside a viewless river
 Whose banks are always green,
For it is the way of prayer;
 Holy Spirit, lead us there.

Oh lead us on, weigh not our merits,
 For we have none to weigh,
But, Saviour, pardon our offenses,
 Lead even us today
Further in the way of prayer;
 Holy Spirit, lead us there.

31. The Word of Pool and Waterfall

It was before our forest house was built, and we had taken a bunch of children to an upland valley about fifteen miles from Dohnavur. But the loveliness of that valley was pierced by the remembrance of those unreached boys, and at last, overcome by the insistence of that thought, we had sent the children off to play in the shallows of the stream and, kneeling by a rock that bordered a quiet pool, had besought the Lord to take away the burden or to show us what He would have us do.

Presently, as we knelt there, soothed by the sound of the water that seemed to flow over us, body, soul, and spirit (and there was healing in its flow), we began to look at the beauty spread about us. The pool was a shining thing; it had a golden floor, for the rocks there, under water and in sunlight, are like jasper, or like amber. On the floor lay a heap of battered, sodden leaves, some still faintly colored, red, orange, yellow, some dull and brown like shadows of leaves. And now and then a current moving gently would slip under the heap and carry some of the leaves through golden gates, where, caught in a scurry of white, the bruised things would be broken up and swept swiftly down the stream. Poor marred things. But were they poor? They were on their way to make others rich. The forest and the glory thereof, the fern by the riverside, the little flower, the moss, live on the food that the dead leaves give.

Presently, idly as a child might have done, I tossed a handful of newly fallen leaves into the pool. They danced off like bright shells, like fairy boats, or, gathering in glowing heaps on the surface of the water, lay contented. Sometimes there was a little rustling sound as though they were laughing. Not for them yet the bruising and the burying.

Holy places which are the figures of the true—this private room in the forest was a holy place; we had seen a figure of the true; we had seen one of the invisible things which from the creation of the world are clearly seen, being understood by the things that are made. There is no life except by death—this was the invisible thing clearly seen that day. "Always bearing about in the body the dying of the Lord Jesus, that the life also of Jesus might be made manifest in our mortal flesh," that was what we had seen in a figure.

Broken, battered, sodden leaves—these that were ready to sink out of sight and be dealt with in any way, all choices gone, they were near to becoming life to the forest. The fairy boats were not yet ready. "Learn to obey, thou dust, learn to meek thyself, thou earth and clay."

Another year passed, and still we could not begin. Baby boys were said to be very difficult to bring up, and we had no doctor. Above all, we had no men, except our faithful Arul Dasan; and well we knew that, though women could mother little boys, the day would soon come when men must take over. Everyone thought of Dohnavur in terms of Lotus Buds; what man would ever want to come? Because of the command concerning the pattern which was shown us in the mount, we were constrained to ask for those who were compelled by the law of their being to follow that same pattern. Where were such to be found? We did not know. So there was nothing to encourage us, much to discourage and forbid the thought of such a venture. As we thought of it, difficulties piled up like heaps of stones tossed from a wall that is being pulled down.

And forebodings that we had never known when we began to save the girls oppressed us. We knew more now than we did then of the inwardness of this to which we must set our hand. "The fire shall try every man's work of what sort it is." Were we ready for that? Was our reputation ashes to us? This was a curious question that came again and again. What if our hopes fell in ruins about us like a child's castle of cards?

Josephine Butler says that she felt a kind of triumph in that beautiful arrangement by which God has chosen the weak things of the world to confound the strong. We felt no kind of triumph, but we knew that her words were true: "It matters nothing at all what we are," she wrote, "provided we are entirely willing to be made the instruments of His will, His agents in this world. I do not think we know the meaning of the word strength until we have fathomed our utter weakness." We fathomed ours. We wondered whether she had ever felt as weak as we did then.

Sometimes now, looking at the scores of boys in their crimson homespun cotton, darting in and out among the trees like hips and haws alive, or careering down the wide path on palm-leaf motorcars, we think of those questions that like rending lightning disclosed the recesses of the soul. And we thank our God that He did not let us carelessly venture on this new thing.

I was in the forest again when at last the word came which settled all for me and brought assurance to the comrades at Dohnavur. The house was being built and the day was full of mundane matters; but the men's dinner-hour was free, and then the river called. After the clamors of the coolies and the shattering racket of hammers on stone and wood, the quiet of the river was the very breath of peace. But as by the golden stream, so now, there was a piercing.

I was standing by a waterfall, which we call by a Tamil name meaning Great Joy, when the question broke forth again, Lord, what of the little boys?

> Oh, there are heavenly heights to reach
>   In many a fearful place,
> Where the poor timid child of God
>   Lies blindly on his face,
> Lies languishing for light divine
>   Which he shall never see,
> Till he goes forward at Thy sign,
>   And trusts himself to Thee.

But, Lord Jesus, where are the men?

There was no answer that I heard. I was looking at the answer, the wonder of the ceaseless flow of water. Then the sense of it came. And I heard a voice from heaven, as the voice of many waters, *Can I who do this, not do that?*

Spiritually, in that hour, the work for boys began.

32.

Nothing strikes me so much in a life of great sorrow and trial as the deep *humanity* of the Scriptures, and of Him, of whom the Scriptures testify. Hymns and most human compositions of a devout kind breathe far too pure and difficult an air, rise to far too sunny and unclouded a height for my struggling soul to breathe and live in; only in the Divine Book do I find the deep, human cry; only in the Psalms of David, and in the Word made flesh, do I find what suits my struggling humanity.—Ellice Hopkins.

32. In Vain?

Our chief traveler during those years was Frances Beath. She was ready at any hour to start on a long journey to save a child. Her journeys covered many thousands of miles—we ceased to count the miles. The changes at crowded stations, at midnight or in the early hours of the morning, made these journeys difficult, and the packed carriages were tiring too. But nothing mattered if only she could return bringing a baby with her, sometimes two or three. They were so tiny, often so pitifully fragile-looking, that to the casual eye it seemed much exertion for little profit. But when they had grown into sturdy, jolly, dancing "tedlets," as many of them did, even the most doubtful felt it worthwhile.

For years the care of the babies had fallen chiefly on our nurse, Mabel Wade, and it was a relief when our first doctor, Gladys Webster, came, answer as we then believed to our prayer of years. But she had hardly settled down before she had to return home with what was thought to be tubercular trouble. It was the first of those strange crashes of hope for which we had been prepared.

But the most prolonged trial of faith (it continues to be so) was the baffling ease with which again and again the

enemy forestalled us. "Yes, a man from the dramatic company was here, and he took two little boys back with him.
I had seen them playing in the courtyard the day before,
but I did not know that anyone was trying to get them."
This sort of thing became a dreadful commonplace. There
was always someone on the ground before we got there.

But I do not know how to gather up into a page or two
anything which will give an insight into the nature of this
wrestle with visible and invisible foes for these who are
being drawn into the vortex of the dramatic companies.
Scouts are everywhere. Those scouts are like creatures
with tentacles. They close around the child and suck it in.
"A lost battle is a battle one believes lost. There are three
courses: you can retire, stand fast, attack. I forbid the first.
You can take your choice of the other two."* With this in
mind, I will tell of a battle not won yet.

It was Dass of Money Town, a hard, worldly-minded
place like its name, who told us of two little brothers who
had been bought by a woman in Travancore and offered to
the dramatic company just then performing in one of our
temple towns. The elder, a boy of nine, was in training.
The little one, a beautiful child of four, was promised to
the company. No one but Dass would have dreamed of
trying to save them. But he was of the kind that dares
anything, a man created for forlorn hopes.

So he set out. He meant to try to get a chance to make
friends with the boys in spite of their guard. Such children
are very carefully guarded. Men attend them wherever
they go. They are not allowed to have casual speech with
strangers. This is not to be wondered at, when their value
to the company is considered. We were offered over a
hundred pounds—it was brought and definitely tendered
to us—for a baby boy whose beauty made him desirable.

Somehow Dass managed to reach the boys and see them
alone. The elder one responded wistfully. Yes, he would

* *Marshal Foch*, Sir George Aston's Life of the Marshal.

like to come, but *she* (the so-called mother) would never let him. The smaller boy munched his sweets contentedly, and was as friendly as four years old can be with a big and wonderful brother who buys sweets in the bazaar. Dass longed to carry them off then and there, but had to keep his promise and return them to the "mother."

It was the first step, and then, having received a fresh touch of God upon his spirit and full of a bright hope, Dass went again. I cannot remember any time when we, who were left to think of him as he went upon this errand, were more filled with hope, for our God does do such wonderful things for the encouragement of those whom He has lately drawn into His sanctuary.

After he left, a disquieting thing was shown to one of us as in a picture—even Dass returning home sadly, deeply discouraged. The woman had gone off with the younger child—so it appeared in that showing. The older one could not be found. A note of this that had been shown was written down and dated, though there did not seem to be much use in it.

Next day Dass returned. He told us that he had gone to the house where the woman and the boys had been, but found that she had gone away with the younger boy, and the older one had been given to the dramatic company and was quite out of reach. The company had left the town. No one knew where it had gone. Dass had then traced the woman to a city a hundred miles distant, and had followed, and found her, and with all his heart, so newly moved in love and longing, he had pleaded with her not to doom this lovely boy to destruction.

And into her mind a fear had crept. What if the Great God had sent this man who said that he was His messenger? What if He wanted the child? Deep in the heart of India, if only one can pierce to it, is a sense of God. Many a child is here because of that sense. Let our thoughts be tender when we think of India. The fiercer our fight against the unclean power whose nature is summed up visibly in certain of the symbols of Hinduism, the gentler let our thoughts be of the soul of this people who might be so different. The woman had wavered. At last, "You may have him," she said, and she pushed the boy towards Dass. "Quickly I went to the bazaar, he running alongside. He had many gold chains and bangles on his wrists and ankles, some that only a goldsmith could get off. The goldsmith was filing through a bangle when suddenly I heard an angry voice. It was the woman. She rushed in raging and seized the boy. Her sister had discovered what she had done and had reviled her and cursed her in the name of the gods. She could not stand against that. So she had come for him, and she snatched him up and carried him off." Deeply dejected, Dass sighed.

Then he read the note, which told in a few words just what had been, and his eyes cleared. Go to the depths of a wood on a dull and heavy day. Look up, see only dark treetops, look round, see only dark and crowding leaves. Listen and hear the sullen roar of a cataract, and the cold noise of unlighted water, and feel the clinging, wet mist. Then suddenly see the flashing of sunbeams everywhere. A wind is blowing in your face. It has scattered the mist. The water is sounding joyfully now. You look up through the leaves. They are like windows of transparent emerald. Far above the treetops you see blue sky.

Make Thy face to shine upon us and we shall be saved— that must have been written out of doors: it has the feel of the sun and the wind. Just such an illumined moment visited us now. Dass read the note, knew that he had not stood alone in that street, gone into that house alone, traveled alone in the train, been alone when he talked to that woman. One who saw all, heard all, had been there. And that same One had been here. This note showed that. And just to know it for certain brought light.

While he was still in the glow of a recovered gladness Dass went to another town for another child and saved him, spreading everywhere a sense of the reality of the

Unseen, so that a missionary, working in a very difficult city, hearing of this so recent touch of the Lord on common life, was strengthened. Then he went to the town where the woman and the little boy were living, sure that this time he would return with that child, and perhaps his brother too. Meanwhile we had been praying that the fear of the living God might come upon that woman so that she would not dare to refuse the boys to Him.

And indeed the fear of God had come upon her "Take the child; he is yours for the taking," and she pointed to a little bundle in the corner of the room. It was the four-year-old boy. He was covered with smallpox and blind.

"Safe from the drama now," was Dass's first thought—the dramatic people do not want marred faces—but what a piteous way of salvation. "Come back for him, he is yours," said the hoarse, anguished voice of the woman. "I promise him to you." And she poured out torrents of invective on the sister whose curse had changed her purpose and led to this great misery. And again a few weeks later Dass went for him, but he could find no trace of him. Is that little boy playing in the Father's house today, a happy child, not blind? We do not know. The impenetrable silence of India has swallowed up that woman and those boys.

A sad story, and so different from the kind we all like best—the kind that ends happily, and leaves us content. In some moods, such a story is unendurable. But we are not left uncomforted. Are not two sparrows sold for a farthing? And not one of them shall fall on the ground without your Father. Were not these two little brothers of more value than many sparrows?

And a story of comfort comes to me, as I think of those little brothers and of others over whom we would write "In vain" if it were not for that glorious "*Not* in vain in the Lord" that cannot be refuted by anything that can ever happen.

Soon after our work began, and before it was quite

understood what kind of child we were commissioned to save, people sent us children who were not in temple danger, and our nurseries were filled, and the strength of our few workers was exhausted, so that we came very near to our limit; and what if we passed that limit and could not take the child whose peril haunted our dreams? Then several fellow-missionaries who were carrying on work for children in other districts offered to take some from us, and we knew that all would be well with them. Some of them proved to be delicate or difficult, or both, but they kept them. "When we take a child, it's for better or worse," they said. And we blessed them, for it meant that more room was left for these others threatened by the temple.

Indian Christian families also asked for little girls to adopt and bring up with their own. This seemed a good plan. In every case the adopters brought assuring letters from missionaries and pastors, and we went to see them ourselves and did our best to make sure all was well. There were some very happy adoptions, but the greater number were unsatisfactory; too often all that was wanted was a cheap slave. We had to retrieve most of the children, and, as they had learned the evil talk of the streets by that time, they were, and for years continued to be, a problem. Some had been cruelly treated; one child had over thirty marks on her face and body caused by cutting or burning. It was months before she recovered. Her adopting father was of such respectability that he would have been elected as an official in his church if it had not been for the missionary who helped me to retrieve that child. (He took me in the sidecar of his motorcycle to the house, and we carried her off together.) But one child—her name was Heavenly One—we hopelessly lost. Her adopters left the city of Madras and no one knew their address. After searching its lanes and byways (the city covers an immense area and numbers over half a million) we gave it up. Little Heavenly One was lost.

Then one day by chance we read in a missionary magazine of a little girl from South India being found in a bazaar in Poona. The Z.B.M.M. missionaries had taken her into their children's home. Could it be Heavenly One? It was. We wrote to Poona, and to our relief heard what assured us that it was that very child. Lonely and neglected, she had wandered about in the strange city to which her adopters had taken her. She did not know the language. She could not explain anything to anyone. But she was not lost; she was not forgotten. Not one of them is forgotten before God. The Z.B.M.M., God bless them, found her. They tended her lovingly, but before long little Heavenly One flew away to the country where all the birds sing.

At the end of the day, shall we not find them all? Will not all our forlorn hopes look different then, all our winters turn to spring, all our nights to dawn? In this fight for the souls for whom Christ died, may we ever say, "In vain"?

33.

By faith we pass beyond the utmost range of sight. To act in faith—whether the action be of thought or of feeling, within our own heart or in relation to others—is to venture beyond what sight will warrant; to let go the obvious and tangible supports to which we might cling within a closely bounded field, and to commit ourselves to principles which sense cannot certify, to lines of action on which sense will not accompany us, to a sustaining power which sense has never promised.—Bishop Paget.

Lord Jesu, I ask Thee, give unto me movement in Thy love withouten measure; desire withouten limit; longing withouten order; burning withouten discretion. Truly the better the love of Thee is, the greedier it is; for neither by reason is it restrained, nor by dread thronged, nor by doom tempted.—Richard Rolle (1290-1349), *The Fire of Love and The Mending of Life.*

33. Transparent Incidents

And after we had found the boys, all was not plain
sailing. Sometimes we had three or four who were in need
of skilled treatment. Neyyoor was always willing to help
us, but once for some reason it was impossible to go there,
and we tried another house of kindness in Madura, two
days' journey distant. We had by this time the great help
of our V.A.D., Mary Mills, who took the little party. It was
strange to be taking a baby boy to that city, famed for its
underworld life of both temple and drama. The boy was
the one for whom a hundred pounds had been offered to
us when he was an infant; he was one year old then. There
were men in that city who would have given much more
to get him. Such a charge is no small responsibility, and
we kept the shield of prayer around him all the time,
asking that no spurious relatives should suddenly emerge.
We had sent two little girls to that hospital once, and they
had been tracked; so there was cause for care. Arul Dasan
was one of the party, and his little son David, whose
mother is the Jewel for whom that long fight was fought in
the law courts which ended in an order going forth from
the courts of Heaven that canceled the order given in the
court of Tinnevelly.

Arul Dasan was not quite fit himself, but he had said nothing about that, and it was left to the doctor to discover that he needed to have a slight, thought painful, operation. But he had gone to help, not to be ill, and he earnestly tried to persuade the doctor to do it without an anesthetic, so that he might not have to take a day off to recover; he could never understand why the doctor decidedly refused.

All went well with the babies, and with Arul Dasan too, and they returned in safety to find us in the midst of one of those confused times that come in every work where there are too few workers to do all that must be done. Several were away on furlough or on holiday, and, naturally, there was some pressure. But one day—a very thronged day—this rested us: "The Lord of peace Himself give you peace always by all means, peace at all times in all ways, peace continually whatever comes, peace in every sense, peace always, under all conditions."* "Go amidst the whirling" is Wordsworth's translation of Ezekiel 10:2. Just then it was the word to us. But what a difference it makes if, when we have to go amidst the whirling of the busy wheels of life, we find peace waiting there for us.

Meanwhile the life of the day went on with its decisions and provisions. We were building new nurseries and in those days had no one to advise or superintend them, so to build meant many labors. But, as we have told elsewhere (*Nor Scrip* tells most of this), there were such continual touches of our Lord upon the common work of our hands, such manifold helps, that the last of the first set of boys' nurseries was gratefully named, Answered Prayer.

In looking through our private records to find the transparent incidents of the time that let the spiritual situation appear, I have come upon one, a note in an old journal torn up for the most part.

It belongs to that same year, 1920, which began in straitness and a general uncertainty about the future, for if the

---

* 2 Thess. 3:16—A.V., R.V., Moffat, Weymouth, Way.

exchange fell further, who could say what would happen? We had all along thought of whatever funds were entrusted to us as intended for the children only. Nothing had been used for English workers. All who had joined us, either had enough to live on without charge to the work or had friends who supplied their needs. But now offers began to come from some whose circumstances were different, and this opened a new question. What did our Father wish to be done about it? Understanding what the will of the Lord is—Lord, give Thy servant an understanding heart—these words, and others like them, were much with us, and on March 15, 1920, relying on His sure promise for those whom He sends forth, this note was written: "Resolved together to accept all who offer who are manifestly called of the Lord to join us, whether they have means or not."

Soon after that time, out of five hundred pounds sent to us, two hundred and twenty-one pounds were lost in exchange, and before long even more. (It seemed to drop into the sea on its way out.) At the same time the cost of living doubled. There were days when it seemed impossible to go on. The children were in faded garments that year instead of the usual cheery crimson and blue, and we ourselves did without everything we possibly could. "May you obtain strength and support to walk in paths unworn, at the edge of precipices where God alone can keep us in safety," Didon wrote from his prison in Corbara. How salutary such a walk must be to the soul, for look where one will, in books and in life, those unworn paths are trodden. Unworn? That is not a true word. Never do we go far on any path of perplexity or pain without seeing the footsteps of Him who is invisible, leading on before.

Is it not always so? Has any spiritual fabric ever been built except upon invisible foundations? "The steps of faith fall on the seeming void and find the rock beneath"; but the rock is hardly ever seen till afterwards. Just when the step has to be taken, coils of blinding, smothering mist descend upon the path, and yet the word persists. And the foot that seems to step out on nothing finds rock. In the years that followed we walked on rock.

> Beloved, should the brook run dry
> And should no visible supply
> Gladden thine eyes, then wait to see
> God work a miracle for thee.
> Thou canst not want, for God has said
> He will supply His own with bread.
> His word is sure. Creative power
> Will work for thee from hour to hour,
> And thou, with all Faith's host, shalt prove
> God's Hand of power, God's Heart of love.*

It was just then, before we had reached the rock, while we were, as any sensible person would have truly said, with one foot over the precipice, that we came to know that a sum of money which had been kindly sent to us under a misapprehension must be returned. It was a large sum to us, and we hardly knew how to do without it; but we had no liberty to keep it. It was twice returned by the secretary of the society which had sent it to us as a grant. In the end he accepted it, "As you have apparently more money than you know what to do with," and we were clear of that entanglement.

But so little was coming in just then that we found ourselves short of ready money for food. Stores had to be bought in large quantities for the sake of economy, grain had to be bought in the same way, and because of the loss in exchange and the general difficulty of the time, we prayed for some ready money—money in rupees. The prayer was dated in our logbook, March 1. And in our private letterbook there is a letter dated March 2, from an old friend of the work. "I smile as I write. I wanted to lie down, but something or someone said to me, No, you have put it off for two days. Go and do it at once." And she

---

* Margaret E. Barber, Fukien.

sent us forty pounds in rupees. This gift tided us over the immediate need. Only once again during that year did a gift so large reach us in rupees. But our Father had more for us than this. Under date April 30 there is another note—"Closed [the month] with God's refund of the money paid to X"—which meant that all bills were paid and there was as much over as we had returned.

I think this incident is transparent. Not because it snows our Father's provision—it does that, but so does every day of every year. There is something different here. Only twice in thirty years of looking to Him for our children have we been directed to return money, and each time the command came at a lean time, when to the natural man it looked like sheer folly. And after we had become willing, there was the inevitable voice in our ear, "You will be misunderstood." But it was the voice of flesh. No one travels far on the road of faith without hearing another voice clearer, more austere, "Walk before Me and be thou perfect." Before Me, not before Sarah. God knew, whether "Sarah" did or not, just how things stood with us, and our affairs were His. He did not tell us to explain things to anyone, but just to obey. And he Himself knew what He would do. What He did we shall tell later, to the glory of His name who never fails the child who trusts Him.

That same year saw us borne along in a new direction. We were wakened in the middle of a stifling night by a fresh burst of the thumping of the tom-toms, and the various noises of the demon-worship that goes on all over this district on Tuesdays and Fridays, from late evening till just before dawn. Presently a cry pierced through the mad racket. At first we thought it was the cry of the one who has received the afflatus, but soon we distinguished a different note. There was a terror in it like that of a tormented animal, and this cry lost itself in distracting wails. We could not listen and do nothing. So we got up and went to the village, passing the group around the fire with its gyrating worshipers and its tom-tom players, till, following that other sound, we found ourselves outside a barred door; we knocked and after a minute's hesitation— for everyone knows that bad spirits can knock at doors at night—someone let us in. On the ground in the middle of the courtyard lay a young man tied with rope. A big man with a polished stick in his hands stood over him, thrashing him vigorously, while all around men and women stood awestruck and silent. They burst into speech now. They told us that the pig-demon had seized the young man when he was a child. It often became violent, and now it was being beaten out of him. We told the big man (he was the boy's grandfather) to untie him, and he did so. Then we called upon the name of the Lord, and our Saviour set the poor lad free. We left the household in peace.

On the other side of the mountains lived a Hindu priest, a seeker after God. A guru had told him that if he would gaze with the eyes of the mind very steadily on a great light, like the manifold lights which surround the image of the god in the inner shrine in the temple, he would see the world in its proper relation to eternal things, and thus he would receive a vision of God. This sounded a possible way to find Him, and so he sought to follow these directions, but was constantly pulled back by thoughts of the world and the things that are in the world, and he gave up, disheartened; he could not find God.

About this time—it was early October, 1921—a man called Pilgrim, then an ardent young convert, was staying with him. One day a crowd of people in great excitement came to the door of the priest's house crying to him to hasten, for a demon had seized one of their clan, and he was needed to cast it out. He was an exorcist by profession, and often cast out demons, or attempted to do so, and he rose at once to go with them. Then Pilgrim stopped him, told him of the true God and of Christ His son, and of how He had cast out demons, and had empowered His servants to do the same. He was much struck by this, and he came to Dohnavur to hear more. It happened that just then the man from whom the demon had been cast out came to give thanks. He laid the big polished stick which his grandfather had used to beat the demon out of him on the low table at the end of the room which we then used as a prayer room, and beside the stick he put the coil of stout rope that had been used to bind him; his grandfather had sent them, he said. And he raised his hands above his head, "The Lord Jesus cast out the pig-demon. To Him be praise!" The exorcist heard him, and was greatly impressed; he returned soon afterwards to his own country, and told what he had seen, and we heard, too, that he had confessed his faith in the Lord Jesus Christ.

After that, many people came, hearing that there was help for them. Some who were tormented by evil spirits came (we are telling a simple tale, and are not careful to guard it even by such words as "or imagined themselves to be so"—for though we know there can be deceptions and hysterical conditions which simulate the other, we believe that there is that other too). Many sick came— pitifully suffering people. They came at the time the children assembled for prayers, and we were all blessed and drawn into a new tenderness, a new awareness of the Presence in our midst. Sometimes Hindus from distant places came to look and listen. "I never imagined that He whom you worship was in the world today," said one, a Government official, as he stood looking on. Others said the same, and soon there was a buzz of talk, and colored stories flew all over the countryside—A place of healing! Miracles! Come, let us see! For still the multitude loves a spectacle.

We searched our Bibles then, to find our Lord's thought about this matter; and we read the scores of letters that came from the ends of the earth, each urging upon us some new view of divine healing. There was a day when we asked Him, if He willed it so, to give us the gift, the *charisma*, that had been in apostolic times. Would it not glorify His name? And what a joy it would be to see pain

instantly relieved—for though we did see a putting forth
of power, there was not anything comparable to the healing of the first century. The *charisma* was not given. Why
was that most blessed gift not given in its fullness?

> Go, and the Holy One
> Of Israel by thy guide
> To what may serve His glory best and spread His name
> Great among the heathen round.

We know not what we should pray for as we ought. Not
our poor thoughts, but the counsels of the Holy One, be
our guide. And the story of how He guided us through the
Green Valley shows another transparent incident.

34

Behold how green this valley is, also how beautiful with lilies. . . . In this valley our Lord formerly had his country house; he loved much to be here; he loved also to walk these meadows, for he found the air was pleasant. . . . This is a valley that nobody walks in but those that love a pilgrim's life. And though Christian had the hard hap to meet here with Apollyon, and to enter with him a brisk encounter, yet I must tell you, that in former times men have met with angels here, have found pearls here, and have in this place found the words of life . . . and they that go through it shall sing, as Christian did, for all he met with Apollyon.—John Bunyan.

In the shadow of Thy wings
I will sing for joy;
What a God, who out of shade
Nest for singing bird hath made.
Lord, my Might and Melody,
I will sing to Thee.

If the shadow of Thy wings
Be so full of song,
What must be the lighted place
Where Thy bird can see Thy face?
Lord, my Might and Melody,
I will sing to Thee.

34. A Green Valley

The glamour that the East flings on all that appears mysterious was still upon us, and our name was drawing crowds, when abruptly our feet were turned off this path into what we think of now as a Green Valley. Not that it was green at first. Is such a place ever green till the pilgrim has gone almost all the way through? ("Over that valley hang discouraging clouds of confusion.") In that valley we were drained of all that we had to give of strength and spiritual energy; and before we were back on the highway, everything that had led to popularity had been left far behind. Now that medical missionaries have been given to us, we have seen greater things than we saw during those days; but everything is quieter, and we understand. The Kingdom of God cometh not with outward show. "And it pleaseth that Spirit of Jesus to blow His sweet wind through a piece of dry stick, that the empty reed may keep no glory to itself."

It was just then that a friend gave us a gift with which to buy land at the foot of the mountains, and wanted to add to it a rice field which was near. It was harvest time, and the beauty of the carpet of gold, tucked into a nook among the hills close by the lovely Lotus Water, drew the imagination. One day three of us went to see the place. Harvest was over by that time; on the threshing floor, at some distance from the land, bulls were treading out the grain, snatching mouthfuls as they plodded round and round. Winnowers, with their fans, were winnowing it. Straw was piled in pale yellow heaps.

There was something alluring in a scene so peaceful and patriarchal. It might have been the field of Boaz. Then, because someone else wanted it, and we were not sure what we should do, we paid an advance on the special understanding that it would be returned if we did not buy, and when we decided against buying (for we were not sent to South India to buy the field of Boaz) we had difficulty in recovering the money. This difficulty was our Father's loving rebuke to us, for we need not have been in doubt.

But one day when we were thinking regretfully about our mistake, someone reminded us of what happened that afternoon. For as we stood by the Lotus Water, suddenly, shattering all illusion, from behind some rocks nearby broke three outlaws, each with his gun over his shoulder, and we had a talk with them. There are unseen doors that lead out of the familiar landscape of life into another entirely unknown. Such a door opened then. And we walked straight through and did not know it.

There are two sources of limelight in India. Do anything which greatly appeals to the people and they flood it full upon you. Do anything which Government recognizes as for the social uplift of the people and, however little you desire it, you may find yourself asked to receive the kindly praise of man. (And it is as true as ever it was that a snare lies near that praise.) To all that can be said for welcoming it, we can offer only the fifty-third chapter of Isaiah and certain familiar passages in the Gospels and Epistles. That lighted place was the last we would have chosen; but we were certainly moving thither when, in that hour by the Lotus Water, as though a hand had touched a switch, the light was turned off.

For that talk with the three outlaws led to a struggle with the powers of darkness for the soul of the chief of the three who had appeared so suddenly from among the rocks of the foothills, and, because that man rightfully belonged to the law and not to us, there were entanglements. In part we failed; we wanted him to give himself up, and he did not do so. But it was not all defeat.

Raj, the brigand chief, was killed; his friends were swept off to jail. Things happened in the process of netting them that are of no account in the East, but they were fire in our bones. We found relief in a litany that we dug from the prayers of men who had been scorched by that same fire. "Who is offended and I burn not?"—The words echo on from age to age.

But, sooner or later, prayer forces out into action. "Open thy mouth for the dumb in the cause of all such as are appointed to destruction. Open thy mouth"—the words came with the drive of a command.* Let any man, anywhere, however detestable all that is involved therein may be to him, obey that command, and uncover some hidden sore of his day and generation, and he will find himself in the pillory. The pillory—it is an uncomfortable word and it is an uncomfortable place; but it is a wonderful place, for all that. No one can have any idea, till he finds himself there, what fine companionship will comfort him, and delight him too. He will never be lonely there. The place is bright with unseen presences, and brave words sound about him like trumpets, "For the love of God thou oughtest to suffer all things, labors and sorrows, temptations, vexations, anxieties, necessities, infirmities, wrongs, obloquies, reprehensions, humiliations, confusions, corrections and despites. These things helpeth to virtue, these prove the knight of Christ, these make the heavenly crown." "He said not, Thou shalt not be tempested; thou shalt not be travailed; thou shalt not be afflicted: but He

---

* Obeyed in the writing of *Raj, Brigand Chief.*

said, Thou shalt not be overcome."* And crowds of others, now companions of immortals, spoke their singing words like flutes among the trumpets, and there were living men and women too who were not in the least afraid of pillories, and they came and stood with us there.

So that soon we began to think of the place as full of distilled sweetness. "Behold how green this valley is: also how beautiful with lilies." One of these lilies was the story of Mimosa. She came to us on a day when faith, long strained about Raj and his affairs, was very weary, and we could not help sharing the comfort that she so unconsciously brought to us. Another flower of joy was the opening of new work in the villages.

Near the foot of the last spur of the Western Ghats lies a little village, buried in the depths of the country. The people there belong to the clan of the brigand chief. The overlord of the place, he who first set Raj's feet in the downward track, forbade the preaching of the gospel. But light cannot be forbidden, and at last a few rays penetrated that village. There was persecution from the first, and the people begged us to live among them. Arul Dasan and Alec Arnot, who joined us about this time, went to prospect, and found that the call was genuine. So some of us went week by week, after the Sunday morning's work was over, spent the afternoon and evening in the village, and returned in time to be ready for Monday morning's duty; the Ford car made this possible (we had just been given a car). At last, being sure that there was a true desire, we built a small house there, and Edith Naish, our chief pilgrim, and May Parker, a keen evangelist who had joined us in 1919, and afterwards Elsie Towill, who had been doing the unselfish work of housekeeper for us in Dohnavur, have made the little place a center for widespread ministry. A tiny dispensary held in the verandah of the house has served and comforted in simple ways many ill and troubled people, and sometimes there have been

---

* Julian of Norwich.

healings that nothing could account for but the presence of the Lord Jesus, whose touch has still its ancient power.

All along the overlord has threatened to ruin us, "The house shall be burned down, the mat church shall go up in smoke." But they are still standing. "I will disperse the people by means of a lawsuit," and he claimed the whole village; a large bribe in the right quarter won his case. But the people moved across to a field on the other side of the mission-house and rebuilt their cottages. "I will snatch their converts from them." In this he has sometimes succeeded. But persecution winnows the grain; we do not want a church of chaff.

Four or five years after Raj's death, a young magician came with his magic books and furniture and burned them in our House of Prayer. He had been a policeman in Raj's time, had found him in the forest, fraternized with him, brought him tobacco. Suddenly Raj's conscience had awakened. "This is not playing the game," he said in effect. "The Government pays you to catch me, and here you are bringing me tobacco. You must not come again." And he had sent him off. The lad had resigned from the police force and had become a magician. One day by the roadside he found a torn tract and read it. "This is what Raj told me; it is what he read out of his Book," he said to himself. The end of that was his visit to us to burn his magic tools.

And there is Linnet—God's song, as her name means— the sunny-hearted Widow of the Jewels, and Kumar, the boy whom Raj influenced for good. He is in charge of our farm, and is the happy possessor of a delightful baby daughter whose Lotus Bud mother helps in one of the nurseries. There are others—we come across them up and down the country—who were turned from sin to righteousness through the message heard or read—rich harvest from that poor seed-sowing. But that is our Lord's way. Our courteous Lord, as Julian of Norwich calls Him, is a very generous Master. And the Green Valley is indeed a very fruitful soil, and doth bring forth by handfuls.

35

Oh, bring them home—what though their faint desire
Falter and fail before the piercing sword?
Or in the wind, or earthquake, or in fire,
      Come to them, conquering Lord.

Or in the sound of gentle stillness, come,
Comforter, come. Let thought of us be far:
Not ours the light that leads them safely home,
      Not of us sun or star.

Dear Lord of Love, so boundless and so deep,
That all Thy heart could yearn for us, accurst:
O Lord of Love, great Shepherd of the sheep,
      Give unto us Thy thirst.

35. Sadhu and Tiger

From this time forward we were led out in new ways. Does the Green Valley always open upon fields which turn to fields of battle? Sometimes among prisoners, sometimes in remote villages, sometimes in the temple towns that stand like little forts under the western hills, sometimes at festivals, different members of our Fellowship have had the joy of the soldier on service, and no one who knows what that can be of Divine companionship would exchange it for any other joy.

Which of the untold tales will show us least, and the Lord, the Doer, most? We have asked ourselves the question as we traveled from point to point over this lately trodden ground. And the story of the sadhu who was called by His name, though he had not heard of Him, comes to mind.

Far in the forests that climb the mountains lived a sadhu with other sadhus, one of a company of followers of a noted guru who had many disciples all over the South. The sadhus come down to the plains, wander from place to place, and return for meditation to their caves on the hill called Mountain of the Great King. Among them was one who was so devout in all his ways and so ardent in his fasts and austerities that the guru called him to his feet and said, "Thou art a God-lover, and among the greater gods is one of whom I have heard, called Yésu. I shall call thee Yésu-Nésan, Lover of Yésu." He did not hear the name Yésu again till he met Marut, a lately converted herb doctor, who taught him a few sentences of a prayer which he thought of as a charm. It was to the Father of Yésu, who is also called "our Father" (so his perplexed ears heard), and it began like this, "Thou who art in the heavenly world, our Father, Thy name, may it be hallowed." He said the curious sentence over and over, using his Saivite rosary with its one hundred and eight berries, mixing the new prayer with the Sanskrit prayers and charms which he had already learned.

One day the quiet of the forest was broken by the big, hearty laugh of a man in a cave, and Lover of Yésu, surprised, went into the cave and made friends with the man who laughed and sang and shouted like a free man, regardless of who might hear. And yet he was not free—he was being hunted. A foolish man, thought Lover of Yésu when he knew him better, disconcerting and hard to take care of, for he left his tracks uncovered in a queer, casual way.

This man, Raj, taught the sadhu, reading to him from a little book which he carried in a goat-skin bag. And the sadhu began to understand and, being in earnest to attain this new knowledge, he decided on a forty-one days' fast. Sitting in the cramped position ordained for meditation, he fasted till he fell into a trance. "But Him I never saw. It was darkness within."

He came out of that fast and that trance with shaken views about various matters. For example, he did not now feel it a sin to take life, and he wanted a tiger-skin. (Sadhus sit on deer-skin or tiger-skin, but they never dream of shooting deer or tiger themselves.) So Lover of Yésu went off to stalk a tiger.

He had been a hunter in his youth, but he was not a

good shot now. He wounded the tiger, which rushed upon him and got his arm and shoulder between its teeth. "I knew in that moment, I cannot tell how, but I *knew* that no one but the Lord Yésu, of whom Raj had told me, could save me from the tiger, and to Him I cried." Then somehow he got his free arm around the beast and shot it.

While he was being healed of his wounds, we were brought into touch with him, and he read the Gospel of St. John. Then he came to stay with us, and our hopes kindled. What might he not do for his Lord? But the wanderlust—that fatal wanderlust of the sadhu—would not let him stay long enough to be taught. He would float off without a word. He was there an hour ago. We looked, and he was not there.

Then tales drifted across the plains of a strange sadhu, a lover of Christ, who had been heard speaking of Him in the mighty temples of the South, in whose innermost halls he had sat and whose priests were his friends; and we heard of him on the mountains among the ascetics, steadfastly holding out against their allurements, for they tried with every art they knew to draw him back. Then a tale came of his being worshiped as a god and garlanded with flowers—but this was in Ceylon. How could he be there? He was there. "*You* must buy a teekut. *I* can go in any train without a teekut," he had told us, and we knew, of course, that he could, for train, motorbus, bullock cart, even steamship, seem to feel alike about holy men. But this talk of the garland of flowers? It was true, too. He had prayed for the recovery of a child; it had been granted; the people had wanted to worship him, and they had run to him with flowers, and he had fled. He was at a festival now, near one of our sacred waterfalls, and the money they had poured into his hands he had used to give a feast to some Christian boys who had gone to see the waterfall. He witnessed to His Saviour everywhere, and showed to all who would look the marks of the tiger's teeth on his arm.

But those same marks seem to confuse his judgment

where baptism is in question. Or it may be that his many fasts and rigorous austerities have clouded him a little so that he cannot understand. "Nay, what need is there for that, have I not this?" And he touches one of those white scars. Or he will say, "Am I not just now going to enter a period of fasting? I cannot stay for that yet." And his mind, as wandering as his feet, moves him to restlessness, so this is only the first chapter of his story. I have told it partly with the hope that it may lead the thoughts of the reader beyond the fugitive figure of Lover of Yésu to those other wanderers, the sadhus of India, for some of whom a true conversion would mean indeed the piercing of a sword.

36.

Art Thou not marching to music, Conquering Christ?
Hark to the trumpets and bugles sounding afar.
Welcome the glow in the east that declareth the
    Morning Star.

All souls are Thine, not the foeman's, Conquering
    Christ,
Passeth, like dream of the sleeper, dark heathendom.
Hasteth the jubilant hour when Thy Kingdom, O Lord,
    shall come.

Praise waiteth for Thee in Zion, Conquering Christ,
Crowned shalt Thou be and belovèd and reverenced
    then.
Thine is the Kingdom, the power, and the glory for ever.

Amen.

36. Pavilions and a Festival

Among our little ones there are some (fewer, thank God, than might be expected) who are disabled in some way. Several are deaf; several, because of some inherited twist, need specially careful training.

Just over the border of the Native State of Travancore, there is a patch of rocky hillside overlooking the place where in ancient days the three kings of Travancore, Madura and Tanjore used to meet in council, and so it was called Three Pavilions. The pilgrim road to Cape Comorin, the extreme end of the Great Trunk Road of India, skirts the hillside, and within an evening's walk little villages lie in pockets among trees, or strewn on the plain. Standing on the rocks you can see the blue line of the Indian Ocean; from that sea, from April till September, the southwest wind blows over the rocks, and from September till April they are swept by the colder northeast wind, so that to be there is like being on board ship in a perpetual gale. The calm days are few. It is a wild place given up to elemental things—glories of wide views of sunrise and sunset, mountains magnificent in cloud and storm, a tumble of wild rocks looking out upon an empty world, with wild winds racing over it.

This hillside, some sixty acres, in part rock, in part fallow land, was offered to us unexpectedly in 1925. The price was three pounds an acre. We bought it, we signed the check on our knees; there were times in the five years that followed when the remembrance that we had done so was comforting, for from the first there were difficulties. When it was known that we were considering the place, there was a burst of angry protest from the priests in a small roadside temple a mile or so from the rocks. They sent a petition to the Government of Travancore asking that we might not be allowed to buy, and the Hindus who owned the fields on the lower levels were afraid that a blight would fall on the crops if Christians looked down on them all the year round. (This was encouraging, however, for the devil does not waste ammunition.) The old head priest became our friend eventually. Poor old man, he told us that he had served his god for forty years and gained neither joy nor peace nor hope. And a plentiful rain that first year turned the fear of curse into assurance of blessing, so the landowners round about welcomed us. The difficulties that mattered most were different.

We built a house for workers and a delightful nursery school, and sent our delicate little ones there in charge of faithful accals, and the children throve. "If ever you turn this place into a T.B. sanatorium, let me know," said a doctor who went out to Pavilions, before we had built much there. Illness is practically unknown on that high land, and the battle with the wind seems to put new life into the children. (One day, when it blew a smaller one over, a tiny boy indignantly struck out at it with his fists. The wind was a person to him.) Tired girls for whom we planned quiet rooms, and who found among the rocks the blessed solitude of a cave, came back refreshed, and talked of the wonderful feeling of spaciousness after our crowded Dohnavur; they found Pavilions enchanting. Some convalescing after operations were sent, and all came back well.

And yet there was something lacking. No one living

there, except the small children, thought of the place as home. Even the married Lotus Bud, whom we hoped would settle, as she had her husband and baby, felt banished; the accals were strangers in a strange land, and, true to their Tamil nature, they were one and all chronically and hopelessly homesick. Different members of the Fellowship stayed there and did what they could, and we went out from time to time and tried to pull the scattered units together, but we knew that they would drift apart before we could return. What Pavilions needed was to have two of its own.

But they must be a special Two. Not any Two would do. The place might be the Door of Heaven (in the glow of a golden sunset one of the colony wrote that name in Tamil on a signboard and put it by the road, whereupon an able-bodied beggar passing, thinking such a name could only mean food for nothing, came up, and was disappointed, and on returning smashed the notice board); even so, it was what some would call lonely, and it was certainly windy. The Two must be able to enjoy wind. And one must be a homemaker by instinct, not only peaceful and happy herself, but knowing how to draw others into peace and happiness. And because some of our tired ones needed more than beauty and fresh air, she must be one to whom it had been given to be a repairer of broken walls, a restorer of paths leading home.* Our forest houses are not possible at all seasons, nor is Joppa (the house we were afterwards given by the sea), but here, within easy reach, was a place to which we could at any time send those needing rest. If only we could have someone who would make home for them and the others there, the place would be like the pleasant arbor about midway to the top of the Hill Difficulty, a house of comforting to body and to soul.

And the other, was it too much to ask for a trained teacher for the deaf and backward, and more than that, a

---

* Isaiah 58:12 (Rotherham).

true lover of such little ones and perhaps unlovable older
ones, too? Lord, what is Thy will about it? What is Thy
will for these children, for this place?

> Lord, by the riches of Thy grace,
>   Open my eyes that I may see,
> And in the shining of Thy face
>   Reveal Thy will to me.

And all the time He who worketh for him that waiteth
for Him was working for us, and in an English vicarage
and in a Scottish parsonage He had chosen and was preparing the two of our hearts' desire. For in the English
vicarage a mother was training her daughter in those
home-loving, homemaking ways that cannot be learned
anywhere so well as in such a home as Vivien Tomkins' is.
And when she came to us in 1930, almost our first thought
was, "She is the one for Pavilions." But the language came
first, and we said nothing till she was ready for her first
examination. And then we knew what God had done; for
to her had come "the feeling that is evidence" that Pavilions was the place of His choice for her.

And the year that we signed that check for Pavilions saw
Jean Ewing in the University of Edinburgh. And to her already it had been given to care for the shut-in, deaf children
whom she had seen Sunday by Sunday in her father's church;
she knew how much they were missing. So, after taking her
degree, she had gone into training, and had become a
skilled teacher of the deaf and a lover of little hurt things.
Her mother had called their home in Bute *Dohnavur*. There
had been prayer links for years, and the sympathy of
purpose which unites hearts; but we had not even heard of
this gift that was being prepared for us till the close of
1930. Then in His time God moved, and the gift was given.
And lest we should ever question this that He had done,
remembering other and far larger spheres, He granted a
certain assurance both to her and to us, so that her call
should be among the things that cannot be shaken.

One moonlit night we were returning late from Pavilions when a long string of men in white, looking ghostly in the white light, passed us, traveling south. They were pilgrims bound for a festival at Siva's temple by the sea, and they were crossing the fields by a shortcut which runs near our house. On such nights the people of Pavilions have opportunities for scattering the imperishable seed, and to some of us the chance is given to follow those pilgrims to the festival.

A festival is a thing that words cannot show. The outward scene is merely the colored shell of something hidden but very powerful. The Prince of the Kingdom of Persia withstood the angel for three full weeks; the Prince of the Kingdom of India (his is the power within the colored shell), for how long will he withstand? There is a sense of such a withstanding. You feel as though you were being pushed back and thrust down by unseen hands. And yet you cannot let yourself be pushed back and thrust down. After a while you begin to feel very tired: a day feels like a week. Is it because of that strange pressure? Does spiritual resistance exhaust the whole being? It would seem so.

But following that string of pilgrims to that festival we come to something that may be partly shown.

There are two temples in the town; the greater one belongs to the god known as Siva's son, the smaller, at the further end of the town, to his wives. In the favorite wife's shrine the light is bright, in the lesser—that of the goddess Divānie—it burns dimly. From this comes a proverb: to burn like Divānie's light is to be discouraged, discountenanced. These two temples are connected by a street which at festival times is converted into a matted corridor. In this one street there are scores of houses devoted to sin. A friend had engaged a shop-front for our brothers, and in this enclosure they sat in turn, talking with those who came in, giving away tracts, selling Gospels and books to any who would buy them. Between them and the door of the house a couple of sacks were hung, and the life on the other side of the sacks was like that of the other houses. One day, as they sat in their shop, a hand was pushed around the sack; they put a Gospel into it, and afterwards, through the open door of the house opposite, saw a woman sitting reading (for these women can read). But later, when we went to visit that house, a man came between us and the woman; he would not leave us for a moment alone with her, and she dared not speak in his presence. I leave the picture with you—a woman in captivity sitting on the floor reading the Gospel, a man who has power over her, determined to hold her in her chains.

Visiting in that town is like diving into a cesspool; the heartbreak there is to see children, babies like bright flowers, as it were, on the edge of that pool. "There are changes being made in the law: they will not be allowed to dedicate children to the gods while they are so young," said an old man. "But what of the law? They will do as they choose." And, remembering those houses with rooms opening one upon another, unlighted, secure, and remembering, too, the courts of the temple, its maze of halls and cloisters and low, vaulted recesses, we could imagine we heard the devil laugh at our sanguine credulity. For how can law change a custom which can be continued in secret? Reading certain pages of *Things as They Are* after years of slowly won knowledge, I wonder at my early hopes. We are thankful that some are working for a better law. It is a move in the right direction, but we put not our trust in princes or any powers of this present age. The coming of the Lord of Righteousness is the one hope, as we see it, for this land.

But it *is* the hope. As we walked between the temple and the sea, we saw heaped-up piles of granite pillars, the sculpture of base and capital often perfect, and there were vast masses of cut stone lying about everywhere. The temple is so rich that it is continually pulling down and rebuilding, and this mile of tumbled stone making a wall by the sea is the result. "So it has ever been: so it will ever be," said a Hindu who stood near us and had observed us looking at the fallen masonry. We told him then of the time when the towering walls above us will be like these scattered piles. The thought of some beautiful pictures shown by a guest to our children just before we left home, pictures showing prophecy fulfilled in history—the cities of old days with their palaces and temples overthrown—was a great stay through those days in the midst of the visible and apparently impregnable fortresses of heathendom.

That Hindu took us to a temple shrine carved in the face of a rock. It was evening, and not many pilgrims were about, and no Brahman priests; so he did what I do not think is often done (if ever)—he brought us inside, led us through a narrow passage cut into the heart of the rock, to a square hole halfway up the wall, through which we crept and found ourselves in a small, dark, clammy cell. There by our flashlight we saw the idol. Standing there, shut in by walls and roof of rock, with the sound of the sea murmuring far away, in the presence of that usurping thing, we stood together and claimed the Town of Siva's Son for the Lord of heaven and earth.

Meanwhile our brothers were at work in the streets, talking one by one with men and boys, "as ambassadors beseeching," as *Daily Light* had it on one of the days we were there. Once a lad came to the little shop-front. He wanted to escape for an hour, he said, from the pernicious life around him, and he found his way to the one clean place in that town as to a city of refuge. *"Without shedding of blood is no remission"*—these are among the words that a knowledge of this town underlines. The blood of Jesus Christ His Son cleanseth us from all sin—*all*, even this that we must meet in towns where the Spirit of Uncleanness visibly reigns. These towns are Jerichoes. And not one wall of any of them has been shaken yet, much less fallen down.

We found an unexpected welcome in a house where an

old musician whom we had met before happened to be staying. We spent an hour or more there, and to get our opportunity had to listen to a younger singer chanting a long, plaintive song which the old musician accompanied on his little harmonica. It was kindliness and courtesy which made them offer this, but as we sat together on the floor of that front room, with the feel of the night life of the town about us (for the streets were full of sound and movement), and the old lady of the house beat perfect time to the intricate music, we longed to get to something that mattered far more. In the end we had a chance, and next day we were with them again. But they were too excited to listen then. Their ear was intent upon the rumble of voices in the street. That long strip of straight street was like a herbaceous border, gay with women in crimson, orange, yellow, purple, blue, sometimes sun-washed or water-washed to lovely harmonies, sometimes bright from the loom. Soon the rumble grew to a roar, and there was the blare of a band and the shout of the elephant's escort, and the great beast came with state. Just in front of our house he stopped and knelt, while a naked brown baby, kicking hard, was hoisted up and set astride upon his neck. Then he curled back his trunk, and we saw a tangled-up struggle, for the child was shrieking with all its might (not a sound, of course, could be heard above the noise) and something it held was being forced out of its hand into that waiting trunk. This done (it was inarticulate with indignation by this time), it was handed back to its grati-fied parents, and the procession moved on. It had been ill, and this was the fulfillment of a vow.

But the intense moment came later. The roar of voices increased. The herbaceous border had vanished—not a woman was on the street; it was now a solid mass of men. A few policemen flicked what looked like dusters in the faces of those who would not let themselves be pushed out of the way; for now, in the midst of another dense throng, led by another band in a sort of uniform, came the idol's palanquin, carried on the shoulders of many bearers who staggered under the load. All down the long street at regular intervals, stone pillars, grooved so as to allow the carrying-poles to be placed on them, were set for the help of the bearers. But, even so, they stumbled with weariness. Then the whole street burst out in acclamations. A forest of brown arms flung up hailed as god that which our Holy One calls an abomination.

"I am the Lord: that is My name: and My glory will I not give to another, neither My praise to graven images. Thus saith the Lord, the King of Israel and his Redeemer the Lord of Hosts, I am the first, and I am the last, and beside Me there is no God. Is there a God beside Me? Yea, there is no God: I know not any." Words like these move and breathe at such times.

The idol was set back in the palanquin so that it could hardly be seen. Heavy wreaths of flowers hung round its neck, and we had been told that it was covered with jewels. "Next time his adornment will be emeralds," said our old friend. "Today he wears all manner of precious gems." On one side of the idol, hidden by the draperies of the palanquin, was a young girl, on the other side a young man. They received the people's offerings. The procession passed on, the flower-bedecked palanquin swinging, as the men who bore the poles swayed beneath it. The hoarse, strong shouts of thousands beat about us like the waves of a rough sea. The visible representative of the Prince of the Kingdom of India passed on to the temple of his wives.

But now, for our eyes are towards the morning, here is a fragment of a story that is linked to that same temple by the sea. It looks back for a moment to an earlier day, to a day when we were out in the villages and nothing seemed to have been done.

It was years before we knew that a child of twelve, who had heard once at one of those village preachings, had been taken to Siva's temple by the sea in the hope that her newborn faith would be shattered by the amazement of that show. See her, then, eagerly searching through the courts and innermost shrines of the temple, with one of her relatives who has entrance to all the corners of that great mysterious place. Nothing escapes the scrutiny of this ardent child. "Gods?" she is saying to herself. "No, they are dead idols. There is no life in them." Still she searches, knowing what lies behind, paying no regard to the tinsel that tries to look like gold. "Vain, vain, it is all vain," is her verdict, and her thought flies back to a well-side in her own village, to a little group standing there; to words about a living God that arrested her and held her kneeling upright on her mat all through the night that followed; to a song learned in a tent where one who had been in that group was singing to the children who gathered in the tent; to the sense of peace and certainty that came when she spoke with that living God. And in her heart of hearts she knew that Him only she must serve.

Months passed; she was delivered from the enfolding Hinduism, then carried back into it, threatened, struck and, far worse, spat upon. (She will never forget what it was to hear that He, the Holy One, had suffered that indignity.) And at last she was given back to us to be beloved child, fellow-warrior, dearest friend. For that child was Arulai.

37

The verse which you want more than any other, and which you had better make your whole Bible for the present, is that wonderful passage in Deuteronomy: "I led thee, and *suffered thee* to *hunger,* and fed thee with food that thou knewest not, to teach thee that man does not live by bread alone"—no, not by what you and I think a necessary of life, that without which we cannot live—love, success, fulfilled desire—"*but* by everything that proceedeth out of the mouth of the Most High," whether that word ("thing" in the Revised Version) be failure or success, love or heart-hunger, uselessness or abounding labor—by *that* does man live. Our life is distinctly a supernatural life, and we are always longing for a natural life, and God has let us go hungry of the natural life in order that we may enter into the supernatural, and our wish be taken up into His.— Ellice Hopkins.

Thou art the Lord who slept upon the pillow,
   Thou art the Lord who soothed the furious sea,
What matter beating wind and tossing billow
   If only we are in the boat with Thee?

Hold us in quiet through the age-long minute
   While Thou art silent, and the wind is shrill;
Can the boat sink while Thou, dear Lord, art in it?
   Can the heart faint that waiteth on Thy will?

37. The Only One Whom We Know There

On July 6, 1925, we resigned our connection with the Societies to which several of us had belonged. This did not affect our ways of working; but it came to us as a new call to faith, because some of our friends at home could not see that we were right to do so. If the worst came to the worst (perhaps they felt like this), there was the Society to fall back upon. If we cut away from that solid institution, where were we? It sounded very unsafe. Two of us who had for many years been connected with Keswick continued that connection, as it was one of prayer only; but this did not satisfy some who, caring for us lovingly, felt that we required the shadow of a greater name than our own. They have been reassured; there hath not failed one word of all His good promise. Perhaps it was that to most of the lovers of our little children, the Name that is above every name was enough. And there was no break in affection; we were very thankful about that.

That year ended with the beginning of something new and good, although we did not recognize it for what it was. It appeared to be only a letter from Mrs. Webb-

Peploe, mother of a guest who had stayed with us for a
few days on his way further east. Now she wrote that a
visit was possible. She and her elder son, a doctor, would
come to us on their way to China. (That letter was like the
moss rosebud of old home gardens that is hardly to be
recognized as a rosebud at all. What buds of joy are in our
hands now, I wonder, folded up like that moss rose, that
in the happy years to come will open into flowers? But in
the East we always have rain before roses.) Our guests
came and went; to that mother we gave an Indian name by
which she is known and loved by all our household now—
Aruthal, which means Comfort, and we were in need of
comfort then. It was not for nothing that fiery questions
had searched us before the boys' work began. Now, eight
years after its beginning, we saw no way for the training
and education and guidance of the boys. The assurance
given by the waterfall in the forest never forsook us. That
word stood, and we stayed ourselves upon our God. But
new questions came: "Are you prepared to perish with
Me, to be counted a fool and worse than a fool by your
own world, your missionary world? May I deal with every
shred of your reputation just as I choose, and will you be
silent? Are you willing to obey in everything, every time,
everywhere?" It was like hearing over again the word of
the withered leaves in the pool, the word of that far-off
Keswick day:

> There is no life except by death,
> There is no vision but by faith,
> And that eternal Passion saith,
> Be emptied of glory and right and name.

There were months, especially towards the end of this
period, after our new friends had gone, when we could
not see our way at all. Faith does not ask why, does not
even wonder why. Faith accepts, and often when the sea
was most unquiet and the boat most tossed about, song
came. There are always new sailors on this sea. The songs

were given for them too. "What matter beating wind and tossing billow if only we are in the boat with Thee?" There are questions whose answer is comfort, the comfort that has not to go away, and that comfort leads to peace.

But the world outside did not hear the songs, and a violent noise of words fell upon us. To listen would have been to lose heart, for the words always talked of defeat. We found then that the only way of peace was resolutely to refuse to listen, to know not the voice of strangers. "Fear not, little flock, for it is your Father's good pleasure to give you the kingdom"—that was the voice we knew and loved. "Neither be ye of doubtful mind"; live not in anxious suspense about these needs that press so heavily: your Father knoweth: Fear not, fear not. And, just then, we were offered land adjoining our own. It was partly wooded, partly open, as though created for homes and schools and playing-fields.

Cross out the invisible and such a purchase appeared folly and presumption. It pledged us to far too much. But that which cannot be seen with eyes of flesh is the rock of our heart and our fortress forever. On September 23, 1926, a new leading came: "Decision to go on and buy land for boys' compound though no help is in sight" was the private note of the day, and in the margin of *Daily Light*: "New land for boys—first advance paid. Help will come. Our God hath not forsaken us." I do not think that anyone observing us and knowing just how things were would have felt it a wise thing to commit ourselves so far as to buy land at that moment. But "Faith is not intelligent understanding; faith is a deliberate commitment to a Person where you see no way," if, deep in your heart, you know that He is directing your goings. "A foreign land draws us nearer God. He is the only one whom we know here. We go to Him as to one we know; all else is strange," that was how Robert Murray McCheyne felt in the unknown world of Genoa; and in life, I think, we often find ourselves in a foreign land. We have not gone this way before, and we do not know the way. And we do not know the people. He is the Only One whom we know there.

But He is enough. The day after that decision, while we were holding out against those assaults upon the spirit which so often follow an action which nothing visible justifies, something happened in China which changed everything.

For on that day, September 24, as we heard months afterwards (for the joy of even the faintest whisper of it was not given then), there was a liberating touch on the life of the man of His choice for our boys. While we were waiting upon our God in our extremity, He was working, He was leading; "whoso is wise and will observe these things, even they shall understand the loving-kindness of the Lord."

We were building a little house by the sea about that time; we called it Joppa, because we wanted it to be a place of heavenly vision for all who stayed in it. Often as we watched the rough fishing-rafts pushing out to sea, we found ourselves elsewhere, thinking thoughts that shamed us and yet lifted us up. Peter did not seem to think it a strange thing to walk on the sea, nor did his heavenly Master say one word about its being unusual to expect to be able to do so. He, the Lord of heaven and earth, was there; the unnatural thing was not to do it, to sink.

But a time came when we were spent out. We had to make a pause for united prayer. Things were crowding so upon us, and we were in such inward distress about the great need of the boys, that nothing short of such a day would meet the case. It was difficult to arrange for it, but the hand of our God was upon us. "Seek ye My face," He was saying to us, and our hearts were answering, "Thy face, Lord, will I seek."

We had no revelation of His purpose that day. Next day things were as they had been, and yet somehow there was a difference, and from that day on we were never once moved to pray for a leader for the boys.

Meanwhile much was happening of which we knew nothing. Till December 15 we knew nothing; then in a blinding flash of joy we knew: Godfrey Webb-Peploe, a man tried and proved on the battlefields of the spirit, he who had met his Lord in prayer for the children in peril on the hillside above a temple of Southern India and had heard Him say, "The task is hard," had gone to China to work for His Master there. But he had been ordered out of the country by the doctors. And now, on December 15, 1926, eight years and three months after the work for the boys began, he joined our Fellowship. So the boys had their leader at last, and we were delivered from all our fears. That night when we went to bed after a full day (for the marriage of a Lotus Bud had been one of its incidents), our hearts singing with relief and thanksgiving because of the comfort that filled them, we found this in *Daily Light*, that little book of "isolated texts" that are so often strangely related to the circumstances of its readers—"Be ye steadfast, unmovable, always abounding in the work of the Lord, *forasmuch as ye know* that your labor is not in vain in the Lord."

It was in gentle, generous, patient ways like this that we learned not to fear any strange land. Even if He is the only one whom we know there, He is enough.

38.

Ring'd around by Satan's power,
    Ceaselessly at grips with sin,
    Battle-stained and faint within—
    "Father, save Me from this hour!"

Nay it was for this I came!
    Heard afar God's trumpet-call,
    Heard and answer'd, rose, left all—
    "Father, glorify Thy name!"
                    —Frank Houghton, C.I.M.

When hosts of hell encompass me
And fears upon the soul advance,
Open my eyes, dear Lord, to see
Thine armies of deliverance.

The heavenly hosts the mountains fill,
O Leader unto victory,
Lead through the long day's fight, until
This land shall know Thy liberty.
                    —Godfrey Webb-Peploe.

Wars and battles, shocks and heartbreaks,
Weariness and hidden scars,
But a vision of the triumph,
Glorious glimpses of the stars,
    Wounded, let us rise and sing
    Welcome to our Coming King.

Sunrise, sunset, fling their carpet,
Gold and orange, grey and rose,
Welcoming His royal footsteps—
Every heart that loves Him glows.
    Joyful, let us rise and sing
    Welcome to our Coming King.

38. The Love of God Suffices

Tamil is an old language.* It is also difficult. Comparisons are hardly possible, because few know several languages well enough fairly to compare, but a discouraged student was once immensely cheered by being told that, in the group of the six hardest languages, Tamil marched with Arabic. It is rich—there is not a thought that cannot be expressed either by word or phrase, hardly a shade of thought—and its idiom is a shoreless sea. To win what is charitably called "a working knowledge of the language" is usually the chief duty of the first two years. And this time, to the eager and the loving, holds a trial of its own: "Shall I ever be able to have any time to help you, or will it always be Tamil? Will the time ever come for being useful?" wrote the first dear comrade in 1908, and each one afterwards felt much the same. There are trials of depression too: "It is really rather dreadful sometimes when I think of how frantically feebly I press on." But a lovely word from the preface to the seventh edition of *The Spirit*

---

* In 1 Kings 10:22 there are three transliterated Tamil words, *danta*, *kapi*, *togai*: ivory, apes and peacocks. "Before the principal basis of the English had a written character, Tamil was a highly polished language."—Dr. Winslow.

of Discipline exactly meets the need of such humble, earnest hearts:

> There is, I think, in the spiritual life an experience somewhat like that of which a trawler in the west of England told me. He said that sometimes through a dark night, when on the deck the air is dull and heavy, and there seems to be a dead calm, there may be wind enough astir, not many feet above the sea, to catch the topsail and carry the sloop along; so that at daybreak it is found farther on its course than the men, for all their keen sense of seafaring, had ever thought it could be.

With us, if possible, after laying a foundation, the student goes out and lives with an Indian friend in a Hindu town to learn something of the thought behind the speech, and the language of allusion, which often says more than the direct. Sometimes we rent a house, or it may be possible to stay with a Hindu family. Once a Hindu friend lived with one of us in our little house in Holy Town. For, after many years of waiting, we were able at last to buy a house in that old-world place, and so have a foothold in the town. Life in such an atmosphere, with a trustworthy guide to open doors and windows into the meaning of what is seen, is wonderfully revealing, and there is no real intimacy possible without such an experience. Learn one little town as you learn to know not only the face of a friend but his heart, and you know much more than that town.

It is the same in the villages. Under the mountains to the north of Dohnavur is a big, cheery, rackety village called Sky Wisdom, quite different in tone from the aristocratic little Holy Town to the south. In that village we have friends who are ready to let us lodge in the upper part of their house, where a wide balcony looks out upon a glorious half-circle of mountains. Several of our Fellowship have lived there at different times, and to visit Sky Wisdom now with one of them is to see how affectionate village-folk can be. But even so, they returned feeling dazed; and this sense of being set as a naked soul alone in a new air is something that can test the spirit. "But some way or other my principal grief was, and so it has continued to be, that I grieved so very little," said the missionary Ragland long ago. Some of us often feel like that. I well remember the look on the face of a new worker, Olive Gibson (now our Home Secretary in England), when for the first time she was aware of our encompassing atmosphere. Her shock of surprised grief (for, though she had heard and read, to see was quite different) reminded me afresh of heavenly values. God forgive us that we can ever be dull to that which touched our Lord so much.

That "feel" of the land, as we call it, has often deep within it a haunting sense of impotence. Imagine a snow-flake falling on the Great Pyramid, melting and vanishing as it touches the hot stone; imagine a feather borne on a wandering wind against the keep of some mighty castle, and you see what we appear to be, as for the first time (or for the thousandth) we find ourselves standing by night in the doorway of the temple, with the sculptured pillars about us, monstrous in the gloom, and the lights glittering round the idol shrine where no alien foot may tread, and the throb and clangor of drum and cymbal bursting forth like a sea, to subside and suddenly burst forth again in deafening uproar.

Here is no petty structure of vague imaginings. Here is force, something with spirit behind it and within it. And spirit is stronger than flesh. Our warfare is not with flesh and blood; but flesh and blood can quail before the awful power of that which stirs and whispers, and with ghostly fingers all but touches us as we stand there. It is a deadly mistake to underestimate Hinduism; the statistics upon which the sanguine are fed do not affect the matter, for they deal with a different problem. They hardly touch Hinduism as the temples of the South understand the word.

But with us is the Lord of Hosts—like a challenge the words peal forth. Not in vain in the Lord, not in vain do we stand by that temple door. For we stand in the name of the Lord of Hosts, the Lord of all the earth. And He has His own way of reinforcing faith.

This is how He did it for Kathleen Grant, a young missionary, out alone for the first time:

> As I passed house after house in the streets of that town, barred as it were against the Lord Jesus, Satan's power had never seemed more real. But I think those weeks have brought one thing home to me more than ever before. It was this: God is faithful. However black things may look, however great the opposition, His love and faithfulness stand, and if we look up and tell Him that we believe in Him in spite of circumstances, then He Himself creates in our hearts that peace which makes us able to hear His voice and to know and carry out His will.

For Geoffrey Webb-Peploe, too, there was a first experience of life in the midst of these things:

> I was coming home from a walk one evening just as the procession had gone inside the temple, and as I looked up the Brahman street I could see the torches and the crowds around their god, framed in the arched entrance gate. Above it rose the great temple tower of the inner gateway, and it seemed in that moment as if the devil reigned here at least, and the shouting of the crowds was like the laughter of the prince of evil, as he saw our feeble efforts to dislodge him from his throne. But I raised my eyes and looked above and behind, and there stood the mountains calm and strong, and over all the blood-red afterglow of the sunset sky, and I knew that He must reign, for He spoke of victory: "And they overcame him by the blood of the Lamb and by the word of their testimony."

And yet, though the strain upon faith at such times can be sharp, a sharper test, I think, comes later. After long prayer and toil, a soul has been led to Christ. By a thousand little signs you know that the miracle is happening

for which you have waited so long. Then other influences
begin to play upon the soul. Some Demas, once trusted
and beloved, snatches at the chance to wound his forsaken
Lord, and injects poison. The one who lately ran so well
falters, looks back, goes back.

Then comes a terrific temptation to regard that Demas
with eyes which see only his Demas qualities. And, as
imperceptibly as water oozes through an earthen vessel,
power to expect his return to peace and purity begins to
pass. And when the next new inquirer comes there may be
a fear to meet him with buoyant, loving hope.

But this is fatal. Better be disappointed a thousand
times—yes, and deceived—than once miss a chance to
help a soul because of that faithless inhibition that grows,
before we are aware of it, into suspicion and hardness.
There is only one thing to be done. It is to realize that in us
there is no good thing, nor faith, nor hope, nor even love;
nothing human suffices here. All that we counted ours
shrivels in the hot winds of disappointment: "Thy servant
hath not anything in the house." But the love of God
suffices for any disappointment, for any defeat. And in
that love is the energy of faith and the very sap of hope.

39

O Father, help, lest our poor love refuse
For our beloved the life that they would choose,
And in our fear of loss for them, or pain,
Forget eternal gain.

Show us the gain, the golden harvest There,
For corn of wheat that they have buried here;
Lest human love defraud them, and betray,
Teach us, O God, to pray.

Teach us to pray remembering Calvary,
For as the Master must the servant be;
We see their face set toward Jerusalem,
Let us not hinder them.

Teach us to pray; O Thou who didst not spare
Thy Well-Beloved, lead us on in prayer.
Purge from the earthly, give us love Divine,
Father, like Thine, like Thine.

39. Highways Are in Their Heart*

This that we have told is something that we know many of our comrades have experienced. There is something else which they have shared with us, and we in our turn are now allowed to pass it on to others. One day a letter came from a missionary in China: "Does that great love of His that flows through you find its main satisfaction back in Him again, with only just the occasional flash of gratitude from an unexpected place? There is my difficulty—the loving seeking until He find." And about the same time this came from an Indian missionary on furlough:

> X has been the means of opening up a part of God's Word which has always puzzled me. You know that passage in which Paul writes to the brethren at Corinth and says something like this: "I think that God has set forth us the apostles last, as it were appointed unto death: for we are a spectacle before fools. Ye are strong, but we are weak; ye are honorable, but we are despised. We are made as the filth of the world and the offscouring of all things." It had puzzled me as to why there were two sets of Christians, and what it meant for us. Well, there are certain people

---

* Psalm 84:5 (Kay).

who are rather criticizing X at the moment. They think she is a little unbalanced. And I was wondering over this and thinking what a pity it was. And suddenly God turned me to those verses, and I think I understood. This is to be our reward when we follow Christ. At first, on the whole it brings honor and respect to us, as He was honored in the early days of His life. But if we choose to go further, we find ourselves classed as unbalanced, for His brethren thought the same of Him, and we become too a spectacle to God, and angels, and men. And if we still hold on, we shall be despised and persecuted and looked on as the filth of the world and the offscouring of all things, and so be truly in fellowship with Christ who was despised and rejected of man. It's a great life, isn't it?

There is a strip of carved teak on a teakwood partition in my room. On it is painted in blue, *He saved others, Himself He cannot save.* We know that we have not sounded the depths in these words. But many of our comrades know more. One from the borders of Tibet told us that for some in China there is a trial of patience now that passes the seventy times seven. Is it that, as they follow so hard after their Lord, their feet are pierced by the thorns that fall from His crown of thorns? We did not feel worthy to be called missionaries as we thought of these, His nearer followers. And we asked then that we might never count on the roses of life (the comforts and the courtesies) as something to be expected: "I will show him how great things he must suffer for My name's sake"; no hint of roses there.

"Bow down, that we may go over": and you have laid down your body as the ground, and as the street, to them that went over. "Bow down"—it was spoken by the enemy to wandering Israel; it is spoken many a time to the soul that follows a rejected and crucified Lord. We have come to know this through letters more than through anything printed in missionary magazines or books. We have come to live, as it were, alongside a friend whose face we have never seen, and we know that, for many, a life that is like a trampled road is appointed.*

But we have come to know, too, that it is their happy choice. Somehow, somewhere in their soul's history there was a day when they were free to choose or to refuse the selfish luxury of a spiritual privacy. They refused. They followed Him whose very garments were stripped from Him. One long look at Calvary, and they chose loss, any loss; they were changed from what they might have been and were made into mere steppingstones for their brothers caught in some slough of despond or despair. They did not belong to themselves any more. Name, reputation, experience of the devil's power and of the magnificence of their Saviour's deliverance, His private tenderness, His intimate touch on the reins of the spirit—all was theirs only for others. To the flesh this can be abhorrent, for it often leads to painful hours that would never have been tasted had the choice been otherwise, but it leads past pain to joy.

"As the filth of the world, and the offscouring of all

---

* Just as *Gold Cord* was going to press, this, which so perfectly fits the thought of these pages, came from M.W.-P. of our Fellowship, who was on furlough then.

> Blasted rock and broken stone,
>   Ordinary earth,
> Rolled and rammed and trampled on,
>   Forgotten, nothing worth;
> And blamed, but used day after day;
> An open road—the king's highway.
>
> Often left outside the door,
>   Sometimes in the rain,
> Always lying on the floor,
>   And made for mud and stain:
> Men wipe their feet, and tread it flat,
> And beat it clean—the master's mat.
>
> Thou wast broken, left alone,
>   Thou wast blamed, and worse,
> Thou wast scourged and spat upon,
>   Thou didst become my curse—
> Lord Jesus, as I think of *that*
> I pray, make me Thy road, Thy mat.

things"—read in polite, perhaps beautiful places, these crude words may sound almost musical. But the filth of the world is not music, it is mud. We trifle with truth when we imagine that we come near to understanding such words while all the time we are leaning back, well out of the way of the smirching finger, the scourging tongue, the reproach of Christ. The power to help others depends upon the acceptance of a trampled life. "Thou hast caused men to ride over our heads; we went through fire and through water, but Thou broughtest us out into a wealthy place." And generous then is the sharing. There is the brokenness of a life that has no rights. "What shall be thy dress?/He clothed me in emptiness." "As poor, yet making many rich."

It was the way the Master went who, though He was rich, yet for our sakes became poor, that we through His poverty might be rich. If there had been a better way, would He not have shown it?

It is the way of the Psalmist, who shows us a cross section of the life of the man in whose heart are the highways to Zion. Highways are open roads. Roads are not made for admiration, but for traffic. "God breaks up the private life of His saints and makes it a thoroughfare for the world on the one hand and for Himself on the other. No one can stand that unless he is identified with God," said Oswald Chambers, who gave his all in sacrifice and service. "Let God make you broken bread and poured-out wine in His hand for others."

This, then, is what we have learned from those slaves of the Lord whom He turns into highways without fear that they will misunderstand Him, or even wonder why. More and more we want to live that life, as part of a company passing through an unexplained discipline. To what end? "Eye hath not seen it nor ear heard, neither hath it entered into the heart of man." Only this we know, oh, healing and immortal joy!—"His servants shall serve Him. And they shall see His face; and His name shall be on their foreheads." But when? Perhaps sooner than we think:

Do we not hear Thy footfall, O Belovèd,
    Among the stars on many a moonless night?
Do we not catch the whisper of Thy coming
    On winds of dawn, and often in the light
Of noontide and of sunset almost see Thee?
    Look up through shining air
And long to see Thee, O Belovèd, long to see Thee,
    And wonder that Thou art not standing there?

And we shall hear Thy footfall, O Belovèd,
    And starry ways will open, and the night
Will call her candles from their distant stations,
    And winds shall sing Thee, noon, and mingled light
Of rose-red evening, thrill with lovely welcome;
    And we, caught up in air,
Shall see Thee, O Belovèd, we shall see Thee,
    In hush of adoration see Thee there.

40.

There is nothing that God does not work up into His perfect plan of our lives: all lines converge, all movements tend to do His will, on earth as in heaven.—*Francis Paget, Bishop of Oxford, His "Life,"* by Stephen Paget and J.M.C. Crum.

O God of stars and flowers, forgive our blindness;
No dream of night had dared what Thou hast wrought.
New every morning is Thy loving kindness,
Far, far above what we had asked or thought.

So under every sky our alleluia,
With flowers of morning and with stars of night,
Shall praise Thee, O Lord Jesus, Alleluia,
Till Thou shalt fold all shadows up in light.

40. Several Dates

I have told how from the earliest days there was a sense upon us that our Father had a special purpose in saving these children. It had cost lives. Sacrificial giving lay behind what had been accomplished. Some had given not of their superfluity but of their very living.

And out here Agnes Naish and her colleagues, to whom was committed the work of teaching and training, had answered Andrew Murray's question, asked long years before, about the possibility of making consecration the foundation of education, with an earnest "It is possible." And the children had also the great gain of many friendships. From almost all the countries of the world guests have come to this remote little place, and they have told us of their fields and their people, so that the children's interest had been already aroused and enlarged. All this lay behind. What was to come of it?

Scattered about the country there were those who had been married. Sometimes the girls were the only Christian women in their villages. Most were living bravely in spite of every kind of odds; but all were heavily handicapped, and some had gone under. These were our griefs. Thank God there were so few sorrows among so many joys. But we looked at them all, our best and our worst, and with mingled feelings from time to time parted with our girls, for we could never be sure that any (except those whose husbands were our fellow-workers) would not be far more hindered than helped. And we looked at the several hundred growing up about us, and sought for light. A number were sure of what they were meant to do. They knew of the peril that threatened so many of India's children. They wanted to live to save them as they had been saved. They knew of the poor and the suffering. They wanted to serve them too. "For I have seen His face," said one of them. She was thinking of the words that we sometimes sing,

> I have seen the face of Jesus;
>   Tell me not of aught beside.
> I have heard the voice of Jesus;
>   All my soul is satisfied.

It was not so with every one, but it was so with most, and it would be so with many more, for our God does not mock us when He moves us to prayer, and our hearts' petition for years had been that we might leave behind us faithful lovers of our Lord. We, whose very own these dear children were, knew their limitations, but we knew, too, that they could offer truth, willingness for hard work, a freedom from the dominance of money, and very loving hearts. We missionaries have not yet tapped the deep springs of pure and passionate love that lie in the Indian nature. We have given too little and asked for too little.

So here we were, as so often in our story, unable to move until the way opened. The Muhammadan and Hindu towns and villages offered the neediest fields, but the young could not till those fields; the customs of India forbade them. To what end, then, were we to shape these lives? Our nurseries, schoolrooms, workrooms and home hospital would ask for a growing number. We could not have gone on taking children if it had not been for the help the older ones gave. But beyond? Lord, what is Thy thought? If it be *this*, this that Thou knowest comes to us again and again, let it not melt away like the little white cloud-thought of years ago.

On the evening of January 30, 1921, eight of us stood together in the sunset, looking over the plain. We could see many clusters of trees, each telling of a village; to east and south and north we saw temple towers; behind one little conical hill lay a small fortress of Islam, place of many frustrations. At that time no gospel preaching was allowed in the streets of that town.

There were hospitals in Travancore on the other side of the mountains and in two S.P.G. centers, at that time two days' journey distant. Heat doubles the toil of a journey, and the alternative may be heavy rain. (Motor traffic shortens distance now, but the very ill cannot sit on the roadside waiting for a possible seat in a crowded bus.) And we wondered why there was no medical mission in this part of British India specially bent on reaching those who are practically unaffected by the gospel.

Was it because Christians at home heard chiefly of the successes of the South, of the crowds swept into the visible Church, of the villages clamoring for teachers? Was it that they had not ever really understood that the castes to whom the great temples belong are still Hindu to the core? Those who are hardest to win for Christ are not being won. Nor have they the least desire to be won. They are either antagonistic or indifferent. As we looked upon the plain, now in shadow, and thought of the pain that we knew was there, hidden away in little shut-up rooms in little shut-up towns, and of the need of those Christless hearts, the need of which they were so unaware, it was as though there swam into our view a Place of Healing, furnished with all that was required for the help of the people, and we saw the work of the place led by one in whom were the instincts and convictions and the glad abandon of the spiritual pioneer; and the long patience, too, for some of the things that we saw as we looked were new, and the new needs infinite patience. The place was served by a company something like the early Franciscans in the gaiety of their spirit. They were lovers of their Lord and servants of His sick; they loved one another fervently, and money had no power over them. We had seen nothing anywhere except in the pages of our New Testament to give us hope that such a thing could be. But it was there, and so why should it not be here?* As we stood there thinking over it, a new soft radiance stole into the air, and this brightened till the west was dust of gold, and flames, and little feathers of rose and violet, and the east was a commingling of all the blues that ever were dreamed. It was so beautiful that it moved us like great music, and when it passed, and the stars dropped one by one through the still, transparent depths—"flowered" is the Tamil word for this coming of the stars—we found ourselves wishing just one wish: Oh, that we had something as lovely as this blossoming sky to offer to the Lord of all beauty.

That evening was not the first time that the hope of a Place of Healing served in this way had come. But that evening we had put it into words and written it in our logbook, and signed our names to a prayer for its fulfillment.

"The vision is yet for an appointed time: though it tarry, wait for it; because it will surely come; it will not tarry," was the word when, again and again, it was delayed.

But was it a spiritual vision, or only a dream of desire? In the *Confessions*, St. Augustine writes of his mother, Monica, "She saw indeed certain vain and fantastic things, such as the energy of the human spirit, busied thereon, brought together; and these she told me of, not with that confidence she was wont, when Thou shewedst her anything, but slighting them. For she could, she said, through

---

* Ten years later we read it all in Chapter 15 of *Guinness of Honan*, by Mrs. Howard Taylor.

a certain feeling, which in words she could not express, discern betwixt Thy revelation and the dreams of her own soul." There is nothing to add to these true words. "Through a certain feeling" we too knew.

Our thought that evening had been only of a hospital for women and children; but we could not always refuse men, and we had our boys now to think of. They, too, would want to share this service with their sisters. So Dr. May Powell, who joined the Fellowship in 1924, and we who had long been inwardly waiting for light, agreed together as touching this thing, and we asked for a man for the general leadership, one to whom the same heavenly vision had been shown, so that he could not be turned back from it or caused to doubt what he had seen.

This mattered very much, for it would be sharply contested. Only one who was so mastered by his convictions about building in gold, silver, and precious stones could hold on through what was sure to happen when there seemed to be no material of that sort at hand and the driving "must" of apparent necessity to accept wood and hay and stubble was upon him. But when convictions are inwrought by the Spirit of God, they are not conquered by opposition, or shaken by criticism of failure, or broken or weakened by disappointment. The leader sent by God would not lose heart.

For him we prayed persistently. Where was he? Who was he? We did not know. And there were times when we seemed to be asking for too much. At such times every valiant word struck from the anvil of life that we heard or read came with power to our soul. "I am full of confidence that God is, in His own way and time, step by step, going to unfold to us the blessing He has in store, and the kindness He is going to show us. So you can think with such a prospect, I feel as if I have but one lesson to learn better, and I am learning it: just to sit and adore and say to Divine Grace that there is nothing I cannot expect His wondrous kindness to do." Andrew Murray said that, and it often helped us.

We have told in *Meal in a Barrel* of how, on December 16, 1924, leading came to build the House of Prayer, and of how to the question, "But, Lord Jesus, what about the hospital?" the answer was, "When my House of Prayer is finished, I will provide for the hospital." And we have told, too, of how, just after the House of Prayer was finished, He did begin to "provide for the hospital."

Dates can be worth regarding; so also can the words that come in our ordinary reading on such dates. On January 30, 1921, we were caused to pray in a new way about this new work. On January 30, 1926, he who, unknown to himself or to us, was the appointed leader for the new work arrived in Dohnavur for a visit. He came and went, and we continued to wait on God, for His thoughts were still folded up in silence, but the word we had read on those two evenings was, *I know the thoughts I think toward you, saith the Lord, thoughts of peace, and not of evil, to give you an expected end.*

On August 25 of the next year, the House of Prayer being finished, a gift of one hundred pounds came for the building of the new hospital, and the word waiting for us then was this: *No good thing will He withhold from them that walk uprightly.*

We heard of that good thing in the forest, for we had gone there with a guest (he who had been with us in January 1926). We were on the steep path that leads up to the house when we heard hilarious shouts and laughter and saw, dashing down through the green trees like a blue waterfall, a torrent of children whose cries of welcome were mixed in a jumble of English and Tamil. "One hundred pounds, one hundred pounds for the new hospital."

There we stood in a gay knot on the path and heard of how they had seen in a home paper this gift from one who signed herself X.Y.Z. "A hundred pounds, Amma! A whole hundred pounds!" I see it all again—the dancing blue-clad children, the forest path bright with orange and crimson leaves, the tall trees on either side, the tall man leading our thanksgiving. And he who led us then was he to whom, in the counsels of God, the leadership of this that was now at last begun was to be committed.

41

It is not far to go,
    For Thou art near;
It is not far to go,
    For Thou art here,
And not by traveling, Lord,
    Men come to Thee,
But by the way of love;
    And we love Thee.

This method of divine leading—by the hour and by the moment—leaves the soul free and unencumbered, and ready for the slightest breath of God.—Madame Guyon.

O Radiant Lord, as morning dew
    Thy freshness meets us everywhere;
A faith that never dares the new,
    Unhazardous and wavering prayer—
Oh, do we choose this dust, that we
    So often offer it to Thee?

Oh, lift our soul to higher things,
    And lift our thought to Thy desire;
Give us the faith that mounts on wings,
    Give us the love that burns like fire,
The love that leads to Calvary,
    Not less than this, we ask of Thee.

41. Dipped in the Brim

On January 30, 1928, we moved forward. The date was
not noticed by us at the moment, incredible as it now
appears that we could have been so blind. For weeks one
or two of us had walked in a clearness of spirit that allowed of no hesitation. We knew by some sure token that
the time had come, and Arul Dasan had begun quietly to
inquire about some land near our compound suitable for a
hospital. But it was not enough that some were sure. The
immediate effect of obedience can be apparent disaster;
we must be one if we are to go through all that may follow
such a step in peace and in confidence. So we gathered
together with the definite intention of considering the matter in the light of what had been already shown to us, and
in seeking to know, as a Fellowship, the mind of the Lord.

We met in a room built off one side of the old bungalow.
A path runs past the windows, and for a while all sorts of
distractions conspired to disturb us. Coolies on their way
home made the usual coolie noises, village children just
out of school shouted shrilly, bullock carts trundled past,
bullock bells jingled. But presently the noontide stillness
fell on the world outside, and a deeper stillness fell upon

us; "Thou that dwellest in the gardens, the companions hearken to thy voice: cause me to hear it."

It was a solemn time. It is never a light thing to press towards the innermost place of His sanctuary. "Put off thy shoes from off thy feet, for the place whereon thou standest is holy ground." To our newer members, it was the first occasion of shared responsibility in prayer. To all there was a burning sense as of being searched and purged. Had the habit of the soul been so careful up till now that it was trained to recognize the voice of its Beloved? We are so ready to slip from under the power of a New Testament warning by relating it to the evangelistic meeting; but that day the words, "Take heed therefore how ye hear; for whosoever hath, to him shall be given; and whosoever hath not, from him shall be taken even that which he seemeth to have," took on a new power. Yes, in the hours when we most deeply feel the poverty of all that we have to offer there is the beautiful word in Revelation ready to reassure us. Thank God for the angel having the golden censer to whom was given much incense that he should offer it with the prayers of all saints (even the least who are called to be saints) upon the golden altar which was before the throne.

To buy land for a hospital implied a belief that doctors and nurses would be given. All along the thought had been that, instead of calling evangelists to enter the doors unlocked by the medicals, they themselves should use the key already theirs (for he or she who has eased pain has a key that no other has). If each were to have time for the double ministry, then more medical workers would be needed than the number usually considered enough. Had we ground for our confidence that they would be given?

And it meant that we had no doubt about the coming of the leader who would find his Pattern on the Mount, not only for the bricks and mortar but also for the house not made with hands. Had we that leader or any *human* hope of him? No, we had not. There was nothing at that hour on the human side to give us even a little glimmer of hope. But then, who said that we were to live on the human side of miracles? And yet, who were we, the least of all, that we should ask for so great a thing? But the Lord did not set His love upon us nor choose us because of anything in us, so our littleness was of no account.

We had no sign; we saw no rod lifted up and stretched over the sea. But we had been steadily driven past every natural hope to the place where we now stood. In the overshadowing of His Presence we found rest to our souls, and in His Book we found sure direction. The story of the crossing of the Jordan was His word to us that day. And we read from a letter that had come that same week from a friend at home: "The Lord is in your midst, I know, and working in seen and unseen ways. Someone has given me a thought today from Joshua 3:15, which I pass on. 'Dipped' here means 'plunged'; and we too have so often to make a plunge, not just the slow, cautious step, but the plunge in faith—and then things happen."

Again in that living silence that can only be when the Lord is near, we hushed our hearts before Him. At last there was thanksgiving, and the singing of hymns. When we rose from our knees we were pledged to faith, and we all knew it and were one.

A gift large enough to cover the purchase of the land required was the first confirmation of that afternoon's leading, and we paid the first installment in February 1928, but the second was not paid till a year later, so slowly do such matters move in the East. And, as though our Lord wanted to make quite sure we should remember that the Place of Heavenly Healing was to be begun, continued and ended in faith, and must be subject to the standards of faith, not of sight, we had to buy all the little plots round about the center before securing the center. The land around that central plot was broken up into numbers of holdings, and for a long time the owners had been unwilling to sell; and when at last they agreed, they had cheerfully tried to get as much as they could out of the deal. This had delayed the purchase, and had given the man at the center a thrice blessed chance to exploit us. But again the impossible happened. The surrounding owners began to jeer: "Have your cows wings that they can fly over to your portion in the middle?" and no Tamil likes to look ridiculous. The middle plot owner came to terms at last, and we walked over it singing in our hearts.

But the day that saw the waters divide according to the promise of our God had come a little before that final purchase. On November 15, 1928, a letter was posted from the R. A. Mess, Meerut. It was from Dr. Murray Webb-Peploe. Our Unseen Leader had given to him the charge of leadership.

"I had fainted, unless I had believed to see the goodness of the Lord in the land of the living. Wait on the Lord: be of good courage, and He shall strengthen thine heart: wait, I say, on the Lord."

42.

For they were pricked, that they should remember Thy words; and were quickly saved, that, not falling into deep forgetfulness, they might be continually mindful of Thy goodness. For it was neither herb, nor mollifying plaister, that restored them to health: but Thy word, O Lord, which healeth all things.—Wisdom of Solomon, 16:11–12.

Lord Jesus, Thou art here with me;
 I do not need to cry to Thee
To come with me, my loving Lord,
 For Thou art with me in the ward.

And though I may not see Thy Face,
 Yet, as I go from place to place,
There is a hush upon my day,
 That would not be, wert Thou away.

When in the still white room I stand,
 Thy viewless hand will guide my hand.
Dear Lord, what joy, what peace to be
 About Thy healing work with Thee.

42. The Door of Health

And now a rather lovely thing began to be. The story of how we had good hope of being able to do more for the people passed out far beyond our borders. We met it in surprising places. One day when two of us chanced to be together in the bazaar of a Hindu town a big burly bazaar-man suddenly said, "You are going to have a hospital at Dohnavur—so we hear," and he smiled all over his face. "You will make it Paradise." It was so unexpected a phrase from that unknown Hindu's lips that for a moment we must have looked our surprise as well as our pleasure, for he added emphatically, "Yes, Paradise."

> If Jesus built a ship,
>   She would travel trim:
> If Jesus roofed a barn,
>   No leaks would be left by Him:
> If Jesus planted a garden,
>   He would make it like Paradise:
> If Jesus did my day's work
>   It would delight His Father's eyes.

And if Jesus, our Lord Jesus, built a hospital, what would it be like?

But our first hospital, apart from our little home hospital, was not in the least like Paradise. It was a henhouse—Buckingham Palace, we called it. Its first inmate was a little old lady, terribly gored by a bull; we called her the Duchess. The Duchess was exceedingly grateful, and as she felt with regard to her doctor much as an affectionate grandmother might towards a beloved and very young grandson, he was occasionally quite glad that he was well over six feet high and so (without hurting her feelings) out of reach of her embraces.

We soon found it necessary to build four mat huts, and shortly afterwards turned an Indian house just outside our walls into a little *pro tem* hospital. This house in its earlier days had been called the Zoo, for it had been the home of a jolly mob of boys. Now it became the *Suha Vāsal*, Door of Health.

In rural India, the first thing a patient and a patient's friends want to see is the kitchen. The ward may be the merest hut (our henhouse, for example)—that does not matter. Nor does it matter whether it be what we consider comfortable or not. If it has a private lean-to, or a kitchen of some sort, it is acceptable. So the little Door of Health shot forth minute cooking-cells, made as secluded as possible, and the people were fairly satisfied. Only fairly, for as the cells were under one roof, "The fishy smell will come over the wall," one disgusted lady remarked—she being a Saivite, a strict vegetarian, her neighbor of another cult. (What one may or may not eat is, of course, a question of religion here.) But somehow they settle down, Muslim and all varieties of Hindu—except where food is concerned, a friendly family. Often we are astonished by this friendliness. Perhaps it is a reflection of the friendliness of those who take care of them.

There was never any difficulty in making our guests feel at home; and our medicals appreciate this very much, but there are limits; they draw the line at poultry, even when the hens are tied up tidily in a corner or under a bed.

Our sick like to be ill in private (except for relations), and their instinct for privacy is respected. For rich and poor alike, some sort of device is arranged so that they may feel alone with their own families. The house is supposed to hold eight or nine cubicles or matted verandah rooms, but as many as can possibly do so tuck themselves in. From a missionary point of view this is perfect, and in spite of the lack of hospital decorum, good and vital things come to pass in that crowded little Door of Health; not only, not chiefly, healings of the body, but that for which we continually pray—eternal healings, too. It is here that our younger children find their opportunity. They have seen their Sitties and Accals and Annachies doing loving things all the time, ever since they can remember, and it is natural to want to be like them. So Barbara Osman and Beatrice Taylor who carry on the kindergarten (Helen Bradshaw and Frances Nosworthy having long ago gone over to the boys' and girls' schools) have the happiness of taking these little ones to sing to the sick people. On special evenings they take colored lanterns. Colors are a wonderful help in this color-loving land. "Now I know what heaven is like," said one of the patients after such a colored-lantern hour.

Often, when the doctors think it would be a cheer, they send a message before an operation begins and a group of singers gathers outside the window of the operation room and sing till a sign from within tells them that the patient is asleep. This custom was brought about by a frightened little boy who said, "Please sing me to sleep," and many grown-up patients, Christian, Hindu, and Muslim, have found it very comforting to be "sung to sleep."

There are times when something poignant brings home to us that we live in a suffering land. The mind faints before pain-smitten millions; and because the subject is so overwhelming, presently it does overwhelm, and crushes out even feeling. But just as where spiritual wrong is concerned, so it is here: lift one single suffering thing out of the mass, one small tormented child, and look at it, and the mind is numb no longer; or endure in your own flesh for a while the sharpness of acute, unrelieved pain, and you know how divine a thing the touch of the healer is.

We are set in one of the most conservative districts of India, and nothing seems to shake the faith of the people in their ancient customs. A tiger bites a man, and the wound will be packed with a dirty mess and carefully closed. A person breaks a leg, and he will be pegged down on the floor and the leg bandaged in tight bandages gummed over with white of egg. "Devils are upon me!" cries the maddened man after a day or two of this treatment, and he tries to break away; but the pegging is well and faithfully done, and there he lies writhing in spirit but held fast in body for perhaps fifteen days.

Fifteen days was the time set for seven-year-old Mardie to endure this anguish. There was some talk of bringing her here, but, true to custom, the parent delayed. "The bandages will come off on the fifteenth day. Then we shall see." They saw, and for ten more days they used their own time-honored poultices, and gangrene set in. At last, almost too late to save her life, the mother laid the agonized little form across her shoulder and brought her in.

We have a great hope that our *Parama Suha Sālai*, Place of Heavenly Healing (the name was chosen by an Indian friend), may become largely a children's hospital. And when we see how the sight of our own little ones encourages the poor distracted mothers, and when we hear of how stories about doctors' and nurses' ways with them, when they are ill, spread all over the countryside, we think that this hope will be fulfilled.

Already we have had many child patients in the Door of Health. Everyone knows how often help given to a child is a key to the parents' hearts. But there are some who come to us too late. And yet there is something that can be done. Prayer can follow. Here is a story of succor to a little Christian girl who lived a day's journey from Dohnavur.

She was sent to us by a fellow-missionary who had hoped that we could do something; to hear her story is like looking through a window into a truly Christian home. The story begins sadly enough, for the child was dying of inoperable cancer, and her father took her away. After her death the friend who had sent her to us wrote to our doctor:

> For the last five days she had no pain and she insisted on getting up on her feet and with her father's help she walked about the house. For those five days she knew that she would go home on the fifth day at three o'clock. The Lord had told her so, and she was full of joy; so our prayers for peace and trust were answered abundantly above what we asked, for she was even merry. She longed to go to the beautiful place ready for her, and was impatient of being delayed by fond parents. She made them promise to be cheerful and not grieve, and said they must give her up willingly to the Lord.
>
> She sang many hymns and laughed at her father for singing in wrong time and sang for him. She said many verses, especially psalm 23, and was glad and happy, and comforting all her friends up to the last fifteen minutes.
>
> The parents cannot grieve. They are full of wonder at God's doing; so the mystery of such suffering for a child is to some extent solved. She is a witness once more that Christ tasted death for every man.
>
> When she walked round the house, her idea was that it was a journey. As Christian had been told, so she had been told to be ready, and she declared that she must walk all the way home, and that was why she was so happy when she was walking; she was really (she felt) on her way home.

There must be many who have been compelled to leave someone to suffer and die, perhaps in circumstances that seemed to forbid peace, and how much more, joy. Thinking of such, we let this story give its cupful of sweet solace. For it is comforting that we have a Saviour who is equal to any kind of forbidding circumstance, even the death by cancer of a little child.

43.

Lord, make of this our pleasant field
  A garden cool and shadowy,
A spring shut up, a fountain sealed
  For Thee, Lord Jesus, only Thee.

And fill it full of singing birds,
  On every bough of every tree,
And give the music and the words
  That will, Lord Jesus, pleasure Thee.

And as from far untrodden snow
  Of Lebanon, the streams run free,
Dear lord, command our streams to flow,
  That thirsty men may drink of Thee.

Array thee in the joy that always finds favor in God's
sight and is acceptable with Him: yea, revel thou therein.—
From *The Shepherd of Hermas,* quoted by Bishop Paget in his
preface to *The Spirit of Discipline.*

O Splendor of God's will,
  Clear shining mystery,
I worship and am still,
  Hushed by the thought of Thee.
Thy great and noble ways,
  Lowland and mountain know,
Fair flower-bells chime their praise,
  And to Thee the waters flow.

O Will most lovable,
  Young budding trees aflame
And all things beautiful
  Illuminate Thy name.
Far hast Thou passed my prayer,
  Good hast Thou been to me,
Thy lover everywhere,
  Blessed Will, make me to Thee.

43. Exalted Days

The work in the Door of Health, in the dispensary, and of course among our children, has for a sort of visible center the House that stands in the midst of the life of the place. Blue flowers climb its tower and look into the windows of its upper room, and in the cool season its roof to the north is covered with purple passionflowers. To the east is a little raised place, like a chancel. It is always full of green things. A large blue Persian carpet, gift of our fellow-missionaries in Persia, is spread on the tiles below. On this carpet he whom the people for miles around call their Doctor Annāchie (elder brother) stands Sunday by Sunday at a certain point of the Tamil service, while any who have been healed and want to bring a gift come from different parts of the House; and then he offers thanks for them, and prays for the sick by name. Their relations (each patient has several) often go to the service. One day I was sitting with a patient in the Door of Health during the service and was there when those who had gone returned; it was amusing, but touching too, to see each relation go straight to his or her sick one and say, "The Doctor Annāchie said your name. He prayed for you. *Mé thān!* (true indeed). He said your name to God."

On the day of the dedication of the House, Alec Arnot, to whose faithful toil it owed so much, was married to one of the children's beloved Sitties, Gwen Jones, and though a few years later they had to return home, they continue to belong to us in spirit. In the evening of that day our friend and bishop sat on a low seat with little children at his feet and on his knee, and we sang all the old sweet children's songs. There were some who thought that hour the dearest of the day.

We have many special days, exalted days,* to use the word of the old text. Each Sunday is such a day. We have long months when our green withers and our poor flowers become discouraged; only a few blossom bravely all the year round. But in this corner of India we have two monsoons, the southwest in June and the northeast in October, and in the freshness of a day after rain the burning months are forgotten. We choose such a day now, and begin at the hour when the moon sets large and bright over the hills just as the dawn breaks in that most lovely light, half silver and half gold, and drenched trees lift up grateful flowers, and all the lesser flowering things, dewy and sweet, are stirring—for it is then the children waken and each little nursery and room becomes a busy place. In the dispensary and surgery too there is much to do. In the House of Prayer, flowers are being put into big bowls and vases, and the red-tiled floor is being washed again, for however clean it may be the children are not satisfied unless it is washed just before the service. They often sing as they sweep and wash. There is a sound of singing everywhere. And the birds sing, too. The magpie-robin has a song of sustained sweetness. Often in the part of the worship which is given up to thanksgiving, the one who is

---

* "Why doth one day excel another, when all the light of every day in the year is of the sun? By the knowledge of the Lord they were distinguished; and He varied seasons and feasts: some of them He exalted and hallowed, and some of them hath He made ordinary days."—Ecclesiasticus 33:7–9.

leading pauses as he gives thanks for the flowers and the birds, that we may hear the dear birds sing.

On Sunday we have three services, one English and two Tamil. The brothers, Indian and English, lead the first two of the day. In one there is much thanksgiving as well as intercession, and there is always a space for adoration. The other is the evangelical opportunity of the week—at that time especially the floor of the House of Prayer is like a wide garden, crimson and cardinal, purple, mauve, blue, with yellow and white here and there: such a gay garden. At the moment when every small child stands up (while all the rest are sitting) and each waves its flag, or, failing a flag, the frond of a fern, it is so living and so gay that we wish we could share the brightness with all for whom life holds more fog than sunshine.

Sometimes the front porch of the House is reminiscent of the porches of the pool of Bethesda. One of the brothers drives the Ford car up with its impotent folk, and they are helped in. There are low chairs at the back for those who cannot sit on the floor, or a mattress is carried in and the sick one lies on it.

One small boy, who had suffered so much from mishandling in his village home that at first he had to be given chloroform before his wounds were dressed, was for many Sundays one of the cheeriest in the House, as he lay on his cot with its blue coverlet. No one who saw that bright little face would have known that under the blue was a frame to which he was fastened. He used to watch eagerly for the moment when a psalm or lyric set to an Indian tune was given out, and the band played (cymbals, tambourines, brass bowls struck with a knitting-needle, a big earthen vessel hit sharply over the mouth to make a drum), and there was a flutter of flags all over the House; for in the flutter he would join with a happy triumph. In his hand, clasped tight all through the service, was his own blue flag.

New Year's Day is one of the special Giving Days of the year. Two big baskets are brought to the House and set on the Persian carpet. And long processions of children come up to the front, each affectionately clutching some cherished toy, and these toys are put in the baskets for the sick children. Afterwards there will be that great event—a feast for the child patients of the year, who are allowed to bring a limited number of their relatives. This feast needs the greatest care in the kitchen arrangements because of the variety of castes, but the father of a little patient, who says that he can never do enough for those who helped his boy, sees to everything for us. After the feast a Christmas tree is dressed by our Friedenshort Sisters. This tree is for the hospital children, and it gives to ours the thrill of the season, for then they see their very own presents given away. And so to these little ones, on whom so much love has been poured by lovers of children all over the world, is given the joy of giving.

"But I will not give anything," remarked a youth of five to his friends, when this plan was first proposed. "I shall keep all my sweets and all my toys, and when you have given yours away, I shall sit in a corner and eat my sweets one by one and play with my toys."

His accal (the little Leela of *Lotus Buds*), aghast at this discovery of greed, did not know how to meet it, and wisely looked up quickly for an answer. Then she said, "Very well, but of course you will not be able to go to the House of Prayer with the others on New Year's Day." This was a shock, but Servant of the Crown stuck to his purpose, and there he sat in his corner, his tears dropping one by one as he ate his sweets one by one, and played (or tried to play) with his toys. And there the happy toyless ones found him on their return. So we are far from perfect yet.

But we must not be tedious. Easter Day shall be the last of our exalted days. It begins before dawn with singing from the tower, and we meet with the glorious greeting, "The Lord is risen," to which the other answers, "The Lord is risen indeed," and both say together, "Alleluia." Then we go to God's Garden. This is an enclosed space in a corner of the garden towards the east, where palms and lilies grow (lilies that open in twilight after rain) and oleanders, the flowers of the Lake of Galilee. We go there at sunrise and sing our Easter hymns.

By the entrance to that garden there is an ancient tamarind tree. It used to be a place of demon-worship and revelry. Now under its green shadow stands a rough-hewn cross of the granite of these hills. Many a broken hour has found us sitting on the stone by the foot of that cross. The very touch of its rough surface seems to bring home the spiritual significance of the symbol. Eternal things have grown clearer then, and things of earth dimmer. We stand under that tree after laying some dear child to rest in God's Garden, and sing something triumphant. We try to make such occasions festival, not funeral in feeling, and sometimes, when people who do not know Him who is the Resurrection and the Life are with us, we find a rich use in such an opportunity.

But under this happiness and peacefulness there is going on ceaselessly a hand-to-hand fight with malevolent powers. Many an hour, even in our exalted days, is spent by one and another in what St. Paul calls wrestling. For the devil and his myrmidons are never off duty; souls lately plucked from their grasp are assailed and plots are formed for their undoing. There is need for us to be sensitive to the approach of the enemy. We should know, before the wolf cometh and teareth the sheep, that he is near and threatening. There is something the hireling can teach us here: he seeth the wolf coming:

> O Lord, make me aware
> Of peril in the air,
> Before the wolf can leap
> Upon the sheep.
> Give me the eye that sees
> When he is threatening these
> Who are so dear to Thee,
> So dear to me.

And so, because deadly things can be attempted even in our quiet compound after the chimes have played "Abide with me," we do not find the long silence of our evening Communions too long. For the hour is full of silence, broken only by the voice of our Tamil pastor, and by versicles of adoration and worship, sung kneeling. The House is white then, and the whiteness of the Indian garments and the stillness, and the very gentle movement and the singing, have a ministry of their own, and often there is a sense of a Presence manifest and all but visible.

That Presence draws so near that loving little things like this can happen: one sultry evening a worshiper, almost too tired to kneel, thought of the first Supper—Now there was leaning on Jesus' bosom one of His disciples whom Jesus loved. "Oh, that I might!" It was not a prayer, hardly a formed wish, only a little tired longing to lean; but One is with us who is closer than breathing, and there was a sudden sweetness, and then, "You may."

And after the hymn that closes our Communion had been sung (it is always that perfect hymn, "Jesus, Thou Joy of Loving Hearts"), and the soft sound of bare feet walking softly had passed, that tired one, refreshed as a withered flower by heavenly dews, went out, to find a Hindu friend waiting near the door. This friend had often wondered whether our Lord Jesus spoke to us in words that we could understand. And just as a hidden fragrance finds its way out into the air, so does a private sweetness. So his question was answered then.

44.

If the labors of so long a voyage, the care of so many spiritual illnesses, this life in a land so subject to sins of idolatry, and because of the great heat so hard to live in—if all this is undertaken for whom it ought to be undertaken, it brings refreshment, and many and great comforts. I believe that for those who delight in the Cross of Christ our Lord, such labors are rest, and the ending of them, or the fleeing from them, death. What death is so great as after having known Christ to leave Him and go on living in the pursuit of one's opinions and likings? There is no toil like that. But what a rest to live seeking not our own but the things which are Christ's.—Francis Xavier.

Make us gay troubadours of God,
  Loyal and guided, strong to dare,
And free to ride the world light-shod,
  Living to love, and lift, and share.
                    —Murray Webb-Peploe.

44. With the Shepherd When He Finds

Half-an-hour's walk from Dohnavur there are reaches of water fed by streams from the hills. They are only grassy or muddy flats during the hot season, but after the two monsoons they are lakes. On these the boys paddle their canoes, and from time to time we have baptisms there. But, more entrancing still, an hour and a half's walk distant, there is a nook among the hills, watered by three streamlets. One of these flows among rocks by a shady old banyan tree where the pilgrims cook their food, for on the top of the rock near by there is a shrine and (to the children most exciting) symbolical animals, bull, horse, elephant, cobra. Three miles farther on up the hill, near the mountain river that divides into the three streamlets, there is a temple in the woods; it is known far and wide as a place of healing. To this temple, when it is possible, some of us go at festival times, spending a long day under the trees which all must pass who go there to worship; and to the lovely little valley of the streamlets our children go sometimes, setting forth an hour before dawn and returning after sunset. Seventy or eighty go at a time; they walk up to the temple, give Gospels to the priests who serve in courses, bathe in the river for hours, and climb the rocks and trees as they will, and, no matter what they do, nobody says "Don't," for "God made that rat like that." (The saying dates from an examination paper of years ago, which asked many curious and, as Chellalu considered, irrelevant questions about a rat. She did not know the answers, so she wrote firmly across her sheet of paper— *God made that rat like that.* What examiner could ask for more? So now if a foolish grownup should want to know the wherefore of any madness on such a day, somebody is sure to answer, God made that rat like that.) But our first association with this wild and charming place was a baptism. Because it was so beautiful we chose it for that pearl of joy.

No one who has followed our story so far, understanding what it is that we have been called to do, will expect to hear of us in connection with numbers. We cannot be happy about mass-movement work, though we do appreciate the faithful toil of many whose line is different, because we know how often the Hindus and Muslims are hindered by the lives of nominal Christians. But we are not called to judge or to criticize (What is that to thee? Follow thou Me), we are called to lead to the Saviour of men one by one those whom His love attracts to true surrender and devotion. So neither the lake-like water nor the little stream sees a large number going together to confess our Lord in baptism. But how precious the ones and twos are, no words could ever tell.

They have been from all classes (for we are sent to all), but especially from those communities which stand farthest aloof and for whom conversion means tremendous things—the loss of all that made life to them before, sometimes almost life itself. It is frequently said that no one in India loses life for Christ's sake and the gospel's. This is, unhappily, fiction. But in this land life is not taken with the publicity of martyrdom, it is stolen away in secret.

God only knows the bitter secret martyrdoms of India. It should be understood that no young man or woman in the most antagonistic castes, or among Muslims, is allowed to live openly as a Christian at home in any of the towns and villages in this part of South India. Here and there we hear of a Hindu widow with independent means (whose life is of no special importance so far as her caste is concerned) who is allowed to continue to live in her own house, but even that is rare. It has never been done in this country-side. True conversion does not mean peace, but a sword, and that sword can cut to the quick. Only those who have gone through this severance with a loving, sensitive Indian brother or sister can even begin to imagine what confession in baptism costs. There is nothing in literature that shows it except our Lord's own words. It passes man's. So there is nothing careless in the joy of these baptism days, and yet joy triumphs. Again and again we have seen the Lord of Life victorious in the place where His foe is most strongly entrenched, and the wide waters under the mountains, and the little shining ford have seen—can we doubt it?—companies of angels rejoicing with Him and with us, as we stood, sometimes in a rich flood of sunset color when His glory covered the heavens and the earth was full of His praise.

Happily, there are other and less exclusive castes and, as medical work serves all, we have sometimes a happiness like one so recent and so pleasant that it stands apart, a separate little bright thing in the minds of those of us who shared it—a lorry load of boys, a Ford car full of girls, and Ronald Procter and John Risk, who drove us. It began in this way:

One day a man badly mauled by a tiger was carried to Dohnavur to be mended. He was converted and went back to his village to witness. Soon a messenger came asking our doctor to go out to tell his friends more of the gospel. So the doctor and some other brothers went, and found a large quiet courtyard prepared for them. Men and women

were sitting in expectation on the verandahs. They would
have listened all night. "It was like going to the house of
Cornelius," said our brothers when they returned. There
was some persecution, enough to test the converts, but
they stood strong, and were baptised, and united to the
little church in the village. We had now gone to see them
and to pray in the house of Cornelius, swept clean of all its
idolatrous pictures (Cornelius himself had built a shrine
hard by, which had been recently turned into a cow barn).
One of the chief pleasures of that day was the welcome the
people gave to the young nurses who had nursed some of
them when they were in the Door of Health; and as two of
the boys spoke briefly but bravely to the friendly villagers,
we saw, not by faith only, as so often we had seen in the
past, but by sight, how great an opportunity has been
given to us in the gift of our children.

The ways of Francis Xavier are not ours, but God grant
that the spirit that inspired him may inspire us: "Many are
the potential Christians in these parts," he wrote, "they
lack only those ready to occupy themselves with devout
and holy things. Often I have had a mind to go to your
universities and shout aloud like a man who has lost his
sense, above all to the University of Paris, and tell in
Sorbonne those who have more learning than will to make
use of it, how many souls through their negligence fail to
go to glory." There are times when we hardly know how
to endure the thought of what thousands of the Lord's
lovers are missing today—the joy of being with their Shepherd when He seeks—yes, and when He finds—His sheep
that were lost.

Among us are many who taste that joy. Our Syrian
Christian brother, Koruth, is often out in the villages and
hamlets which lie between the temple towns, called to
them, now by a pastor earnest about his flock, now by
someone drawn towards Christianity—and him he seeks
to draw to Christ Himself. And he always comes back
from these days and nights (the nights are often spent on

his knees) with a look in his face which tells us with whom he has been walking on our Indian roads.

45

For even as love crowns you so shall he crucify you.
Even as he is for your growth so is he for your pruning.
Even as he ascends to your height and caresses your tenderest branches that quiver in the sun,
So shall he descend to your roots and shake them in their clinging to the earth.
Like sheaves of corn he gathers you unto himself.
He threshes you to make you naked.
He sifts you to free you from your husks,
He grinds you to whiteness,
He kneads you until you are pliant;
And then he assigns you to his sacred fire, that you may become sacred bread for God's sacred feast.—Kahlil Gibran.

I thought I heard my Saviour say to me,
My love will never weary, child, of thee,
Then in me, whispering doubtfully and low,
How can that be?
He answered me,
But if it were not so,
I would have told thee.

I thought I heard my Saviour say to me,
My strength encamps on weakness—so on thee.
And when a wind of fear did through me blow,
How can that be?
He answered me,
But if it were not so,
I would have told thee.

O most fine gold
That naught in me can dim,
Eternal Love, that has her home in Him
Whom seeing not I love,
I worship Thee.

45. Ye Shall Ask Me No Question

The Friends of the Fellowship who wanted this book wished to have something more than the husk—they asked corn in the ear, our Lord's more private ways with us, the very gold of our gold. "We cannot show that," was our first response. But if it would help another, it is not ours to keep. "He hath caused the arrows of His quiver to enter into my reins. And I said, My strength and my hope is perished from the Lord." "Whoso that loveth knoweth the sound of this voice," Thomas à Kempis says, writing of love. Whoso that loves and has lived knows the sound of the voice that must speak now, if this writing is not to be froth. Deep calleth unto deep, not bubble unto bubble.

After many difficult years we had received much help. A good wind had filled our sails, and we had appeared to be about to speed along as never before, when suddenly we found ourselves in the midst of bewildering confusion, and, instead of making headway, we seemed to be caught in crosscurrents, hopelessly set back and greatly hindered in helping others.

The saving salt in a household which is the center of various activities is that, whatever the preoccupation of the hour may be, the duty of life goes on oblivious of feelings. Just then friends at home were sending us a number of old books to distribute among English-reading pastors and teachers, and when the postman staggered up to the house laden with a sack of book packets and poured them out in a heap on the dining-room floor, we had to unpack them and put them away. Somehow one went astray, and reappeared later on my table, a thin, small book in faded brown, Adolphe Monod's *Farewell*, published in 1873. It was not attractive—in fact it looked distinctly stodgy. I opened it without enthusiasm. It was the hot hour when the mind moves sluggishly; mine drowsed, till suddenly, startled, I came upon this:

> And if among the trials* that you are called to bear, there is one that seems, I do not say heavier than the others, but more compromising to your ministry, and likely to ruin forever all the hopes of your holy mission; if outward temptations be added to these coming from within; if all seems assailed, body, mind, spirit; if all seems lost without remedy, well, accept this trial, shall I say, or this assemblage of trials, in a peculiar feeling of submission, hope and gratitude, as a trial in which the Lord will cause you to find a new mission. Hail it as the beginning of a ministry of weakness and bitterness, which the Lord has reserved for the last because the best, and which He will cause to abound in more living fruit than your ministry of strength and joy in days gone by ever yielded.

The words pierced to the heart of things in a way no other words had done.

Would it be truly so? Would what had seemed only hurtful to our ministry turn to blessing and power and joy? Was this something to be accepted with hope and gratitude? And now He who guides even to the sending of books caused a friend to lend us one just then which gave us this:

---

* In the French, "cross." We venture to change the word; the cross denotes something different.

The old nature dies as He died. That which we were by nature, peacemakers, centers of happiness, dies as the corn of wheat dies, or rather appears to die as it passes out of sight, in order that it may reappear in a glorious resurrection form. If by God's help we hold fast in humble submission and childlike trust to our Lord while the dying is being accomplished, then our prayers for others have a tremendous power in His name, and either here or hereafter we find that we, like our Lord, have lifted up those for whom we prayed by His own resurrection force.*

It is the eternal in books that makes them our friends and teachers—the paragraphs, the verses, that grip memory and ring down the years like bells, or call like bugles, or sound like trumpets; words of vision that open to us undying things and fix our eyes on them. We are not here, they tell us, for trivial purposes. We are here to prove to angels and to men

> That life is not as idle ore,
> But iron dug from central gloom,
>   And heated hot with burning fears,
>   And dipped in baths of hissing tears,
> And battered with the shocks of doom
>   To shape and use.

We are not here to be overcome, but to rise unvanquished after every knockout blow, and laugh the laugh of faith, not fear.

And so, as week followed week, the vicious whisper Why? lost its power, and peace flowed in and filled every crevice of our being, till at last a day came when, awed and almost broken by so great a gladness that we could only worship and wonder, we saw what had been bitterness in the cup turned into sweetness, even into the very wine of joy.

---

* Bishop Wilkinson. He speaks, too, of our Lord's giving to us His Cross in the very form which He knows is a real cross to us.

We understood then why our Lord said to His disciples, "In that day [the day of revelation] ye shall ask Me nothing." "Ye shall ask Me no question; the mysteries that now perplex you will have been illuminated." Already, indeed we asked Him no question. "With the Lord, we shall forget even the Gospel of John."

And yet the immortal will remain. Life cannot die. We found a seed of immortality in the poem which a guest who stayed with us soon after our morning of joy had dawned gave to us.

> Who packed thy wallet, friend?
> One whose love shall never end—
> What therein was laid?
> He put in bread and wine and stayed.
> What said he thereon?
> "Wilt thou want more than these when thou art gone?"
> How didst thou answer him?
> I begged a candle, for mine eyes were dim.
> He bent on me his gaze
> Clearer than a thousand days,
> "Thou shalt need no light
> (Quoth he) by any day or night."
>
> Then said I, "My fear
> Was of a blackness when no hand was near."
> But he this word let fall:
> "I shall not leave thee when thou leavest all."
> And wilt thou take a staff?
> Of his cross he gave me half.
> *What shall be thy dress?*
> *He clothèd me in emptiness.*
> Dost thou need no book?
> His face is all whereon I crave to look.
> Hast thou no map or chart?
> I know my road, it leadeth to his heart—

In this short chapter I have packed the fine gold of many years, but instead of the word "submission" in the far-reaching thought of the French teacher I should write *acceptance*, for more and more, as life goes on, that word opens doors into rooms of infinite peace, and the heart that accepts asks nothing, for it is at rest, and the pilgrim of love does not need a map or chart: "I know my road, it leadeth to His heart."

And so we, in common with all the Father's children who abide under the shadow of His wings, have proved that the darker the day the more illuminating are His words of delight. But my words are frosted windows. What would be seen, if only they were clear glass, would be a loving-kindness that is better than life.

And now something learned in a later year may end this record of succor in distress; it belongs to a time of pain and weakness. A mauve net curtain hung in front of a door in the room where the disabled one lay. Beyond were green trees. In dull weather every fold of the net curtain showed, but when the sun was shining on the trees the curtain was all but invisible. It was still there (in that lay its parable) but it was transparent. It could not be seen for the glory of that light. And often, during those months, the singers of the Fellowship used to gather outside another door leading into that room and sing to sweet and haunting music:

> "I could not see
>   For the glory of that light"—
> Let the shining of that glory
>   Illumine our sight.
>
> Things temporal
>   Are transparent in that air,
> But the things that are eternal
>   Are manifest there.
>
> Jesus my Lord,
>   By the virtue of Thy grace,
> In the shining of Thy glory
>   Let us see Thy face.

46.

Duties are ours, events are the Lord's. When our faith goeth to meddle with events, and to hold a court (if I may so speak) upon God's providence, and beginneth to say, "How wilt Thou do this or that?" we lose ground. We have nothing to do there. It is our part to let the Almighty exercise His own office, and steer His own helm. There is nothing left to us but to see how we may be approved of Him, and how we may roll the weight of our weak souls in well-doing upon Him who is God Omnipotent.—Samuel Rutherford, 1637.

For the love that like a screen
Sheltered from the Might-have-been;
For that fire could never burn us,
Deeps could never drown or turn us,
For our daily blessings, Lord,
Be Thy name adorned.

For the gentle joys that pass
Like the dew upon the grass,
New each morning, lighting duty
With a radiance and a beauty,
For our daily blessings, Lord,
Be Thy name adored.

Many a storm has threatened loud
And then melted like a cloud,
Seeking to distress, confound us,
Met Thy great wings folded round us,
For our daily blessings, Lord,
Be Thy name adored.

46. What Mean Ye by These Stones?

When the children of Israel crossed the Jordan, they piled up two heaps of stones, one on the bank of the river, the other in Jordan's bed.

We too have our stones set out in the open—the visible things that our God has done. They are continually before our eyes, and many, looking at them, ask how they came to be there. When they do that, when they say, What mean ye by these stones? we tell them as much as they wish to know. Every stone in the heap has its story.

And we have our stones under water, too, covered from the casual eye, but held fast in our heart's affections—the secret things of our God, the touches of pure wonder. This book has shown a few stones in that heap, and will show one or two more. This chapter shows something of the more evident.

In our part of South India, months are required for collecting building-material. Granite has to be quarried; bricks burnt, carted, tested, counted, stacked; timber felled (or if felled already, chosen) and carted in huge logs from the neighboring State of Travancore, sawn and examined foot by foot. And the thousand sundries that at home are undertaken by experts have to be seen to as thoroughly as possible by one of us. To hand over the work to a contractor saves all this, but it is more expensive, so we do our own contracting. With two exceptions, the House of Prayer and the operating theatre for the Place of Heavenly Healing, all our buildings have been designed and carried through by ourselves.*

The field across the little stream, which in dry weather disappears, was beginning to fill up with granite gneiss quarried from the big rock which makes the frontispiece for *Lotus Buds*, when one day Barbara Osman, who with Joan Roberts was just then in charge of the office, brought me the summary of the previous month's accounts, prepared for June 6, our day of prayer.

She was looking puzzled. We had received a good many gifts earmarked for the Place of Heavenly Healing, but the close of May had found us short on the home side. There had been a good balance in April, so that all was well, but somehow the question had come, were we to continue one family in this (the financial) sense, or must we divide?

We remembered then how similar questions had risen about the boys' work. First as to place—was it to be alongside or, as is usual in this land of segregation, at a distance? We knew the difficulties of including boys in a family like ours. No one could live in India for many years and not know them. And yet it was the natural way. Accounts, too—were they to be divided?

We remembered how the directions for the tabernacle had flooded our minds with light—the loops of blue sewn on the edge of the two sets of curtains, the clasps of gold "that the loops may take hold of one another. And it shall be one tabernacle." We remembered how beautifully the matter of the accounts was settled. There was never any

---

* But one of the latest gifts to our Fellowship is an engineer and building expert. Philippians 4:19 fulfilled again.

difficulty. And now, would not an equal clearness be granted? With that slip of paper covered with figures in our hands, we asked that it might be so, and we wrote the request then and there in the logbook.

Did we expect what followed so soon? "A few minutes afterwards," is the note in the logbook, "there was a check in the mail for two hundred and fifty pounds and it was not earmarked." On June 10, three hundred pounds came, neither was it earmarked. So we continued in great peace. God would guide His givers to earmark their gifts, or to leave them open.

And then, as though to confirm us in that peace, the close of the first three months of 1930 showed a balance of over six hundred pounds which we were free, because all the claims of the older work had been met, to use for the new. "I counted it twice over," said Barbara Osman. "It seemed too good to be true."

Often where funds for the new work were concerned our God appeared to wish to teach new lessons of faith. One day an amazing letter came—a kind of dream-letter. It was from an old Scottish friend who wanted us to tell him what the surgical instruments required would cost, and he asked us not to be "blate," but truly to tell him. So, with feelings that I leave medical missionaries to imagine, the list was carefully made out and sent. Again it seemed too good to be true; but is anything in the kindness of God too good to be true? And a Scotsman's word is inviolate. Then for more than a year we heard nothing. Was it a dream-letter after all? It was not. Our friend had been injured in a motor accident. For almost a year he had been unable to think, or do anything. As soon as he could hold a pen, he sent his check. And then there was a mistake in the date, and it had to go back, and we knew that our dear old friend might not live to return it. But he did.

Some years ago the children who are now our fellow-workers heard that X-rays were needed in Neyyoor, and they gathered their coppers and sent them to Dr. Pugh, who had done so much for us all. With this gift they wrote a loving note, hoping it would be "enough to buy the Ex-Rays." If anyone had told us then that we were to have "Ex-Rays" in Dohnavur, we would have thought it a fairy tale. But the last stone in our heap shall show a kindness that has already helped many. The X-ray installation is not here yet, but the powerhouse is a fact accomplished, and the first time the electric light was used in our little home surgery it was for a badly hurt man who was carried in for operation that night. Only those who have done operations by lamplight can appreciate the value of electric light, and we never cease to bless the givers who gave us this good gift.

This is from Ronald Procter's story of how the engines were kept for us. It was written early in 1930.

Some weeks ago Murray had a letter from a friend, an electrical engineer in one of the large railways, telling him that down in Travancore, owing to the recent state visit of the Viceroy, there were for disposal quite large amounts of electrical machinery and stores, going cheap, but in first-class condition, as they had been used only for the two nights of the Viceroy's visit, for special illuminations. I am afraid I was not in the least bit keen on getting this stuff just then. I did not think it would be at all likely to be the kind of stuff we were wanting, and I was afraid we would be forced into buying something quite unsuitable to our purpose. What we were wanting was an engine and dynamo capable of charging a large battery, from which it would be possible to run lights in the wards of the hospitals during the night, and X-rays, when wanted, during the day, without having to keep the engine running continuously. Obviously this would not be the kind of machinery down there, as it had been used for lighting only for a few hours on both nights. So I told Murray that in the absence of any definite information as to the make and nature of the engines, we would just have to let the matter go. We could not as it were say "Yes" to stuff we knew nothing whatever about, and the reply had to go by return of post.

For months I have been keen on getting a special kind of engine, of well-known make, but quite the latest thing of its type, and running on crude oil at a cost of about fivepence a gallon, thus costing practically nothing to run. I had made all arrangements with the Madras manager of this company for one of these engines, and all that remained for me to do was to run up to Madras, which I did last week, see the manager, buy the engine, and make arrangements for it to be brought down here by rail as well as ordering all the other electrical supplies needed. I called in at the Madras office the other day, saw the manager and definitely ordered this particular engine, about which I had been corresponding with him for weeks and months past, and asked him to send it down to Tinnevelly the same day.

I then went straight along to a large English electrical engineering firm to see about a suitable dynamo to run off the engine I had just bought. I was shown into the office of the manager, and lost no time in explaining what I wanted. "What kind of engine would you be using to drive it?" he asked. I told him the engine, the particular type and the size. He started suddenly. "Have you *got* the engine?" he asked me. "Yes," I replied, "bought it about ten minutes ago." "Man alive, what a pity! I've got a couple of those identical engines, same make, same type, same horsepower, almost brand new. You could have got them both from me for about the price of one engine, as I would be willing to let you have them at a very special price. They have been used for two nights, during the Viceroy's visit." These, then, were the engines we had originally heard about, not knowing their make or size, and they were still unsold. It was unbelievable. We immediately got busy on the telephone, got on to the manager of the engine firm, from whom I had just bought a new engine of exactly the same size and type, and hurriedly explained the position to him.

Would he have any objections to canceling my order, and thus allow me to accept this other offer at a greatly reduced price? "Not the slightest," he replied, "go right ahead. I'm only too glad you have one of my engines— don't care who you buy it from!" *What* a sportsman the fellow was! We then got down to talk it out. If I bought the two engines down there he would let me have them at an absurdly low price, about half of what I would have had to pay for them in the usual way; but if I could take only one, he couldn't promise it to me, for the engines were already under offer to some people down there. Their time limit had expired, but he expected a reply from them any hour now, buying the two. Would I take them? Two engines specially tested and specially supplied from England for this special job, practically brand new, the finest stuff obtainable *and* just the very dynamos we were wanting, for, in spite of the fact that no battery had been used down there, these were battery-charging dynamos, because they had not the others in stock just then. I told him that I would write my answer, one engine was what I had come up to buy, not two. I went out, had lunch somewhere, did a lot of thinking and praying, and then guidance came, clear as a shot—"Buy them." I went straight along, closed on his offer, bought them.

We have two superlative engines and dynamos, of just the very size and type we were planning on, for about the price of one. We shall be able to run them on alternative weeks, always keeping one as standby in case of need, thereby increasing their efficiency enormously. When one thinks that there are probably at least twelve different makes of engines sold in Madras, each make having at least twelve different types or sizes of engine, making a possibility of at least 144 different engines, it seems absolutely unexplainable, on any human grounds, why these two engines should have been the very type, size, and make that we wanted, and not only that, but that they were kept waiting for us for over three weeks without our knowing anything definite about them.

The sequel—I got home last night. This morning I got a letter from the manager of the electrical firm. . . . "You will be interested to know that at four o'clock this afternoon we received a telegraphic order for the engines from another party, so you did well yesterday in deciding to have them." There are some very solemnizing moments when one realizes more than ever how marvelously He leads and undertakes. Don't you think this was one of them?

Has the reader lost the child's sense of wonder? We of this little Fellowship cannot lose it, and we cannot grow accustomed to what may not appear so wonderful to greater people. For years a mud wall stood outside our kitchen; elsewhere mud had been replaced by brick, but that wall stood. We had carried the mud for it ourselves to save a few annas. We kept that wall for remembrance. The gold that comes to us may be coined in mints of earth, but for us it is heavenly gold, and there is a private mark on it, a private light. And we are learning perpetually new lessons of faith as we take these gifts from our Father's hand.

What mean ye by these stones? This is what we mean.

Think through me, thoughts of God,
　My Father, quiet me,
Till in Thy holy presence, hushed,
　I think Thy thoughts with Thee.

Think through me, thoughts of God,
　That always, everywhere,
The stream that through my being flows
　May homeward pass in prayer.

Think through me, thoughts of God,
　And let my own thoughts be
Lost like the sand-pools on the shore
　Of the eternal sea.

47. Out of the Blue—A Diatom

A glance at our book of gifts would show that there are not many rich among our friends. The drafts sent by our secretaries are chiefly made up of a number of small gifts, and the same is true of gifts which come to us direct. These little loving gifts fall like small snowflakes, very quietly, without observation, like the daily little love-gifts of sweet airs and sunshine and cold water that we would miss so much if we had to do without them. And so it is not a usual thing with us to live through chapters like these, and we do not want to convey a wrong impression by putting them together, and yet they came so in real life, and why should we not show the kindness of our Lord?

Early in December 1929 the medical workers talked about doing without a maternity ward in the new hospital. This is such a conservative corner of India that probably it will be some time before such a ward will be fully used. We have always rather grudged money put into bricks and mortar. "We might use one of the other wards to begin with," said Dr. May Powell, eager to economize if possible. But our wise older nurse, Mary Mills, objected, and so did the younger, Jessie Walker, upon hearing of it. She had known what it was to help poor distressed mothers in difficult conditions. "No, it would be ineffective, impossible to run properly"; and the doctor-builder, keen as he also is on economy, agreed. So the matter was left; the Lord would show what He wanted done. And He did.

Among our Dohnavur customs is a happy way of keeping birthdays and coming-days. (A coming-day is the anniversary of an arrival.) When Pearleyes came to us, a much-feted child of seven, she regarded the life of the village church and congregation to which we then belonged with a grave and wondering scrutiny. "Christianity is a dull religion," was her first comment. Fresh from the round of festivals which are scattered through Hindu life, that was how what should be the most gloriously happy thing on earth appeared to her. And I sympathized. Vividly I remembered the time when it appeared just that to me; indeed, I was not at all sure that the time was entirely past. Thereafter in all our plans for the children we let the gaiety of birds and all the young things of God's creation have a place in the scheme of things.

So on birthdays and coming-days the room where the one to be feted lives is dressed with flowers (flowers have always meant much to the children, such dear joys). On great coming-days there is a feast for all in the group to which that one belongs, and on still greater, a feast for the whole family. The food is simple enough. There are a few delectable extras, such as payasam, a sloppy concoction of rice and palm-sugar, or homemade honey cakes, or balls of a nutty and oily nature—something not tasted every day—and these luscious delicacies are thoroughly appreciated, sometimes with an open abandonment, often with a weighty seriousness, for the young Tamil child takes its pleasures with dignity. But one year we had to be very careful; the feast was to be ordinary food with the cheapest of twisted hard biscuits to help out, and we feared that the children would be disappointed. It was not so. "If we may have it all together, and strings of flowers over our heads, and decorations (of flowers, of course), that makes a feast," they explained. And we found that it was so.

We were nearing the end of one of these festivities, held in the open courtyard of the girls' school and in the classrooms around it (the date was December 15, 1929), when a child ran up with a yellow envelope in her hand. She was waving it like a small and stickless flag. No thought that a cable might spell trouble had crossed her mind. But it crossed ours, and I opened it quickly, and read, "One thousand pounds for maternity ward." *One thousand pounds!* For a dazzled moment I stood like Rhoda, and opened not the gate for gladness. A thousand pounds would do much more than build a maternity ward.

Before me on the table as I write is a page from a looseleaf notebook. On it is written a short penciled note, "2.9.29 P.S.S. [the hospital, Parama Suha Salai, Place of Heavenly Healing] £1000. one gift." The note means that on that day, September 2, 1929, a servant of the Lord in Dohnavur, as he waited on his master in the early dawn, was moved to pray for this astonishing thing: "a thousand pounds for the hospital in one gift." "It came out of the blue," was all he could say by way of explanation when he quietly told of it. It is sometimes all that can be said. We do not know enough of these heavenly matters to explain them in earthly language. We only know that they bring us down to the dust at our Lord's feet. But I knew that much lay behind. There was nothing light or facile in that prayer.

Why was it given to him to pray that prayer?

All medical missionaries, and indeed all missionaries everywhere, will understand how unusual, and on the face of it how wasteful, it seems to build a hospital out in the heart of the country. It had been questioned already, and we ourselves would often be tempted to question such an apparent folly. Then, too, in a place where a notable conversion might empty the wards at a stroke, why build at all? Was it that our Father, foreseeing what would be, had sent this thought to His son chiefly because of the word that it would hold? That gift would be another

Gideon's fleece which the winds might play upon as they would but could never blow away. It would assure us that His purpose would be fulfilled, whether by the coming of many patients or few.

We had already proved what He could do among a very few. The Door of Health had been a fruitful field. Was it that He was saying something like this to us: "This gift will say to you not once, but continually, *Do not look at the things which are seen* (numbers, success), *but at the things that are not seen* (the spiritual, that which I am doing in the souls of men and women), *for the things that are seen are temporal, but the things that are not seen are eternal. And these alone are of eternal importance to you*"?

All this, the prayer-note and its inner significance, had not been mentioned in our daily prayer meeting, nor had there been any talk about it. I think that only one or two had heard of it and, so far as I was concerned, it had been pushed to the back of my mind, where it lay, a memory indeed, but not ready instantly to cause recognition of that blessed knock at the gate.

But, like Peter, the words of that cable continued knocking.

"What is it, Amma? One thousand pounds!"—the word flew through the little company as one and another ran up to read it and to handle that wonderful slip of paper. And we felt how good and right it was that into the heart of our festival such a message should come, such a reminder of the purpose of our creation as a family—not to be ministered unto, but to minister.

An Indian feast is unlike anything seen at home. There are no tables, chairs, benches, no china, cutlery, glass, silver. The feasters sit on the floor in lines or circles. Before each is a large, smooth plantain leaf. On this shining satin plate is heaped rice and little piles of curried vegetables, or cakes, if it be a feast of cakes. No one ever gave a thought to the color scheme, it arranged itself; but it is satisfying. Overhead, flowery festoons, pink and white and crimson; on the ground, on the dark green and pale green leaves, white rice and yellow curry, or brown and yellow cakes; and everywhere the children, of course, in their gayest. Presently polished brass bowls are brought in filled with sweetened milky coffee, a treat reserved for feast days.

It took some time to get round the groups, and, before we had explained the cable to all, some who had not been able to come to the feast, hearing exciting rumors, had gathered in the big schoolroom, called the Room of Praise, which opens on the courtyard, and so we met there, old and young, and thanked our Father, and rejoiced with the children who love their Doctor Annāchie. He was out at a case, but would soon be home to be welcomed by this cable, which would be so much more to him than just a cable or just a gift (great gift though it was). But of this they did not understand much yet, for who can understand it but the one to whom our God has shown His thought in secret and for whom He has confirmed it openly? "I could not see for the glory of that light": that shows what such an hour can be.

The gift was anonymous, but some of us were allowed to know who the giver was, and this is from her letter in reply to one from Dr. Webb-Peploe telling her of that directed prayer for the thousand pounds in one gift. "What can I say to that letter of yours, written on Jan. 1? The wonder of the things behind fills me with awe. It all seems so sacred, so entirely of God."

Then she tells how the date his letter mentioned, September 2, when he noted down that prayer guidance, was the first day of a week memorable to her, too, because of a book that she had read. "The impression to do something besides praying deepened, until the Heavenly Father just told me what He wanted, bit by bit, and that He wanted it without delay; and showed how, for at first it seemed impossible—I didn't see how the sum could be got. From the first whisper from Him there was no doubt as to the sum, nor that it was all to be sent at once. That was absolutely clear. But oh, the wonder of it all—and that He should have let one of the least of His children so realize His presence and His wish and guidance, seems almost too much joy."

One evening, a week or two before that happy day of the cable, on our way back from work farther afield, Dr. Webb-Peploe stopped at a little house in Holy Town where he had a patient. The young wife was still very ill, and the small, hot, dark room was full of relatives, but the old grannie, tired out with anxiety, was sitting on the floor of the verandah mechanically chopping vegetables, and I sat beside her and tried to reassure her. She told me the story of those desperate hours. It was not the child they had wanted to save so much as the mother—such a good girl she was—they had tried everything (the list was long and dreadful); at last the barber's wife called for the knife. "What knife?" "Oh, this one." It was the one that she was using to cut up the vegetables.

I looked at it, a crude thing of soft Indian iron, but capable of being sharpened on a whetstone. It would have been cleaned, of course, rubbed on the barber woman's rags, and somehow things grew vivid. No chloroform— and a vegetable knife.

People keen on the study of the diatom know how the finer the lens the more beautiful the marking is seen to be. The eye is bewildered by the beauty of the delicate, the minute, the perfect. The nearest thing that shows it in language is T.E. Brown's,

> Then took I up the fragment of a shell,
>   And saw its accurate loveliness,
> And searched its filmy lines, its pearly cell,
>   And all that keen contention to express
> A finite thought. And then I recognized
>   God's working in the shell from root to rim.

For the giver at home, the reading of her book; for the

one who prayed here, that prayer "out of the blue"; for the three, their talk about economy; for us all, the knowledge of the bitter suffering that may be and often is, formed a lens that brought into relief the perfect wonder of God's diatom.

*   *   *   *   *

Months after the coming of this birthday cable, we heard that a nurse in Lancashire was praying the same prayer as the one that came out of the blue. "In her prayer she told the Lord that she wanted to send you a thousand pounds as a birthday present, but she could not do it. Would He send it for her?" And it came, as I have told, in the middle of the birthday feast. How near Thou art, O Lord.

None of us had ever before, or have ever since, been caused to ask for such a gift, and the more we ponder the matter, now enriched by this lovely little story of the dear Lancashire nurse, the more surely we accept it as confirmation of all that went before. In days when we shall be tempted to put the crowd before the individual, the remembrance of that Sign will hold us fast to prayer that the Lord of the harvest may continue to prepare the soil for the seed ("Thou makest it soft with showers; Thou blessest the springing thereof"), let the reaping cost what it may.

And because to sow heavenly seed takes time, time with God alone, time by the bedside too, and there are, after all, only twelve hours in the day, it is good that we should leave the question of how those hours are to be filled to the Healer and Lover of souls.

It has always been the kind custom of our God to deal with us in some tender, intimate manner before leading us into action for which His word alone was our warrant. "There came again and touched me one like the appearance of a man." He who has felt this touch can go on in quietness: something has happened that cannot be shaken, for it is not of earth. "Fire and hail, snow and vapors, wind and storm fulfilling His word"—that will be his song through life's rough weather, for the loving-kindness of the Lord has quickened him, His loving mercies have come unto him, and his heart has been refreshed in the multitude of peace.

48

Lo, here is felawshipe:
One fayth to holde,
One truth to speake,
One wrong to wreke,
One loving-cuppe to syppe,
And to dippe
In one disshe faithfullich,
As lamkins of one folde.
Either for other to suffre alle thing.
One songe to sing
In swete accord and maken melodye.

Fear not, for those that be with us
    Are more than be with them,
And hoary idols fall before
    The Babe of Bethlehem.
And we shall see them fall. Oh, come
    And let us bravely sing,
For the Crown was given unto Him
    When He went forth conquering.

Fear not; for Islam too shall own
    Our Saviour, Christ the Lord:
In every mosque He shall be known,
    His blessed Name adored.
Oh, let us praise before we fight,
    And sing before we see,
And claim the Muslim for His knight
    Who triumphs gloriously.

48. There Is That Openeth

The year 1927 had seen us formed in legal fashion into a Fellowship with power to hold land and property. The document was so worded that no one could mistake who was in charge of us. It plainly referred to our Unseen Leader. So it was not a usual document, as the legal friend who examined it told us, but that was nothing to us. As soon as this matter was concluded, the C.M.S., to whom part of the compound and the old house of Dohnavur belonged, gave them to us with kind words and benedictions. All along ours is the story of a small thing greatly helped.

In this new arrangement, with its new formalities, we had no thought of becoming a "mission," and Faith Mission is a name we have never called ourselves. To us it seems that all true missionaries are pledged to faith. Apart from that, there is already on the field a mission* working on "faith lines," as the word is generally used. So we continued to be what we were all along—just a family, a Fellowship, free to fill any gaps we can, the gaps which a missionary map of a densely populated country cannot

---

* The Ceylon and India General Mission.

show, for the red dots are sown so thickly on the paper that it looks as though the country were Christian. But it is not so. Between these dots are places where the gospel is still unknown or, if known, misunderstood. And these are the hardest places of all, and call for the longest patience of hope and a love which many waters cannot quench, neither can the floods drown.

South India has long ago been divided among the great missionary societies, and comity is surely the golden law of missions. So when converts are given, our course is simple. If they can live in their own homes, they are attached to the nearest church. If they have to take refuge with us, we adopt them into the Family.

Our first business all along has been to be true to our trust towards the children for whose salvation we were called into being, and as they increased in number we needed, and received, more workers whose hearts the Lord had touched to care for them. There is a peerless joy in comradeship that the years can only prove and strengthen. This joy has been ours. We know that the Lord "who knit us together, shall keep us together." And the old rune which faces this chapter is, as literally as may be, a description of the family as it grew from year to year:

> Comfort and joy meet in this vital union,
>   Shelter in storm and peacefulness in strife;
> Thus to be knit in Thy pure love's communion
>   It is our life, O Lord: it is our life.

The year 1927 saw the medical work open out, and we earnestly asked for at least one nurse to help on that side; and the workroom, where so much that looks secular, but is sacred, goes on all the year round, and where so much of the King's money is spent (and saved), urgently needed someone to take charge.

These two needs were met by two good gifts of that year, Jessie Walker, with some nursing experience, and Margaret Clark, very able in all practical ways. And when

Sister Paula and Sister Erna from Friedenshort came, one a nurse, and later, Lorna Bliss, from St. Thomas's Hospital, London, we were glad, thinking of the suffering that would be relieved.

Friedenshort was to help us more. It is our spiritual twin in Upper Silesia, and its dearly loved Mother Eva and Sister Annie (the one now in the Land of Light, the other still on the battlefield) mean much to our Fellowship. In 1930, in tender memory of its missionary-hearted Mother, Friedenshort gave us four more young Sisters, of whom one, Sister Marta, is a nurse.

I have told how our hearts' desire, trained child-lovers, had been given to us, and now that our fourteen nurseries were filled to overflowing, we asked for one specially fitted to guide the young girls there, and found that she had been already given.

Most of our D.F.s have unusual stories of preparation and call. But only one, I think, heard in a railway train the call that compels. Edith Phillips Jones had been visiting India, and just before leaving the country had come to us for a day or two. We had thought of her as a passing (but dear) guest, and she had no thought of what was to be; but after she left us, as she sat in the train, that which cannot be mistaken for anything else came to her, and she wrote to us. And as we too had clear assurance, we wired to her boat at Bombay, "The Lord bless thy going out *and thy coming in*," and here she was already "come in," and ready to meet that need. In such loving and unexpected ways does our Father answer prayer.

About this time He opened a door that had never been opened before.

Near to us is a small Muslim town called Song of the Plough. Years ago, when a band of evangelists went there, a furious mob of men drove the preachers out of their streets.

Gradually, because of our children (all India loves a child), the town became friendly, and gay bunches of women would come to see round the nurseries and go

home to talk of us with affection. Then came the War, and
the townsmen used to come to see our illustrated papers
and to hear all we knew. They knew as much as we did,
we found. When Turkey came in, that friendliness ended.
The men came no more. Then we were officially warned
that mischief was planned, and were urged to be very
careful, and not to sleep out of doors, as is our wont. But
we made no change in our customs, for we knew that we
were safe. After this, gradually neighborly relations were
resumed, but when we tried to get a little house in the
heart of the town, the whole place closed like a single
door. After months of waiting and negotiations, we all but
secured a cottage on the edge of the town. At the last hour
the owner drew back, terrorized by the threats of his
townsfolk. We might visit the town as often as we wished,
teach as many people as we liked, reopen a school that had
been closed—but live there? "No one in these parts has
ever lived in a Muhammadan town. You are asking for a
miracle," they said. But the creation of a flower is a miracle,
and God makes new flowers every day. So that word
could not trouble us, and we could not give up the hope of
winning that determined little place. At last, when the
medical work had broken down barriers in its own gentle
way, we tried again.

And for a week or two miracle seemed too great a word
for anything so easy as an entrance now appeared to be.
Four houses were offered, but hurriedly withdrawn when
it came to terms. An anonymous petition from the street in
which there was a house suitable for our purpose ex-
horted us to sit down elsewhere, and teach our faith in a
cool and pleasant place more befitting our dignity than
their insignificant town. Behind that there was a settled
firm resistance, so the petition meant trouble for the landlord, and he dared not proceed. But there is that openeth
and no man shutteth; the landlord recovered his courage,
and four of us went quietly in, a gallant old grannie called
Faith, Sister Erna and Sister Elsa of Friedenshort, and

Favor, who had once prayed behind the wings of a theatre, "Lighten our darkness, we beseech Thee, O Lord."

Then an implacable enemy called a meeting in the mosque. Many men attended it. The shops were forbidden to sell, the women forbidden to go to the house, the hooligans of the place (it is famed for them) were to be incited to throw stones and, if that failed to drive the little family out, to set fire to the house at night.

And then this happened: the old mother of the man who had called the meeting had a carbuncle on her neck, and she insisted on being taken to the dispensary which our Sister had opened. Their loving ministrations won her son. Next day he brought her to Dohnavur for an operation, and the last shreds of his enmity fell from him like old rags, when, after his mother's operation, he spent the night with us. Afterwards, when his small grandson was beguiled into joining the stone throwers, he showed him a rope and a stick: "That is to tie you up, and this is to beat you, if you throw stones at those Sitties." Meanwhile, in groups of fifty or sixty at a time, hundreds of women and children had flocked to the house undeterred by the thunders of the mosque, and the shops had taken no notice of its commands. The hooligans grew tired of trying to upset the tempers of that happy little household; there was not much stoning and no firing. And now the town sees, for the first time in its history, a simple friendly Christian life being lived in its midst, and the life is so simple, so loving, so open, and so carefully inoffensive as regards Indian feeling and customs, that prejudice is being broken down, melted rather, by the sun of Love Incarnate.* But Islam is

* "I have never heard of anyone who, after having *bona fide* attempted to become Chinese to the Chinese, that he might gain the Chinese, either regretted the step he had taken or desired to abandon the course. Merely to put on their dress, and yet to act regardless of their thought and feelings, is to make a burlesque of the whole matter. Let us appeal to the Word of God. Consider the Apostle and High Priest of our profession, Christ Jesus, who was faithful to Him who appointed Him and left us an example that we should follow in His steps."—*Hudson Taylor.*

not asleep; a paragraph in an Islamic Tamil newspaper tells us that:

THE EVERYWHERE–SPREADING CHRISTIAN WAY

Four miles from Song of the Plough is the Dohnavur Starry Family [the name the people gave us long ago]. They give away countless small pamphlets, and have a hospital, and teach the Christian religion. It is going everywhere. But what is the use of finding fault with them? Let us Muslims, vain things forsaking, by sweetness make known our holy Islam. Let us scatter Muslim pamphlets. Why do not we come forward to help people? If we do this our good true religion will come forth, and like the dew that has seen the sun all the untrue religions will of themselves perish. Let all the great take notice, we respectfully request.

I have told the story of this beginning in some fullness because to think in terms of millions is not to see things as they are. We have to come down to the little town, the village, the street, the individual. None of us can be in more than one place at a time. One man to so many hundreds of thousands is a phrase that blinds by its very bigness. No man can vitally impress hundreds of thousands, though a wide scattering of the seed—through literature, for example—is part of every endeavor. But it is good, and joyful too, to get an opportunity to stand effectively in even one small town. There are larger towns where the need is very real. One who is at work in a city of over 100,000 said, in speaking of the dearth of evangelists, "Do send someone who is free to seek souls. We have schools; they take up all our time, we have no one to spare for festivals or anything of that sort." And a senior missionary of our own district, to whom we wrote asking about Muslim work, answered at once by telling us of an offer of a plot of building ground in the Muhammadan quarter of one of our towns. That town was the last to which we would have thought of going, for something was already being done there; but to one who knew and cared it was as nothing in face of the great need.

But coming back nearer home, within half a day's car run of this house, besides hundreds of thousands of Hindus belonging to the exclusive castes, who cannot be reached in numbers but must be sought out one by one, there are more than a hundred thousand Muslims living in little scattered communities, like Song of the Plough.

The Lord calls men with the spirit of Epaphroditus. That spirit will be required, for the life of uttermost service cannot be called comfortable. "Comfort, that stealthy thing that enters the house as guest, and then becomes a host, and then master. Ay, and it becomes a tamer, and with hook and scourge makes puppets of your larger desires. Though its hands are silken, its heart is of iron. Verily, the lust for comfort murders the passion of the soul, and then walks grinning to the funeral."* It is true; but it is one thing to applaud it as truth and quite another to *turn* from that lust that murders the passion of the soul, for the sake of these for whom Christ died. But no one who has done so would exchange this way of living for any other.

---

* Kahlil Gibran.

49.

It is possible to sing, "My all is on the altar," and yet be unprepared to sacrifice a ring from one's finger, or a picture from one's wall, or a child from one's family, for the salvation of the heathen.—Hudson Taylor.

You have chosen the roughest road, but it goes straight to the hilltops.—John Buchan.

When the door opens we ought to press in, sacrificing our lives if need be for God, as the Muslims did at Khartoum for their Prophet. . . . Of course it costs life. It is not an expedition of ease nor a picnic excursion to which we are called. It is going to cost many a life, and not lives only, but prayers and tears and blood.—Dr. Zwemer.

Battles are won by teaching soldiers how to die, not how to avoid dying.—*Biography of Marshal Foch*, by Major-General Sir George Aston.

Cape Comorin

There is no footprint on the sand
　　Where India meets her sapphire sea;
But, Lord of all this ancient land,
　　Dost Thou not walk the shore with me?

And yet, a goddess holds her state,
　　Along the frontiers of the sea,
She keeps the road, she bars the gate
　　Against Thy tender majesty.

O Purer than the flying spray,
　　O Brighter than the sapphire sea,
When will she turn and flee away,
　　And India walk her shore with Thee?

49. The Great Undone

On a day of some travail of spirit, a letter came from John Risk (a young Naval officer who joined us in 1928)* who, with our Indian brother Koruth, was spending a fortnight in a pilgrim lodging-house near one of the great sea-temples of the South. There from the floor of Hindu life, seeing, hearing, entering into that which is closed to the casual sightseer, John Risk wrote: "What words can ever tell what the place is like where Satan's seat is? It is like nothing but Satan himself." ("It was as though the flames of hell itself came up and scorched away the daub of respectable missionary Christianity with which our eyes had been blinded and our comprehension dulled," he said afterwards, still burning with that memory.) And he wrote of the sound of feet, feet, feet, that he heard as he lay on his mat at night, listening to the people trooping from the railway station to the temple. "There is no other road there, just the one from station to temple. The noise of their talking, the crying of little children, the sound of the carts and the shouts of the drivers could be heard in the stillness of the night. And the thought came of the gap on

---

* See *Meal in a Barrel*, Chapter 19.

the edge of the precipice, and of how there was only one road, and they were following it because they knew no other, and of how it led them to destruction, to be robbed and spoiled and sent away empty." Who shall measure the grief and the shame as day by day the two men saw the glory due to the Lord of Hosts given to another? In that other's name whole streets around the temple were defiled by the traffic that is bound up in the minds of thousands of worshipers with the very words "temple festival."

"They are sold like little kids, "a pitiful Indian woman had said to us a year before in speaking of the young girls in her own city, a wicked little city in a Native State, where that traffic had flourished for ages. "I have gone from mission to mission asking if nothing can be done for them, the broken things—but no one can do anything. No one can begin anything new now." When she said this, two or three of us were with her by the roadside near a wide expanse of moonlit water; the hills were in mist behind. As we looked across the water we seemed to see the form of One walking there in the mist, seeking these young lost things who had been sold like little kids. And He was quite alone. We were all quiet for a while. There was only the sound of the softly lapping water. Then we promised her that we would not refuse such Broken Things if she brought them to us. And so what is growing into a special work began, and we thanked God, as we thought of those streets around that temple, that we had been given the opened ear that evening. And now we were all to hear another call.

I said that the time was one of some travail. This was because several of us had been driven to pray along the lines of the command, "Spare not; lengthen thy cords and strengthen thy stakes"; and those responsible for the conduct of the work realized what was contained in such a prayer. Our family of about five hundred was only part of that which had been committed to our care. We knew how far we were from doing thoroughly all that should be done, and superficial work is pretense of the worst sort. How, then, attempt more? For those at the heart of things, the spiritual responsibilities of the day did not end with the day, and often the call on strength and time began very early in the morning, so that to get quiet alone with God meant rising too early, so it seemed, for health. How stretch the cords further?

But these Hindus in their hundreds of thousands, these one hundred thousand Muslims all but at our doors, how *not* do more for them?* To do more meant that we must ask for more workers. "Pray ye therefore the Lord of the harvest, that He may send forth laborers into His harvest." If we prayed they would be sent. How could we refuse to pray?

And supplies? We have three funds, one called Comforts (the "baskets" of Chapter 17) not meant for present requirements; another made up of earmarked gifts for the new hospital now being built; and the third a current account which usually holds provision for a few months' life, necessary because foodstuffs have to be bought in bulk for the sake of economy, some time ahead. The accounts of the last six months read thus in rupees, anna, and pies (in English money about £5,000).

	Rs.	as.	p.		Rs.	as.	p.
Gifts	57,752	1	1	General expenses	62,113	12	3
Legacies	6,498	4	1	Land	1,313	6	0
				Passages	822	8	0
	64,250	5	2		64,249	10	3

Gifts and legacies exceeded expenditure by ten annas,

---

* From the *International Review of Missions.* "Perhaps the most startling fact about the unoccupied territory in India from the Christian standpoint is that India's villages number nearly three-quarters of a million, whereas the returns show that no more than 39,727 villages have Christians living there." And we know that very many of the Christians are themselves unlighted candles.

eleven pies, something under a shilling—but how much more than a mere coin was that shilling! And yet one shilling in about five thousand pounds could not be called a large excess. Looked at just as a shilling it was not much to encourage advance, and very little was coming in; everywhere there was straitness and financial confusion, and letters from home were not reassuring. But we have never yet built on any rock of earth, so these forbiddings appeared to us like beckonings. But men and women? We were in touch with none of the kind required for either stakes or cords.

Careless prayer is presumption, commanded prayer is obedience. It was the old word once more, Lord, *if* it be Thou, *If*—

At last, and the time was the evening hour of our Prayer Day, we sang these words together:

> Lord God of all the great undone,
>   They live by faith who with Thee dwell;
> For Thou dost turn the flinty stone
>   Into a springing well.
>
> Lord God of doors we cannot pass,
>   We go where Thou art leading on:
> For Thou dost break the bars of brass
>   And cut the bars of iron.

And then we prayed for men and women to strengthen the center, the stakes ("thy tent-pins make thou fast," is Rotherham's translation), and for others, the cords, to spread forth our curtains (Medical, Muslim, Hindu), and for the funds required for new outgoings. And we asked that none should come save those who were of the order of Epaphroditus.

The date of that prayer was August 6, 1931.

50.

No purer joy can be
Than to be one in Thee;
Bound by one golden cord
Of love to our dear Lord.
Together, together, together,
Made one in Thee,
All one in Thee,
Come let us flow together.

Come let us flow together
To the goodness of the Lord,
Together, together, together,
Alleluia.

Than song of sweet wild bird,
Deep in the green wood heard,
More sweet the melody
Of such a unity.
All singing, all singing, all singing,
Made one in Thee,
All one in Thee,
Come let us flow, all singing.

50. A Second Spring Season

When that brave and patient man, Ezekiel, was told to draw a city on a tile, I wonder how he did it. He must have found it difficult to get the perspective right. In trying to draw our city on a tile I have not attempted any sort of earthly measurement, but have tried to draw it so as to show that interchange of the earthly and the heavenly which makes life: brick and mortar, and between the buildings and inside them too, angels walking. (How quietly they walk—who ever heard the footfall of an angel?) Children and grown-up people, sick and well, good and bad, and everywhere a Presence—strange, invisible movement in that envelope of air that surrounds this world of ours, dark powers and shining powers contending; and through all a sense of triumph. For He must reign; we fight a conquered foe.

And now on a corner of the tile I want to show the last five months, beginning on August 6 with the prayer about the Great Undone, and ending with the year 1931.

Near to us to the north is an old-world country town called Joyous City, which has never wanted the gospel. Education is wanted there—it is desired almost everywhere if practically free—and a little mission school for girls is carried on, and a Bible-woman teaches those who want to learn at home. But when, six years ago, we tried to get a house so that some of us could live among the people, no one would either rent or sell. And for years we waited. But just after that prayer of August 6 about the Great Undone, a deputation from the town came to ask us in, and a haunted house was offered.

It was so dangerously haunted that it had been empty for three years (an advantage from our point of view, as its minor inhabitants would be the fewer for that). And it was perfect for our purpose. It had an upper sleeping-verandah not overlooked by any neighbor, and a fair-sized upper room reached by a ladder; and downstairs there was room for a dispensary. For here, as in Song of the Plough, we hoped to win a hearing from the most opposed by the friendliest way we knew.

The people clearly understood why we wanted to come. "We have such sweet honey that we cannot keep it to ourselves. We have such a dear Friend that we want you all to know Him. If we can help you in your troubles, then just for love's sake you will look when we show you our pot of honey. And when we tell you of our dearest Friend, you will not shut your ears. If only you will look, then you will want to taste; if only you will listen, you will want to know Him"—in some such words we made our purpose plain. For we were anxious to be straightforward, and not even to appear to sneak in under false pretenses, and, after all, we knew only too well what it would cost these dear people should any of them taste our honey and learn to know our Friend. The least we could do was to be honest with them. But they were not afraid of the power of the gospel, because they had so seldom seen it affect one of their own. Never once had a man been converted there, and only once a woman, fruit of the work of our sister missionaries of the C.E.Z. So they let us rent the haunted house, and Margaret Sutherland, a trained nurse who had joined us early in the year, with our evangelist, May

Parker, in charge, went out to open a dispensary.

But the men of the town would have been unreached if it had not been for something that had happened the day the key of the house was brought to us. These men were disdainful, self-contained, and in no wise affected by anything they had ever heard of Christ. The handful of Christians in a hamlet outside the town, of whom one was the tavern-keeper whose story is told in *Raj, Brigand Chief*, might have been at the north pole for all the difference they made in any street in Joyous City. The Brahmans especially were aloof. Imagine King George and his Court strict Hindus, and an uninvited stranger trying to penetrate to the King's private room in Buckingham Palace with a view to the conversion of King and Court. If you can accomplish that feat, you may approach an understanding of the barriers any Christian man not a Brahman would encounter, should he visit a Brahman house. To get access to Brahmans of the Joyous City kind, a courageous and truly heart-converted Brahman was required. And he must manifestly be quite other-worldly. None of us here knew even one of that caliber, except perhaps a dear old pastor, who of course was unobtainable.

But God knew of one; he was hundreds of miles away on the day of our prayer, and we had not heard of his existence, but he was led to us. He came, as it were floated in upon us, on the very day the key of the house was given to us. He seemed to be in every way the man for the occasion, and, full of enthusiasm and hope, he went straight out to Joyous City and things that had never been before began to be. Three months later, suddenly, sorrowfully, all ended. An insidious disease flared up, and so affected his way of thinking that he became quite unfit. His heart was sound, we know that, but his judgment was warped, and our dry heat tried him and accentuated the trouble; so he returned to his own country, and there was no one to take his place.

From Central Africa, M. Coillard, warrior and saint,

wrote words which come to us when life appears to be flowing too easily. "The evangelization of the world," he says, "is a desperate struggle with the Prince of Darkness and with everything his rage can stir up in the shape of obstacles, vexations, oppositions, and hatred, whether by circumstances or by the hand of man. It is a serious task. Oh, it should mean a life of consecration and faith."

And now came the joy of welcoming the first six of the new order of Epaphroditus, and because of the Place of Heavenly Healing, and for the sake of the towns and villages, we were glad that there were nurses—Edith Hope Gill and Helen Chart of St. Thomas's, and Sister Oda Van Boetzelaer of Holland, who came to us by way of Friedenshort. Jean Ewing for Pavilions came too, and the long-watched-for brothers, Philip England, electrical engineer (called by our wonderful God in time to take over from Ronald Procter, who could no longer stand the strain of life in the tropics), and Norman Burns, whose parents are missionaries in Africa. They had only four days with him after their return on furlough, and yet would not delay him, but sent him on with a Godspeed. Such parents are the blessed background of our Fellowship. When the call came to Philip England, it seemed impossible that he could be set free so soon. But we have a God who is equal to anything. He can break the strongest bond as a thread of tow is broken when it toucheth the fire.

So the word by the waterfall is being fulfilled, and life is full of good companionship, and the joyful little Fellowship song which is set to a sort of woodland music tells the simple truth:

> No purer joy can be
> Than to be one in Thee;
> Bound by one golden cord
> Of love to our dear Lord.

Can a life hold a second spring season? There is the

sense of that happy season now. How good it is to see the eager study of Tamil again; the *munshies* (language teachers) with their students, the big, indispensable Winslow's dictionary, the rooting out of old evangelistic weapons of war, now to be used more keenly than ever and increased and perfected. It is good to know that this generation of Hindus and Muslims along this reach of country, who are growing up without a personal loving offer of the gospel, will soon have that offer, and thousands at the festivals too. It is spring again now, and full of renewals of hope.

But the precipice edge? The mountain that long ago suggested this view of the unevangelized world is the great rounded head of the Hill of the Holy Washerman, 4,610 feet in height, which can be seen a day's sail from Colombo, and which is so much ours that it is sometimes called the Dohnavur mountain. On the top is a bare, grassy cap, about a quarter of an acre in extent, and from this cap it drops sheer for a thousand feet or more, and then in shelving slopes finds the plain. There are two heads separated by a deep cleft, but they coalesce in the view, as we have it, and in cloudy weather the precipice takes on a darkness that gives emphasis to its steepness.

Surely no one who loves his Lord and his brothers can regard unmoved the truth that, for vast multitudes who do not know Him, life is sinful and death is fear. "The night is so long for thoughts that dare not dream of sunrise, the night is so dark for eyes that cannot see the stars," wrote a blind and sorrowful man. There are many blind and sorrowful. But though I think a heart that is unmoved by this must be made of frozen mud, yet there is a greater word. It is the command of the Leader who ought not to be disobeyed.

For us of the Fellowship, the gap to which we have been specially appointed is that unfenced place where so many children have slipped and fallen. But we have shown other gaps. Most visitors to South India see the guarded places— they see churches, schools, institutions of all sorts, shepherded souls. They do not see the towns which are wholly Hindu, the crowds that pour like rivers through the byways of the cities. They do not see the real India off the main roads, that hidden India of village and country town, each clustering around a temple often far more imposing than any parish church at home. And they do not see much of the scattered Muslims of the South, three and a half million strong. They do not see that crystal rock which is Islam, whose base is so deeply set, whose surface is polished as though it were a precious stone.

51.

For us swords drawn, up to the gates of heaven:
Oh, may no coward spirit seek to leaven
The warrior code, the calling that is ours,
Forbid that we should sheathe our sword in flowers.

> Swords drawn,
> Swords drawn,
> Up to the gates of heaven—
> For us
> Swords drawn,
> Up to the gates of heaven.

Captain belovèd, battle wounds were Thine,
Let me not wonder if some hurt be mine.
Rather, O Lord, let my deep wonder be
That I may share a battle wound with Thee.

Oh, golden joy that Thou, Lord, givest them
Who follow Thee to far Jerusalem.
Oh, joy immortal, when the trumpets sound,
And all the world is hushed to see Thee crowned.

51. Swords Drawn

In November '31 a Muslim of Song of the Plough confessed Christ openly. He had searched the Qur'án to find the way by which sin could be forgiven. "But I could not find it anywhere, nor could I find One who died for love of me." Then he began to study the Bible. He read it carefully for three years, and he heard the Man of Galilee say to him, the Muhammadan merchant, "Follow Me." He waited for months, pondering that call and, at last, he and his wife, who is one with him in spirit, took the tremendous step of an open avowal of the Lord Christ, crucified and risen and coming again.

Immediately, urged on and backed up by the solidity of Islam (for the news spread like wildfire), Song of the Plough forbade, on pain of fine and other penalties, any Muhammadan to go to our house or to come here to the hospital, and Muslim missionaries came over from Ceylon to preach and give away tracts. If only the town had allowed these, the first converted Muslims it has ever known, to live in its midst, what a glorious witness would have been borne; but the light is banished. The little family (there are three young children) has had to settle with us, and the town has once more closed like a clam shell, lest the power of the Lord enter in.

Soon that which almost invariably happens in the case
of a convert happened. Apart from the spiritual suffering
of the wrench of uprooting came pain to the flesh. "But
put forth Thine hand now, and touch his bone and his
flesh"—it is the old word, the old wile.

Within seven weeks of his open confession, this strong
man, who had never been ill before, had to have two
operations for a poisoned foot. His beloved paragraph in
Romans 8, beginning, "Who shall separate us?" did not
fail him. He came out of the anesthetic speaking to the
Lord Jesus, and apparently hearing His reply, to which he
answered, "Joy, joy!" "It was like listening to one speaking
into a telephone," said Arulai, who was there at the time.
His chief thought (and his wife showed the same loving
self-forgetfulness) was not for himself, but for another
who also had an injured foot, and all his prayer was for
her. What will not India be when set aflame by Fire Divine? Who can wonder that we love her people, and would
give our lives countless times over to lead them to their
heavenly Lover? Then came this song, the first I have ever
heard from Muslim lips:

> The Name of my Lord is the good medicine,
> It is the heavenly medicine,
> I have proved it true, O Lord Jesus,
>
> I am the sinner who committed uncountable numbers of
>   sins.
> It was when I did not know Thee.
> I knelt down, humbly shutting my mouth, folding my
>   arms,
> I confessed all my sins, O Lord:
> There is no sinner like me in this world, I said.
> I cried, I besought and said,
> Lord, save this sinner from destruction,
> Thou didst die for my sins, O Lord,
> Thou wast crucified on the Cross, O Lord,
> I looked at Thy Cross—the burden of my sin slipped
>   away.

I knelt in His presence without moving,
He heard the great sinner's petition;
The Lord has forgiven my sins.
With my inward eyes I saw His heavenly Light.
Where went my burden? Where has it gone?
It went below the depths.
O Father who bore me, I have Thee, so what do I lack?
Thou art the Beginning and the Ending,
The Heavenly Being, immeasurable, who rules me.

This first breach in the Muslim line was followed by the first among the castemen of Joyous City. A young man, a patient in the Door of Health, was nursed by one of our boys who is in training on the medical side, and this boy had the joy of showing his patient "the life of Jesus" (a phrase that came from an old man near Joyous City, who, rather weary of what he thought of as empty talk, asked us to come and "show the life of Jesus").

But our story must stop somewhere, and so it stops facing the morning of our new spring. And, because it is part of the story, here is a note from the office (the room which was the gate of heaven to Ponnamal, the room where she heard the music that lightened her last days on earth, is our office now). After our special prayer about the Great Undone, when we asked for new workers, there was a long, lean season when very little came. The first mail after special prayer for funds brought us two pounds ten, and our average is about two hundred pounds a week. *Now shalt thou see what I will do*, is the word for such times, and we did see, for when very little came from England and Australia, friends of the Fellowship in Ireland, Canada and America sent us help. All through September and October, however, this shortage continued. But on a day in October when we found that we had received about two hundred and thirty pounds less than the expenditure of the month, an anonymous gift came for two hundred and eighty pounds. Then followed another time of shortness; we sought to know if in anything we had run before the

Lord. But He did not show us that it was so, and to all of us
was given a quiet certainty. "Ask me not how it came,"

> I saw it not with eyes,
>   It was not spoken.
> These mysteries
>   Have neither sign nor token.

It was not now as it had been before. There was no sign
nor token, but we knew that all would be well. And it was
well.

In the last fortnight of December it was as though a
hindering power or barrier had been removed. "Pharaoh
King of Egypt is but a noise; he hath passed the time
appointed"—it was like that, and gift after gift came
through. In one week there were thirty-six separate gifts.
December brought us one thousand three hundred
pounds, and other incomings, such as medical payments
and thank-offerings, and book profits, brought the total
up to one thousand five hundred pounds, of which we
were able to set aside seven hundred pounds for the Great
Undone. Could anything be safer than to trust the Lord,
and to take His words to mean just what they say? There
are times when it is not only lack of faith, it is sheer
blasphemy to doubt: "*They spoke against God*; they said,
Can God furnish a table in the wilderness? Behold, He
smote the rock, that the waters gushed out, and the streams
overflowed; can He give bread also? Can He provide flesh
for His people?" He did great things in the past, can He do
such things now? Or will He? *If we are humbly sure of His
direction, then it is speaking against Him to let our hearts ask
such questions, be the finance of the world what it may.* This
word came early in October, when things were at their
lowest. I have told what He did for us at the end of that
month.

And yet there is always a sense of wonder, and, because
we are human and may be mistaken even when all seems
clear, there is need for that pause of quietness of which we

have written before, which gives time for the Lord to give assurance by His further doings. "And the man, wondering at her, held his peace, to wit whether the Lord had made his journey prosperous or not." And this, though the sign that he had asked had been given. The old-fashioned phrase "reverence and godly fear" is much in point here.

And so, though the war of the Lord cannot go on without His gold and silver, the supreme assurance in a matter of this kind comes through the answer to our prayer for warriors. On that Prayer Day in August, we asked for men and women like David's soldiers, expert in war, of the order of Epaphroditus, and as the year closes we hear by cable of the sailing of the seventh. This fitly ends our long and happy story.*

To Margaret Adamson, whose cable told of her sailing early in January 1932, and to her fiancé, Hugh Evan Hopkins, belongs spiritually the Fellowship song, "Swords drawn"; for one of them wrote to the other, "I know that for us two it is to be swords drawn right up to the gates of heaven."

It will be that for them. It is so wherever the wife is as much pledged to the war as the husband. In this case that means language study before marriage, so that the life of these two, who before they met were called to Dohnavur, begins at the right place—the altar of God, their exceeding Joy. How often in the Scriptures we find the thought of sacrifice bound to joy as by golden cords.

---

* A book must end somewhere, and this book ends with the year 1931. But before it returned in proof, our God had given five more, three women and two men, of the order of Epaphroditus, for the lengthening of our cords and the strengthening of our stakes.

52

"Have I been so long time with thee,
And yet hast thou not known Me?"
"O my Master, I have known Thee
On the roads of Galilee."

"Have I been so long time with thee
On the roads of Galilee,
Yet, My child, hast thou not known Me
Walking on the tossing sea?"

"O my Master, I have known Thee
On the roads and on the sea."
"Wherefore then hast thou not known Me
Broken in Gethsemane?

"I would have thee follow, know Me
Thorn-crowned, nailed upon the Tree.
Canst thou follow, wilt thou know Me,
All the way to Calvary?"

So many people go to Communion seeking peace. We go into His presence, whose hands are marked with the nails, and we ask for peace; and we get no peace, because we ought rather to ask for that deeper sense of His presence as He leads us into war. There is always something more in your nature which He wills to mark with the Cross. This is the primary purpose of Communion: that you should learn, in company with Him, to endure; that you should learn to be quite still, as He carries you along on the path, ready to suffer. Only so can He do His work in us. If that were our attitude towards Communion, if we went to Him that we might go back more brave to our work and our warfare, then indeed our Communion would be to us what He means it to be. It would be the cleansing of the mirror of our soul that it might reflect the divine glory in us. It would be the increase of the divine life in us, making us ready for the final revelation, the blessed vision of God.—H. Maynard Smith, *Frank, Bishop of Zanzibar*.

52. Steps Cut in the Rock

We are often asked how we "find workers." We do not "find" them; we pray for them, and we think that our God finds them for us and draws them.

There is no lightness in this prayer. Sometimes it is a burden: the burden that the prophet did see is a word that has kinship with it; and it asks for continuance. There is battle in it, a contending with bitterly opposing forces of which we are only in part aware. "Let no man think that suddenly, in a minute, all is accomplished and the work is done." It is not like that: Moses' hands were steady until the going down of the sun.

There was once a time in the history of our Fellowship when a defined and commanded prayer was charged with a strange distress. It was not so at first. For many hours there was only a sense of awe, a pure and speechless joy. But that blinding sense of the Presence passed (it must if we are to walk by faith), and a torturing fear consumed the soul so lately bathed in wonder. How be sure that what appeared to be a divine command to pray for a certain good was not the human in disguise? The petition that must be offered could not be granted without what appeared to be certain loss to some of the Lord's servants and hurt to others. There was no imaginable way by which the double difficulty could be turned; it was like a barbed-wire entanglement, a forbidding fence. Such a prayer appeared like treachery; how gain by another's loss or hurt? Intolerable thought—could a prayer like that be of God? And it felt intrusive, too, like pushing into a room without knocking. But words are shadows. They cannot show what was.

There was one dark night when something occurred that shattered hope. "It was all a mistake," said a voice hour by hour through that night.

Next day a letter came. It was like the dropping of a lark straight down through the blue air, only there was this difference: one hears the song high up in the air while the bird is only a speck in the blue; that night had passed uncheered by any song. But here was a letter that told of part of that prayer answered. It had been answered in the counsels of God, before the command "Ask now" had been heard and obeyed.

"From the first day that thou didst set thine heart to chasten thyself before thy God, thy words were heard." That first day dated further back than the day of the commanded prayer. It went back to a time of great trouble: "In the day of my trouble I will call upon Thee, for Thou wilt answer me." In a world full of uncertainties about many things, this is certain: prayer is not like a homing bird that is blown out of its course by contrary winds and loses its way in the void or drops exhausted into the sea. Prayer is like a child who knows the way to his Father's house and goes straight there. Or if winds buffet him, he is not beaten back. He wrestles through, sure of his road, sure of his welcome. But sometimes there are hindrances, and then an old story comes to mind: "When he was yet a great way off, his father saw him, and had compassion."

But the command had been astonishing in its largeness. And a fulfillment to its uttermost edge appeared, even on that day of joy and wonder, to be surrounded by circumstances that stood like hills all cliff and impenetrable jungle. And yet the word persisted.

Then vividly, perhaps in the way all the kingdoms of the world and the glory of them were shown to our Saviour, the high places of mission lands were spread out before the mind of the one who was under the hand of God for prayer. And, last of all, like a little heap of red sand piled in a corner, appeared the place to which that prayer would lead the servant of the Lord whom it concerned. It was a place where a corn of wheat might die— there was nothing else to offer there. Wounds lay in that prayer, and a daily crucifixion. And so there was cloudy darkness. How could it be the way of God-directed prayer?

> Whoso hath known the Spirit of the High
> Cannot confound, nor doubt Him, nor deny.

Deep within that tormented heart these words sounded their steadfast note. There was no escape from that prayer, though a way of escape was earnestly sought.

At last strength failed and the troubled one, all overborne, turned from the steep ascent. How climb the face of a rock where no steps were?

The place of this collapse in courage was a wood, very green and still.

Presently, as the soul waited, drinking from wells of bitterness and fear, steps were slowly cut in the face of the rock; and they led up into sure dwellings and quiet resting-places. It is worthwhile to break through the snowfall of silence, and let the track be seen, if to even one traveler in the harder ways of prayer the path may be made plainer.

First, then, came a question, tender, poignant: "You fear to cause loss and hurt to your fellow-servant; would I ask you to do so? You fear to intrude into the life of another; would I ask you to intrude? Have I been so long time with thee and yet hast thou not known Me?" Then like a trumpet call, "Toward the sunrising shall the standard of the camp of Judah be. Open your windows towards the sunrising." Prayer can be mortal strife. Even so, open your windows, keep them open towards the sunrising.

But confusion and perplexity did not pass at once: "Lord, if it be Thou, why this extremity of distress?" And for a while no word was heard, no word was spoken, till gently, imperceptibly, there was a presence,

> How entered, by what secret stair,
> I know not, knowing only He was there.

"Behold I am the Lord, the God of all flesh: is there anything too hard for Me?"

"Ah, Lord God, behold, Thou hast made the heaven and the earth by Thy great power and by Thy stretched out arm; there is nothing too hard for Thee."

"Thus saith the Lord that doeth it, the Lord that formeth it to establish it; the Lord is His name: call unto Me and I will answer thee, and will shew thee great things, and difficult, which thou knowest not."

"Why art thou cast down, O my soul? And why art thou disquieted within me? Hope thou in God, for I shall yet praise Him, who is the health of my countenance, and my God."

There is a place where the human fails, breaks down, turns to ashes. Hope has not a single foothold. In such an hour there is a perishing of everything unless the soul waits in silence for God only.

"My soul, wait thou in silence for God only"—the words whispered through the wood as a light wind blew the leaves on the trees. "Roll thy way upon the Lord; trust also in Him, and He shall bring it to pass." *He will accomplish all that which thy faith has laid on Him.* "And blessed is she that believed, for there shall be a performance of those things which were told her from the Lord."

Does the reader know what it is to find a page of Scripture take life under his eyes? Not letter, but spirit is there, eager to speak to him. He reads and wonders, Have I ever read it before? Yes, countless times, but never as today. On that day, in that cave, such a scripture took life.*

Months whose weeks seemed years passed dumbly—
twenty long months. Is there anything that melts the heart
more than the Lord's patience, His gentle handling, His
tender bearing with our fears, while all the time He is
preparing surprises of delight for us that no storm can
shatter? How often He has shamed us with His kindness:

> Always hath the daylight broken,
> Always hath He comfort spoken,
> Better hath He been for years
> Than thy fears.

And then at last, at last, there was performance, and He
whose name is Wonderful revealed His plan. All through
those silent months His hand had been working at the
other end. The fence that had forbidden—we looked for it,
and to our astonishment it was not there. The hills had
melted like wax at the presence of the Lord, the hills of

---

* The scripture was 2 Samuel 7:18–29: "Who am I, O Lord God? And
what is my house, that Thou hast brought me hitherto? And this was
yet a small thing in Thy sight, O Lord God; but Thou hast spoken also
of Thy servant's house for a great while to come. And is this the
manner of man, O Lord God? And what can David say more unto
Thee? For Thou, Lord God, knowest Thy servant. For Thy word's sake,
and according to Thine own heart, hast Thou done all these great
things, to make Thy servant know them. . . . And now, O Lord God, the
word that Thou hast spoken concerning Thy servant and concerning
his house, establish it for ever, and do as Thou hast said. And let Thy
name be magnified for ever, saying, The Lord of Hosts is the God over
Israel: and let the house of Thy servant David be established before
Thee. For Thou, O Lord of Hosts, God of Israel, hast revealed to Thy
servant, saying, I will build thee an house: therefore hath Thy servant
found in his heart to pray this prayer unto Thee. And now, O Lord
God, Thou art that God, and Thy words be true, and Thou hast promised this goodness unto Thy servant: therefore now let it please Thee to
bless the house of Thy servant, that it may continue for ever before
Thee: for Thou, O Lord God, hast spoken it; and with Thy blessing let
the house of Thy servant be blessed for ever."

The force of these words lay in the fact that the commanded prayer
of the time concerned the future leadership of the Fellowship.

impossible circumstances had melted like wax. "Who shall roll us away the stone? And when they looked, they saw that the stone was rolled away."

And so our wondering hearts had rest. No wrong was done to anyone. (Have I been so long time with thee and *yet* hast thou not known Me?) Nor was there hurt to those whom that prayer had touched. To see a seed fall into the ground and die is not to see it hurt. To see a warrior wounded is to see him crowned. Our temptations are so fierce, because our vision is so limited. We need to pray that the things that are seen shall be transparent like the pavement of heaven for clearness, so that, looking through, we shall see the things that are eternal.

Is the reader for whom this unusual chapter has been written facing some soul-racking responsibility of prayer or of decision? If the war be real, and not a painted fight, it often must be so. We look at one, young, strong, free, beautiful and quick with life and the joy of life. Can we pray a prayer that will loose spiritual forces upon that soul, forces that will sweep it on till its glorious youth is broken on the wheel? Christ did: "I have prayed for thee." . . . "Verily, verily, I say unto thee, When thou wast young, thou girdedst thyself and walkedst whither thou wouldest; but when thou shalt be old, thou shalt stretch forth thy hands, and another shall gird thee, and carry thee whither thou wouldest not." "Who for the joy that was set before Him endured": can we trust God so to set this joy before these for whom we pray that they will not look back to curse us for our prayer? Christ did. It is a solemn thing ever by spiritual influences to move an immortal soul to such tremendous issues. It should not be done lightly, And yet, if this burden be laid upon us by our Lord, it must be accepted. To refuse would be not gain but loss for those for whom we dared not pray. But let us be very sure. Such prayer should cost us all that we are able to know of fellowship with Him whose sweat was, as it were, great drops of blood falling down to the ground.

53

Girt in the panther-fells,
    Violets in my hair,
Down I ran through the woody dells,
    Through the morning wild and fair—
To sit by the road till the sun was high,
That I might see some god pass by.

Fluting amid the thyme
    I dreamed through the golden day,
Calling through melody and rhyme:
    "Iacchus! Come this way,
From harrowing Hades like a king,
Vine leaves and glories scattering."

Twilight was all rose-red,
    When, crowned with vine and thorn,
Came a stranger god from out the dead;
    And his hands and feet were torn.
I knew him not, for he came alone:
I knew him not, whom I fain had known.

He said: "For love, for love,
    I wear the vine and thorn."
He said: "For love, for love,
    My hands and feet were torn:
For love, the winepress Death I trod."
    And I cried in pain: "O Lord my God."
        —Mrs. Rachel Annand Taylor.

"You have gained battles without cannon, passed rivers without bridges, performed forced marches without shoes, bivouacked without strong liquors, and often without bread. Thanks for your perseverance! But, soldiers, you have done nothing—for there remains much to do." So spoke Napoleon to his men, and they rallied to him as leader. But a greater than Napoleon appeals today.

"I am going out from Rome," said Garibaldi. "I offer neither pay, nor quarters, nor provisions; I offer hunger, thirst, forced marches, battles, death. Let him who loves his country in his heart, and not with his lips only, follow me." But a greater than Garibaldi speaks today.

Scott appealed for four men for his perilous Arctic expedition. The response came in thousands. Men pressed for a place, without conditions and without reservations. Nay, some offered to pay their own expenses, no matter how menial the task. But a greater than Scott asks for volunteers today.

It is said of Mallory, who died upon or near the summit of Mount Everest, that "he was always drawn to the big and the unexplored"; that "the great walls that mountaineers set aside as obviously impossible" had a strange attraction for him. And the high places of God's field call today for the love, and the zeal, and the daring of those who will jeopardize their lives for higher ends.—W.H. Aldis in a Note sent out by the China Inland Mission in 1930.

53. For Love, for Love, My Hands and Feet Were Torn

One of the brothers of the Dohnavur Fellowship has a
gallant friend, Clifford Harris of Isfahan, Persia, for whom
the trumpets lately sounded. (I write has, not had; such
friendship is immortal.) And we of this Fellowship were
allowed privately to share a matter which at one time
filled his mind. Should he become a Persian subject so that
he might take the gospel into Afghanistan? He knew what
that might mean (fully to understand, one must know the
East), and after his decision to do so, God leading on, he
wrote to his comrade here, "Now I am quite easy in mind,
having faced up to it." And a thrill went through us who
heard that letter read, for there is nothing so kindling as to
see the soul of man or woman follow right over the edge of
the usual into the untracked land—for love of Him, sheer
love of Him. But that land was not really untracked. Our
Saviour did just that when He laid aside His heavenly
rights and became, not a Roman, but a Jew who could be
crucified.

Clifford Harris would have set his feet in the footsteps
of his Lord; they might have led him also straight to prison

and to death. "Naturally, after making the decision about Afghanistan and being ready for anything," he wrote to his friend in Dohnavur, "I am just waiting to see what the next step will be. What fun [delightful word] to tackle it together!" It was this, the resolve that was in him, that gave iron to the prayer he prayed before his last message to his fellow-missionaries—for his next step was across the valley to Higher Hills. And the prayer was not made of mere beautiful valorous words: "O Thou who art heroic Love, keep alive in our hearts that adventurous spirit which makes men scorn the way of safety, so that Thy will be done. For so only, O Lord, shall we be worthy of those courageous souls who in every age have ventured all in obedience to Thy call, and for whom the trumpets have sounded on the other side; through Jesus Christ our Lord."

But neither Afghanistan nor any other of the big and the unexplored and the high places of the field will look wonderful when the traveler reaches them. Nor will he feel in the least valorous. Again and again he will find that he has need to pray for the simple graces of good cheer, courage, patience, persistence, the will to ignore the clamors of the flesh, the will to refuse the softness that would sink to the easy. God give us climbing souls. ("He died climbing": happy Swiss Guide!) And to climb may be nothing more romantic than a steady trampling on the lust of comfort, a going on, when everything in us wants to stop. And for some to climb will mean somewhere, some time—being reviled, we bless: "I find it is drawing all of us who are going this way nearer to Calvary, to a deeper service of abandon and obedience. God keep us in the dust, mud for Him to use to make men see, doormats for men to wipe their feet on, if only they will come Home to Him, scrap heaps of the religious world if need be, like Paul's offscouring of all things"—this is what climbing meant to one of the Fellowship at home on furlough.

This book is being written in a room that is full of a jumble of common affairs, but today its windows seem to open on a temple tower, pierced by a door one hundred feet high. By that door is a woman—not with violets in her hair, nor with a flute in her hands, but with a rosary of Siva's beads round her neck; she is clad in thin salmon-colored cotton that wraps her scantily. There is not one woman in that crowd of fifteen thousand people who can tell her the way to find Him whom she seeks. But there is, thank God, one man bold enough to speak to her, and to him she is drawn now. He does not know her language, she does not know his, but somehow they feel their way toward each other's hearts, helped by Sanscrit, which is familiar to both; and he tells her of the Divine Redeemer, the suffering Saviour ("For love, for love, My hands and feet were torn"). And she tells him that when she was six years old she was dedicated to the Supreme God: "For sixty-two years I have been on pilgrimage. But I have not found Him yet. Only I know that He is not *there*. I never go through that door [the majestic door through which millions have passed to bathe in the sacred waters within the temple enclosure, and to worship that which is hidden away in the secret cell under the great tower]. It is vanity. I have traveled all over India to Benares, Puri, Hardwar"— she names the sacred cities one by one—"but never once before this day have I met a lover of your God, nor has one who loves Him spoken of Him to me." And suddenly there in the dust of the road the pilgrim prostrates herself, "He of whom you have told me is He whom I have sought."

We do not often see so sudden an enchantment, for we do not often see a soul prepared like that. But sometimes we see them. What dust in the balance any loss appears beside the unimaginable loss of having been about one's own business on some other road when that seeker passed by. What would it be to look back at the close of the day, when things show clearly in the evening light, and see that the Lord who redeemed us was on that road just then, looking for us to say to that soul, "Behold the Lamb of God which taketh away the sin of the world"—and we were not there. Parents, whose children have heard the call, will you not loose them and let them go? Soldiers of Christ, in whose hearts the call is ringing, will you not rise up and obey?

In the years of Armenia's misery, the children of Dohnavur, thinking of the young girls carried off into Turkish harems, sang a prayer for them. It was about

> Little boats, drifting over the bar,
> Little lambs lost in fields afar,
> Where is nor moon nor star—
>
> Far on fell, far on fell,
> Wander the lambs that stray,
> Far, far, from harbor bell,
> Drift the small boats away—
> Open to Thee are the paths of the sea,
> All the world's corners are open to Thee,
> Follow them where they be,
> Call Thy little ones, call Thy little ones home.

Those were the children's words. But for whom have these new words been written?

> Deep to deep, answereth now,
> Dimly I see a cross,
> Thirst, wounds, thorn-crowned brow,
> Stripping and utmost loss.
> Over the bar the fret of the foam,
> Rain on the fell where the young lambs roam—
> Lord, art Thou bidding me
> Call Thy little ones, call Thy little ones home?

* * * * *

Our story is told. Perhaps some thread of a new gold cord has been wrought, even as the pages were turned and the reader let new thoughts speak and new affections waken. We have told our story badly if we have not shown a lovable people; but were they not so, were they cold, indifferent, hard (as indeed even in our dear India some can be), what would it matter? The tender love of God desires them all. His Son our Saviour died for them all. How much do we care that He did? Lord, teach us to care. Give it to us to see beyond the grey street, or the green countryside, or the sparkle of the sea, or the glory of the mountains. Give it to us to love, as Thou dost love all the nations of the earth. Give it to us to give as Thou didst give, holding nothing back.

The Dohnavur Fellowship

The work in Dohnavur still continues, but now the Fellows members are all of Indian nationality. They do not belong officially to any of the organized churches; but in fellowship with others of God's children, they seek to make His love and salvation known to all whom they can reach.

The dedication of girls to the temples is now illegal, but the Fellowship provides a home for children who might otherwise fall into the hands of people who would exploit them in some way.

Girls of all ages from babies to teenagers form a large part of the family in Dohnavur. The need to care for them continues until they are securely launched elsewhere or else have become fellow workers. The aim is still to bring them up to know and love our Lord Jesus and to follow His example as those who desire not to be served but to serve others.

The hospital treats patients from the surrounding countryside. They are from varied religious backgrounds—Hindu, Muslim, Christian. They include rich and poor, highly educated and illiterate. Through this medical work God continues to bring to us the people we long to reach, those whose need is for spiritual as well as physical healing.

Boys are no longer admitted, but the buildings they occupied are now put to full use. In 1981 the Fellowship in partnership with other Christians formed the Santhosha Educational Society to administer a co-educational English-medium boarding school, primarily for the benefit of the children of missionaries of Indian nationality. The buildings provide facilities for over 300 children now studying there. Their parents come from Indian missions and organizations working in many parts of India, including tribal areas.

In matters of finance, we follow the pattern shown from the beginning of the work. Amy Carmichael rejoiced in her Heavenly Father's faithfulness in supplying each need. We praise Him that His faithfulness is the same today.

The Dohnavur Fellowship
Tirunelveli District
Tamil Nadu 627 102

The Dohnavur Fellowship
15 Elm Drive
North Harrow
Middlesex HA2 7BS
England

Index

Index of First Lines

Music for many of the children's songs, and for our prayer choruses, has been given to us by our friend, May Dobson, now in the Singing Land, and by the Rev. K. Procter, and by other friends and members of the Fellowship.

This book was produced by the Christian Literature Crusade. We hope it has been helpful to you in living the Christian life. CLC is a literature mission with ministry in over 50 countries worldwide. If you would like to know more about us, or are interested in opportunities to serve with a faith mission, we invite you to write to:

Christian Literature Crusade
P.O. Box 1449
Fort Washington, PA 19034